This book is to be returned on or before
the last date stamped below.

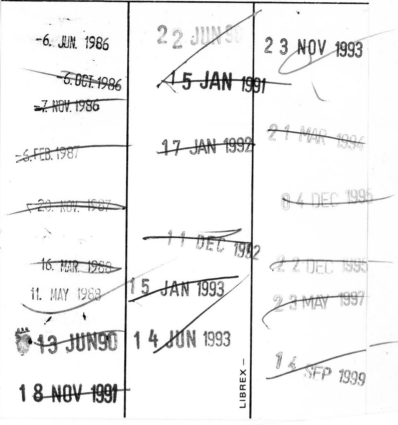

-6. JUN. 1986

-6. OCT. 1986

-7. NOV. 1986

-6. FEB. 1987

23. NOV. 1987

16. MAR. 1988

11. MAY 1988

13 JUN90

18 NOV 1991

2 2 JUN90

5 JAN 1991

17 JAN 1992

11 DEC 1992

15 JAN 1993

1 4 JUN 1993

LIBREX —

2 3 NOV 1993

2 1 MAR 1994

0 4 DEC 1995

2 2 DEC 1995

2 3 MAY 1997

1 4 SEP 1999

The Rise of Modern Urban Planning
1800–1914

STUDIES IN HISTORY, PLANNING AND THE ENVIRONMENT

The Rise of Modern Urban Planning 1800–1914

edited by

ANTHONY SUTCLIFFE

The first volume of the trilogy
'Planning and the Environment in the Modern World'

MANSELL, London 1980

ISBN 0 7201 0902 7

Mansell Publishing, a part of Bemrose UK Limited, 3 Bloomsbury Place, London WC1A 2QA

First published 1980

© Mansell Publishing 1980

This book was commissioned, edited and designed by Alexandrine Press, Oxford.

British Library Cataloguing in Publication Data

Planning and the environment in the modern world.
(Studies in history, planning and the environment).
   Vol. 1: The rise of modern urban planning, 1800–1914.
   1. City planning – History
   2. Regional planning – History
   I. Sutcliffe, Anthony   II. Series 711'.09'034   HT166

ISBN 0-7201-0902-7

Text set in 11/12pt Ehrhardt, and printed in Great Britain by Henry Ling Limited; bound by Mansell (Bookbinders) Ltd., Witham, Essex.

Foreword

While today there is considerable questioning about the future directions of planning, there is a parallel and growing interest in the origins and history of the planning process and its effects on our environment. In this series, *Studies in History, Planning and the Environment,* we intend to provide in-depth studies of some of the many aspects of that history, to reflect the increasing international interest, and to stimulate ideas for areas of further research.

We shall focus on developments during the last one hundred to one hundred and fifty years and attempt to examine some of the questions relating to the forces which have shaped and guided our contemporary environment—urban, rural and metropolitan—and which demand answers not just for critical analysis in the advance of scholarship, but also for the insights they can provide for the future. Planning policy is constructed from knowledge of the *origins* of problems, as well as the *consequences* of decisions. Planning history therefore looks at processes over time; how and why our contemporary environment is shaped as it is. The broad outlines may be known; exercising an interpretative judgement on the details provides a fascinating field of study in which there are not a few surprises and many lessons for academics and practitioners alike.

In shedding light on the recent past we hope to understand the present; in fusing insights from different subject fields we hope to strengthen the synoptic traditions of both history and planning; in being avowedly international we will reflect the different cultural attitudes to planning and the environment over time.

It is right that the first three volumes, which make up the trilogy *Planning and the Environment in the Modern World,* should derive from the papers presented at the first International Conference of the Planning History Group, held in London in September, 1977. Other conferences and meetings of the Group can be expected to provide material for the series, while individual initiatives will release the fruits of personal labour.

Gordon E. Cherry
Anthony Sutcliffe
July 1980

Contents

The Contributors

FRANZISKA BOLLEREY has been Professor of Town Planning History at the Technical Highschool, Delft, since 1978. She was previously engaged in research and lecturing on both historical and contemporary aspects of urban planning and architecture at Berlin and Dortmund. She is author of *Architekturkonzeptionen der utopischen Sozialisten* (1977), and a number of smaller studies and articles on housing history and conservation, some of them in association with Kristiana Hartmann.

PETER BREITLING is Professor of Town Planning at the Technical University of Graz, having previously lectured at the Technical University, Munich. His interest in planning history complements his prime concerns in present-day planning and conservation issues.

DONATELLA CALABI is a Professor at the Istituto Universitario di Architettura, Venice. She has published extensively on the history of German planning and its influence in Italy, and is currently working on the career and thinking of Werner Hegemann.

DAVID R. GOLDFIELD is Associate Professor of Environmental and Urban Systems at the Virginia Polytechnic Institute and State University. He combines an interest in urban history and in contemporary planning. One of the founders of the *Journal of Urban History,* of which he is currently associate editor, he has published many articles and three books: *The Enduring Ghetto* (1973), *Urban Growth in the Age of Sectionalism: Virginia, 1847–1861* (1977), and *Urban America: From Downtown to No Town* (1979).

KRISTIANA HARTMANN lectures in architectural and town planning history at the University of Dortmund, where she is also involved in public participation in planning decisions. She is author of *Deutsche Gartenstadtbewegung* (1976), and numerous articles, some in association with Franziska Bollerey.

HELEN MELLER is Senior Lecturer in the Department of Economic and Social History, University of Nottingham. She is author of *Leisure and the Changing City* (1976), and editor of *The Ideal City* (1979). She is currently working on a major reassessment of the life and work of Patrick Geddes.

P. J. SMITH is Professor of Geography at the University of Alberta, where he has taught since 1959. Previously a research planner with the City of Calgary, he has authored *Population and Production* (1967, 1970) and edited *The Prairie Provinces* (1972) and *Edmonton: The Emerging Metropolitan Pattern* (1978). His work on Edinburgh is a product of his interest in the origin and diffusion of planning ideas.

ANTHONY SUTCLIFFE is Reader in Urban History in the Department of Economic and Social History, University of Sheffield. After work on the history of Paris and Birmingham, he is currently completing a general study of planning in the late nineteenth century.

JOHN NELSON TARN is Roscoe Professor of Architecture at the University of Liverpool. One of Britain's best-known housing and architectural historians, he has published *Working-Class Housing in Nineteenth Century Britain* (1971) and *Five Per Cent Philanthropy* (1972), as well as numerous articles.

WILLIAM H. WILSON is Professor of History at North Texas State University. He made his name as a planning historian with *The City Beautiful Movement in Kansas City* (1964). Recently he has worked more widely in American urban history, publishing *Coming of Age: Urban America 1915–1945* (1975), and *Railroad in the Clouds: The Alaska Railroad, 1915–1945* (1977). However, he is currently researching the City Beautiful movement again, on the basis of a sample of five medium-sized towns.

Acknowledgments

The studies in this volume were first presented at the First International Conference on the History of Urban and Regional Planning, which was organized by the Planning History Group at Bedford College, University of London, 14–18th September, 1977. The Group wishes to extend its gratitude to the bodies whose generous grants allowed the conference to take place: the Anglo-German Foundation for the Study of Industrial Society, the British Academy, the Nuffield Foundation, the Rockefeller Foundation, and the Social Science Research Council.

A record of the discussions at the conference was made by Martin Gaskell, James Read, Stephen Ward, and Madge Dresser for the Planning History Group. This record has proved most valuable in setting the context for the papers collected in this volume, and grateful acknowledgment is made for their hard work at that time. I should also like to express my thanks to the contributors for their careful re-editing of their papers for publication.

Finally, acknowledgment is given for permission to reproduce the following illustrations in the paper by Donatella Calabi: figure 4.2, Archivio Comunale di Venezia; figure 4.3, Archivio Storico Novarese, Fondo Museo; figure 4.4, Museo Civico di Padova.

Anthony Sutcliffe

1

Introduction:
the debate on
nineteenth-century
planning

ANTHONY SUTCLIFFE

Conference proceedings are not always the most enlightening or entertaining of literary forms. In preparing the trilogy, *Planning and the Environment in the Modern World,* of which this is the first volume, the editors were agreed that to reproduce all the forty papers given at the First International Conference on the History of Urban and Regional Planning would make too unwieldy a publication. Instead, we have selected representative essays in order to recreate the vital atmosphere of international debate which was the most exciting product of the London conference in 1977.

Much of the conference's time was spent in discussing what is generally acknowledged to be the foundation period of modern planning, the century of rapid industrialization and urbanization which culminated in the First World War. Of course, elements of planning had existed before industrialization; since ancient times, towns had been laid out by authority, public facilities such as piped water had been provided, and regulations to control private building had been enforced. Without such planning, towns were liable to discourage prospective residents, turn away trade, burn down, and lose their populations in sweeping epidemics. Industrialization, however, brought a new scale and complexity of urban development, combined with the refinement of a new economic and social ideology which blessed individualism and the free working of the market. This ideology, often referred to as *laisser-faire,* was appropriate to the early stages of a productive revolution which freed man from his age-old dependence on the land and destroyed the institutional shackles of feudalism. Progress and growth became ideals as well as practical possibilities. Some seers even glimpsed the demise of a traditional authority and its replacement by a freely-evolving association of individuals based on contract in an age of plenty permitted by untrammelled exchange and expanding machine production.

This new ideology implied that the creation of the urban environment could safely be entrusted to the market. In practice, however, the market proved incapable of regulating the massive conflicts generated within the industrial town by economic forces of unprecedented power and related social divisions within the urban populations. Traditional authority, far from disappearing, regularized itself at the level of the State. Discovering that the problems of the growing towns threatened it more than in the past, the State was inclined to involve itself increasingly in urban affairs, though it was prepared to leave much of the initiative to local administrations generated within the urban communities.

The ultimate product of these interacting private and public forces was what we now know as urban and regional planning. Firmly established as an essential administrative activity throughout the industrialized world, urban and regional planning can be recognized as a coordinated effort, usually undertaken by public authority, to secure an efficient and socially acceptable use of land by a great variety of potentially conflicting functions. This intervention takes two principal forms. On the one hand, public expenditure on the development and maintenance of the environment is allocated and scheduled in order to secure the greatest possible benefits in relation to the resources invested. On the other, the freedom of private owners and users of land is curtailed in order to prevent conflicts damaging to third parties or even to themselves. Both modes of action are subject to the impact of changing circumstances, the changes stemming in part from the fact of public intervention. So both involve an element of forecasting which requires a scientific approach. The alternative to planning, a free conflict of individual interests moderated by the market, is no longer seriously advocated, even in the remaining bastions of capitalistic individualism such as the United States and Japan. In the socialist world, meanwhile, common control of the means of production has in theory allotted full control of the environment to the institutions of planning.

Most of the machinery of planning in today's world has emerged since 1914. The First World War gave a death-blow to *laisser-faire,* and although planning went through a somewhat unproductive phase in the later 1920s and 1930s, it received a new stimulus from the Second World War. In most of the advanced countries of the West, general planning legislation was not passed until the 1940s or even the 1950s, the British Town and Country Planning Act of 1947 being perhaps the best-known example. Meanwhile, in the new areas of the socialist world such planning powers as had existed before 1939 were completely revised. However, much of the terminology, ideology and techniques of planning had been in existence before 1914. The expressions 'town planning', 'city planning', *'Städtebau'*, *'Städteplanung'*, *'urbanisme'*, *'urbanistica'*, *'stadsplanering'*, *'stedebouw'*, and *'gradostroitel'stvo'*, all came into general use between about 1890 and 1914. The institution of the comprehensive development plan, covering an entire city, had already emerged, above all in Germany. Great planning textbooks had been published in Germany and Britain. Prophetic legislation had been passed, such as the Saxon *Allgemeine Baugesetz* of 1900 and the British Town Planning Act of 1909. In fact, urban planning was so firmly on the scene by 1914 that the nineteenth century might fairly be designated as the most crucial period in its evolution.

At the London conference three broad interpretations of nineteenth-century planning were on display—liberal-progressist, functionalist, and marxist—and they underlay much of the debate, even on matters of detail. The liberal-progressist interpretation was the dominant one in that, informing as it does much of the historiography of British and American planning, it appealed to the Anglo-Saxon majority at the conference. Its guiding assumption, that men find better ways of doing things as time passes, is reflected below in the essays of Breitling, Tarn and Wilson. The main challenge to it came from the marxist interpretation, currently well entrenched in continental Europe, and represented here by Calabi, and by Bollerey and Hartmann. For the marxists, planning is neither vice nor virtue; it is merely part of the superstructure of institutions built on the foundations of the economic organization of society. Its function in the nineteenth century is to reinforce the dominance of a ruling bourgeoisie, partly by enhancing the efficiency of their creation, the State, and partly by imposing on the masses values and modes of behaviour which contribute to bourgeois hegemony. As such, the institutions and techniques of planning develop in step with changes in society as a whole and in the level of technology. In the functionalist view, seen here in the work of Goldfield and Smith, planning is a residual activity to which a pluralist society resorts in order to do what cannot be achieved in cheaper, more individualistic ways. On this interpretation, planning does not help lead society on to more enlightened modes of organization, but neither is it systematically exploitative. In fact, functionalist elements can be detected in all eight of the essays, but it is not entirely a coincidence that both Goldfield and Smith are North Americans.

The mode of interpretation affects not only the interpretation of given phenomena but the whole definition of what constitutes planning. The British eye, in particular, has become well trained in detecting evidence of a 'rise' or 'genesis' of planning in the late nineteenth and early twentieth centuries as the defects of the free market were recognized and State activity gained in respectability, while the idea of planning was decked out in an attractive architectural form which promised somehow to marry the urbanity of the metropolis with the calm comfort of the village. British participants at the conference were therefore more bemused than most by a number of papers which purported to discover planning already operational in the middle and early decades of the nineteenth century. The clearest example, among the essays published here, is Goldfield's, which by defining voluntary and even private initiatives as part of planning is able to detect a fully developed planning strategy in the cities of the Old South *in advance* of effective institutions of urban government. Calabi gives him indirect support by identifying as 'planning' the whole gamut of State activity in nineteenth-century Italy. It was, however, Jeanne Cuillier, in a paper not included here, who went furthest along this path by extending 'planning' to cover the apparently uncoordinated provision of facilities such as almshouses by voluntary organizations in early-nineteenth-century American towns[1].

The temptation to dismiss these broad definitions should be resisted. They have been generated not only by distinctive ideologies but by the varying experiences of the national societies in the context of which they have been formulated. Despite the customary use of the term 'Industrial Revolution' to describe it, Britain's modernization process in the late eighteenth and nineteenth centuries was a very leisurely affair. In a country already fully settled, virtually free of feudal restrictions, with a firmly-rooted State apparatus, and in the absence of serious foreign competition, economic development could well proceed spontaneously and organically, ignoring or even eroding the institutions of public administration. In the United States and Italy, on the other hand, a new society was created much more rapidly in the nineteenth century, and in this process both the State and private enterprise adopted roles which diverged from the British experience. In the United States, the main dynamic of economic development, at least during the first half of the century, was provided by the westward expansion of settlement. The Federal government became deeply involved, not only in the regulation of this process, but also in its promotion. In the 1840s it went on to supervise the creation of a railway network to bind together and further extend the new territories. The railway companies, however, remained in private ownership. Entrusted with the exploitation and settlement of extensive land grants, they soon acquired the power to control the destiny of whole tracts of the continent. It was in their reaction to these monopolies that urban communities, according to Goldfield, began to plan. They lobbied for more and better lines, often helping to finance them by public bond issues. Many of those which lay on navigable water improved their port facilities. Goldfield is largely indifferent to the exact status of lobbyists, boosters, and improvers. For him, city councils, boards of trade, and individual businessmen are all equally qualified to promote the interests of the urban community. All benefit from growth, and as growth is clearly sought, a process of planning may be said to be taking place.

Further west, urban government was even more rudimentary than in Goldfield's Old South, a long-settled area. On the Frontier, the very existence of towns was usually the product of the operations of the land promoter, albeit under the general oversight of the land-grant authorities. To attract purchasers, the promoters ensured that streets and blocks, usually in grid form, were laid out before building started, and that certain public facilities were provided. Some even sought to impart to their creations an attractive appearance capable, if only in the long term, of generating extra settlement. In this, they echoed some of Goldfield's examples, seeking to make beauty pay in the constant competition with their neighbours. They also foreshadowed the behaviour of many cities during the City Beautiful phase described by Wilson. That these activities, too, amounted to planning was cogently argued at the conference in two papers which it has not been possible to include here. In 'The forgotten Frontier: urban planning in the American West before 1890', a wide-ranging review of western town plans, John Reps argued that the Frontier had always been an urban one, with founded towns usually forming the first wave of settlement. He was supported by Norman Pressman's study of Goderich, a new town in Ontario laid out by the Canada Company in the 1820s[2]. Reps and Pressman, it must be said, by concentrating on the deliberate creation of an organized layout, had an easier task than Goldfield and Cuillier in convincing their audience that the activities they described, though private, amounted to urban planning.

Calabi's Italy provides a very different context for a similar issue, and comparisons are further complicated by her different ideological stand-point. Goldfield assumes, as does Wilson, that the activities of improving businessmen are generally beneficial. For Calabi, the reforming and modernizing legislation passed in a reunified Italy is essentially an expression of the bourgeois desire to mould the country's economic and social institutions in its own interests. The infant State apparatus is used directly to create the necessary infrastructure, particularly in communications. Complemented by land reclamation schemes and other public improvements, this effort can be regarded as a concerted strategy of territorial transformation, or, regional planning. This argument was more extensively developed in a paper not published here, Alberto Mioni's 'Regional planning and territorial interventions in Italy, 1880–1940'[3]. Surprisingly, however, Calabi goes on to argue that State economic planning *failed* to generate urban planning, at any rate in her sample of medium-sized towns in the Veneto. Perhaps she expects too much; some of the 'instruments' of urban intervention which she dismisses so lightly would have been envied by British planners as late as the early 1940s.

The remaining six papers in this collection are more conventional, in that they focus on widely-acknowledged aspects of, or episodes in, the emergence of comprehensive urban planning in the late nineteenth and early twentieth centuries. Their temporal centre of gravity is that prolific twenty-year period between about 1890 and 1910 in which the idea, if not the achievement, of planning swept the world. The British or American reader will recognize, in the essays of Tarn, Wilson and Meller, original and up-to-date variations on three traditional themes in the historiography of early planning. Indeed, Wilson avowedly sets out to rehabilitate an episode in American planning, the City Beautiful movement, the significance of which has been questioned in recent years mainly, it would seem, because historians have cast around desperately to find something new to say about so obvious an evolution. Tarn concentrates on the equivalent catalyst in the genesis of British planning, residential design, which is so pervasive that even the most iconoclastic historian would hesitate to question its importance. Finally, Meller's discussion of Patrick Geddes emerges from a long-term research project designed to establish the true scientific credentials of a man who had so long been acknowledged as the greatest prophet of early British planning that familiarity had begun to breed contempt.

Breitling's theme, for its part, lies fully in the main stream of German planning historiography. He is right to claim that the planning *competition* has not received the attention it merits, but the subject of many such competitions, the town-extension plan, is recognized as the forerunner of comprehensive urban planning over much of continental Europe. As such, it is beginning to enter a period of reassessment similar to that endured by the City Beautiful movement. Even within this collection, we note Calabi's low opinion of Italian town-extension plans, while Bollerey and Hartmann's account of key developments in residential design in Germany virtually ignores them. At the London conference, however, the extension plan was the revelation of the nineteenth-century proceedings, at least to the British and American participants. Gasps of admiration greeted the extension-plan slides dismissively projected by Calabi and by Bollerey and Hartmann. Their scale and apparent complexity surpassed anything known in Britain before 1914, and they made the grid extensions of American cities look crude. Moreover, Breitling found allies among contributors whose papers do not appear here. Frank Costa's sweeping account of the development of Rome gave full attention to the big extension plans prepared in the later nineteenth century after the capital of a reunited Italy had finally settled there[4]. Manuel de Solà-Morales and Bernard Miller, meanwhile, drew the attention of the conference to an even earlier extension plan, perhaps the most impressive produced during the century— Ildefonso de Cerdá's extraordinary Barcelona *ensanche* of 1858[5].

A paper on the central reconstruction of Paris and other French cities in the 1850s and 1860s might have set extension planning in a more balanced perspective. However, the only contribution to deal with the inner city was Smith's analysis of slum redevelopment in Victorian Edinburgh and Leith. Moreover, it was discussed in a separate session on housing reform and so never directly confronted the extension-plan studies. In any case, Smith's functionalist approach allowed no room for claims that the Edinburgh version of urban renewal was part of a grand progress towards more enlightened planning. Miller, especially, made full use of this opportunity. He portrayed Cerdá as a democratic and even socialistic idealist who sought to convert Barcelona into a new urban form which would reconcile economic efficiency with human demands for personal and social fulfilment, and contact with nature. More modestly, Solà-Morales mainly stressed the technical qualities of Cerdá's planning. Though he established the uniqueness of Cerdá's expertise and vision, he was at pains to point to the pervasiveness of extension planning throughout southern Europe. Cerdá, for him, was the most outstanding planner of his day, rather than the isolated, anachronistic, and slightly warped genius that until recent years he was often understood to be.

Despite their differences, the contributions of Miller and Solà-Morales combined in suggesting to the conference that the theory of comprehensive urban planning was already fully developed in Spain by 1860. That the practice was defective, they both had to admit—indeed, the environment which had evolved in the new Barcelona by the end of the century made the point for them. However, not even the idea of early Spanish leadership in planning *theory* convinced everyone, and some of the muttered Italian reactions to Miller's ecstatic evocation of Cerdá's omniscience were particularly dismissive. Breitling, moreover, knows little and cares less about southern Europe and Calabi clearly identifies Germany, not Spain, as the main source of advanced planning ideas in Italy at the end of the century. The debate on extension planning has a long way to run and it would be premature to try to pronounce on it here. What it reveals, however, is the survival in planning historiography of distinct national attitudes which go back to the very origins of the movement.

The London conference was deliberately planned to recreate some of the atmosphere of the R.I.B.A.'s London Town Planning Conference of 1910. On that occasion, the various national contingents had combined in a great society of mutual admiration. As usual, the British had been dazzled by foreign poise, technical competence, and linguistic ability. The foreigners had been charmed by the British low-density residential planning which they encountered on pilgrimages to Hampstead, Letchworth and other landmarks. Overall, however, German *Städtebau* and the even more exciting brand of American planning represented by Burnham had most impressed the conference. In 1977, an uncanny re-enactment occurred. On the first evening Gerd Albers, addressing a plenary session on the course of German planning, generated much the same admiring reaction as did Joseph Stübben's brilliant lectures to foreign audiences before 1914[6]. Later, the conference was to hear from David Eversley and Stefan Muthesius, descendants of the planning pioneers, Rudolf Eberstadt and Hermann Muthesius, the former of whom had addressed the 1910 gathering. Throughout, a large German contingent made its mark on the proceedings, rivalling the massive American presence. In fact, only in the presence of an important Italian group did the composition of the 1977 conference differ greatly from that of 1910.

In this atmosphere, it was no surprise to observe a regeneration of Anglo-Saxon admiration for early German planning. Less predictable, however, was the renewed expression of the German sense of inferiority to Britain which had been so evident before 1914. Bollerey and Hartmann, for instance, not only explain much of the development of German planning in terms of an effort to emulate, and supplant, a British 'father-figure', but they themselves perpetuate an over-generous assessment of British achievements. Their assumption that the 1909 Act was both mandatory and applicable to entire urban areas is typical of the myths with which German planners drove one another to greater efforts before the First World War. Calabi's admiration of German planning also reflects attitudes prevalent in Italy during the period she describes. It is only in an international gathering that this almost universal tendency to deride domestic planning and view foreign practice through rose-tinted spectacles can be clearly revealed.

It would, however, be quite wrong to dwell on the appearance of perennial attitudes in these essays. They also indicate the penetration into planning history of interpretations and preoccupations developed in recent years in other branches of the historical sciences and urban studies. The great growth of housing history, through which planning's impact on ordinary people can perhaps be best assessed, is reflected in the contributions of Tarn and of Bollerey and Hartmann. The new American desire, sometimes known as 'presentism', to make history directly relevant to contemporary concerns, shines through Goldfield's work. The new, marxist planning history has clearly come to stay, and Britain and America will no doubt have to acknowledge it as fully as continental Europe already has. However, on the evidence presented here, great difficulties in this interpretation remain to be resolved. Ultimately, perhaps, it is the functionalist interpretation which emerges as the most stimulating. It is well represented here in Smith's measured, self-effacing discussion of Victorian urban renewal. In examining a hitherto neglected improvement programme over four decades, Smith is able to detect considerable continuity of aims, methods, and general mentality. Although he acknowledges certain elements of progress, he also finds elements of regression. The end-of-century attitude to slums and slum-dwellers was in some respects less understanding than that of the 1860s. Above all, Smith presents slum clearance as the product of a struggle with a constantly evolving urban organism rather than a novel and instantaneous solution to a problem generated in a specific period of urban growth. Admittedly, he is on the look-out for continuity, for, like Goldfield, he acknowledges the 'presentist' call. However, his methodology raises issues which all nineteenth-century urban historians would do well to consider, and which are not revealed by the more traditional British slum-clearance studies in which emphasis is laid on the expansion and refinement of powers through national legislation and accumulated local experience.

Different though her work might appear at first sight, Meller has much in common with Smith, apart from the Edinburgh connection. She stresses the continuity in Geddes's thinking between the 1860s and the First World War, and through into the 1920s. For her, there is no great Geddesian revolution in planning ideology. On the contrary, Geddes's constant striving to make himself understood reflected his lack of success in doing so. His contorted prose must partly have been the product of his efforts to convey a largely intuitive message. There is a very close parallel here with Le Corbusier, a later planning prophet who drew heavily on biological theories and who constantly resented what he felt to be his failure to secure understanding for his crucial message. No doubt both men's frustration sprang partly from their unrealistic and megalomaniac expectations of a world entirely remoulded by their single-handed efforts, but their own perception of their impact may well be more accurate than the great influence on ideas and events which we are often tempted to ascribe to them. They themselves were more aware than most of the unchanging or slowly evolving structures of society, impervious to the easy solutions of public administration.

The overall message of this volume, then, is one of continuity. Our attention is drawn to elements of 'planning' already present in the early nineteenth century, while the significance of the apparent planning 'progress' achieved around 1900 is questioned. Beneath the veneer of planning portrayed by the authors from an architectural background, Wilson, Tarn and Breitling, we can perceive fundamental and constraining social realities to which Calabi, and Bollerey and Hartmann, specifically draw our attention. All the contributors would agree, however, that planning had not yet gripped the city by 1914. Whether it would do so thereafter, and to what effect, will emerge from Volume 2 of this collection, on twentieth-century planning.

NOTES

1. Cuillier's paper has appeared as: Social organization of urban space, U.S.A. 1760–1820. *International Journal of Urban and Regional Research,* 2 (2), 1978.

The original, entitled 'Urban social planning and mobility: new forms of social order in the early nineteenth century city', has been deposited, together with all the other papers delivered at the First International Conference on the History of Urban and Regional Planning, in the British Lending Library, Boston Spa.

2. Reps' paper was published as part of his *Cities of the American West: A History of Frontier Urban Planning*. Princeton: Princeton University Press, 1979. Pressman's was entitled 'The Canada Company and urban settlement pattern in S.W. Ontario: the case of Goderich'.

3. For Mioni's views on nineteenth-century regional development in Italy, see his *Le trasformazioni territoriali in Italia nella prima età industriale*. Venice: Marsilio Editori, 1976.

4. A version of Costa's account has been published as: The evolution of planning styles and planned change: the example of Rome. *Journal of Urban History*, 3 (3), 1977, pp. 263–94.

5. The interpretation of Solà-Morales is fully developed in his *Los ensanches, (1): el ensanche de Barcelona*. Barcelona: Escuela Tecnica Superior de Arquitectura, 1978. Miller's somewhat divergent assessment can be studied in his: Ildefonso Cerdá: an introduction. *Architectural Association Quarterly*, 9 (1), 1977, pp. 12–22.

6. Albers's paper is published in Volume 2 of 'Planning and the Environment in the Modern World', edited by Gordon E. Cherry. It has appeared in German as: Wandel und Kontinuität im deutschen Städtebau. *Stadtbauwelt*, 69, 1978, pp. 426–33.

2

Planning for urban growth in the Old South

DAVID R. GOLDFIELD

Planning for growth has traditionally been one of the major responsibilities of city planners. There are two major elements in the growth question that planners must confront. First, there is the necessity of formulating and implementing policies designed to stimulate growth. Second, once growth is underway, planners must order and rationalize that growth so it does not overwhelm the city. Ideally, the control of growth will ensure an attractive environment that will, in turn, stimulate more growth. Unfortunately, planners in American cities today are faced with problems of decline, rather than of growth. Instead of working in an environment of abundance, they are confronted with scarcity. Questions of growth policy might seem interesting, but hardly relevant to contemporary urban problems. Yet, planners in some cities, refusing to accept decline as a permanent urban condition, have aggressively sought to expand their community's economic base, attract new taxpaying residents, and restore the vitality of downtown. Growth, in short, is the centrepiece in the urban planning process. It could be instructive, therefore, to analyse how nineteenth-century cities stimulated and ordered growth and to relate their efforts to modern-day planning policies.

The cities of the Old South provide an interesting framework within which to study growth policies for two reasons. First, the traditional image of the antebellum South as 'planter, plantation, staple crop, and the Negro, all set in a rural scene', dominated southern historiography until the mid-1970s[1]. Although there is little disagreement now that the Old South

11

did indeed possess cities worthy of the name, the next step is to analyse the process of urbanization in these communities to determine whether their somewhat exotic locale distinguishes them from urban counterparts in the North. Since the planning process is intimately connected with urbanization, it is a good vehicle with which to observe these differences, if, in fact, they exist. Second, urban growth in the Old South was viewed in the same apocalyptic light as was urban growth in contemporary north-eastern and mid-western cities. In the nineteenth century, the choice for American cities was either growth or oblivion. In the fierce rivalries for commerce— the major catalyst of growth—the winners went on to urban greatness: Chicago, Cincinnati, and New York, for example; and the losers had names like New Albany, Marietta, and Cairo. For southern cities of the period, growth assumed an even greater urgency. The South, locked in a bitter sectional struggle with the North, came to view urban growth as a means of attaining sectional economic independence. As the *Richmond Enquirer* predicted: 'building up Virginia's cities will save the South from an indelible brand of degradation'[2].

The analysis of urban growth planning in the Old South involves three elements. First, it is necessary to examine the planning process; that is, how policies are formulated and how they are translated into implementation. The personnel involved in the process is an obviously important consideration here. Second, it is important to examine the policies designed both to stimulate and to rationalize urban growth. Finally, the relative success or failure of these projects, both in terms of immediate local goals and the larger regional objectives, will be evaluated.

PLANNING PROCESS

The planning process in antebellum southern cities was a simple one. From formulation to implementation, a small group drawn from the commercial elite controlled the process. Although several different organizations and institutions became involved along the way, membership of these groups overlapped sufficiently to ensure a rough continuity from start to finish. Thus, the desire for a particular policy may have originated with some members of the board of trade (the antebellum predecessor of the chamber of commerce), then been discussed at a public meeting and in the local press, and then, if necessary, found its way to the city council which acted upon it. Virtually the same individuals were involved in all of these stages.

The phenomenon of ubiquity was the major characteristic of antebellum urban leadership in the United States. From the counting house to council chambers to churches, the urban elite formed an interlocking directorate. Their influence stemmed not only from their ubiquity, but from a wide range of shared characteristics. Studies of elites in Poughkeepsie,

Philadelphia and Cincinnati, among others, have demonstrated that these men possessed the proverbial stake in the community. They had resided in the city for quite some time; their persistence rates being considerably higher than those of the general urban population. These were men of property who not only owned their own homes but several town lots as well. They lived comfortably, but were not necessarily the wealthiest members of their community. The leaders were family men with children and usually one or two boarders in the household; either a servant or a relative. Finally, these men were invariably native born and Protestant in religion[3].

Southern urban leaders apparently shared these characteristics. My own study of Virginia cities indicates a similarity with the northern profile in all areas, with three relatively minor differences. First, there was a higher percentage of native-born leaders in urban Virginia. This is under-standable since European immigration was much smaller to the South than to the North. Second, Virginia's elite was more overwhelmingly mercantile than its northern counterparts, who counted a few industrialists and financiers among their number. In almost all antebellum cities, however, the economic base was predominately commercial, so this was a difference more of degree than of kind. Finally, the gap between the leaders and the rest of the population was not as pronounced in Virginia cities as in the larger northern metropoli. Property holding was remarkably widespread, with more than forty per cent of the white householders in Richmond, for example, possessing some form of real property: a figure more than four times that of most northern cities. This may be due, in part, to the fact that the vast accumulations of wealth characteristic of the larger northern cities were absent in the less developed South[4].

Despite these differences, the most important aspect of antebellum leadership—ubiquity—was maintained in southern cities. Examples of two southern businessmen typify the range of activities common to the urban elite of that era. James Robb arrived penniless in New Orleans from Pennsylvania in the 1830s. Within a decade of his arrival Robb was a prominent banker and a respected member of local government. He was Louisiana's most prominent railroad promoter in the 1850s. Joseph R. Anderson, born into a yeoman farmer family on the western Virginia frontier, became a leading southern industrialist. By the time he was forty years old Anderson was operating the Tredegar Iron Works in Richmond, directing a major bank in that city, promoting several railroad and canal schemes, serving on the city council, and travelling throughout the South pressing for improved rail connections between southern cities[5].

The broad interests of urban leaders meant, among other things, that they were in frequent contact with one another: on the street, in the commodity exchanges, at social events, and in church. Comprising about one per cent of a city's householders, the elite moved in a fairly tight circle in their communities. Not surprisingly, this propinquity generated a general consensus about the city and helped to speed policies toward implementation. This is not to say that conflict was foreign to the planning process. Merchants adopted different positions from manufacturers, and rival railroad interests clashed at times. When the ward system of representation became predominant in southern cities during the 1840s and 1850s a further divisive element entered the process as councilmen now represented specific constituencies rather than the city as a whole. Despite these differences, however, there was a general commitment to urban growth, even if there were occasional differences as to how to achieve that objective.

The planning process, in addition to being dominated at all stages by a small group of men, was a closed process as well. Citizen participation, a phrase that evokes strong allegiance in planning circles today, was unheard of a century ago. The leaders did not perceive the exclusivity of the process, however. As Michael Frisch has demonstrated in a penetrating study of nineteenth-century Springfield, Massachusetts, and as Carol Hoffecker argued in a similarly incisive analysis of Wilmington, Delaware, during the same period, businessmen genuinely believed that adherence to the interests of merchants in the commercial city benefited all. The entrepreneur was public opinion and public consensus[6].

The fact that the entrepreneur was the most important element in his city's growth reinforced his identification with the city. In the intense competition which marked the pursuit of trade in antebellum America, the role of the urban leader often determined the difference between success and also-ran. As geographer Peter Goheen has observed: 'Behind every successful city lies at least one enterprising entrepreneur'[7]. Historians have amply documented this dictum in their studies of northern cities before the Civil War. The aggressiveness of New York merchants in pursuing European and western commercial connections was legendary. Similarly, the policies of Chicago's leaders designed to make that city a prominent railroad centre ensured victory over rivals Cincinnati and St. Louis. Leaders in the latter cities were more divided, more complacent, and confined their activities to broadsides in the press[8].

The importance of entrepreneurial skill is equally evident, though less well known, in southern cities. With the notable exception of James Robb, the New Orleans elite was content to rely on the river rather than construct railroads to expand its commerce. As a consequence, the Crescent City's share of the western trade began to decline in the 1850s as northern railroads became attractive conveyances for western produce. Houston merchants, on the other hand, perceived the value of rail connections and outduelled better-situated Galveston for commercial supremacy in the Gulf region. The elite in the latter city was more concerned about erecting gaudy mansions along the waterfront than in searching for new trade opportunities. Finally, Richmond boosters transcended their shallow port facilities and transformed the city on the James into an export centre for the

South American trade. Neighbouring Norfolk, however, with the finest natural harbour south of New York, languished as an export facility. As these examples demonstrate, entrepreneurial skill was capable of surmounting the disadvantages of location, while in the absence of initiative natural advantages were insufficient to sustain power in the long run[9].

Given that the leaders dominated the planning process and that their activities within this process were vital to the city's future, the policies they chose take on added significance. These plans, in effect, were blueprints for growth. In the case of the southern city, these plans not only had local impact but regional implications as well.

PLANS

Since commerce was essential to urban growth, leaders naturally emphasized the means to secure that commerce in their plans. New York's Erie Canal had demonstrated that the development of transportation links to the hinterland was the most effective means of stimulating urban growth. By the 1830s the railroad was supplanting the canal as the favourite means to that end. Indeed, urban boosters quickly related growth with railroads and often stressed reciprocal benefits to both city and country:

> Railroads ... are necessary to farming communities in creating a value for their products, in opening a market for them. They explain the rapid growth of cities that are the *termini* of a large number of railroads.[10]

Southern leaders took these precepts to heart and, beginning in Charleston, South Carolina, in 1833, launched railroad building programmes. Though major trunk lines to the West were the ultimate dream of these boosters, limitations of capital and technology kept their early efforts mostly short affairs into the immediate hinterland. By the 1850s, however, urban leaders throughout the region began pushing for longer and more ambitious railroads. The objective was still urban growth but by then other considerations were evident in implementing these schemes. As the Virginia urban booster, William M. Burwell, wrote in 1852, railroads 'will result in the rapid increase of our cities ... and the South will be restored to her former position in the Union'[11]. The New Orleans urban leader, J. D. B. De Bow, predicted that with efficacious rail lines, New Orleans and Norfolk could command two-thirds of the nation's trade and ensure southern economic independence[12].

Southern urban leaders realized, however, that railroads alone could not stimulate growth. Wise economic planning required rail lines to interface with other economic activities to make the railroad an effective commercial carrier. The generation of an export trade meant that produce collected by railroads would not rot at urban railroad depots. While New Orleans and Mobile exported a portion of their cotton receipts directly to Europe, the South Atlantic ports shipped the overwhelming majority of their produce to northern ports for further distribution. It was evident to leaders in these southern cities that direct trade was a high priority in their growth planning and in Savannah, Charleston, Norfolk, and Richmond they sought to implement such a policy. Once again, regional motives were evident as well. 'By showing our determination and ability to conduct our own foreign trade', a Portsmouth, Virginia, leader reasoned in 1850, 'we shall soon lessen the existing disparity between the northern and southern sections of the country'[13].

The encouragement of manufacturing was another programme designed to maximize the impact of the railroad. Industrial buyers offered farmers good prices for their produce. Heavy industry such as iron, glass, and agricultural machinery would enable the railroad to develop a two-way commerce: from the farm to the city, and from the city to the farm. This reciprocal traffic was beneficial to the city and essential to the financial well-being of the railroad. Accordingly, urban leaders sought to encourage investments in manufacturing firms. Unlike the funding of railroads, which came primarily from the cities, and state governments as well, industrial investment was strictly a private affair. Much of the industry that was established in southern cities after 1830 related to the processing of agricultural commodities. This reflected not only the agricultural nature of the region, but also the fact that some of the most prolific investors in urban industries were farmers.

Urban leaders sought industrial development with the same two objectives that framed other economic plans. First, industry stimulated urban growth. 'A large industrial class', the Norfolk *Southern Argus* claimed in the 1850s, 'is the greatest builder-up of a prosperous city'. Second, local industry was a regional weapon in the growing sectional confrontation with the North. A Mobile journal declared that domestic manufacturing was 'the only safe and effectual remedy against Northern oppression', while a Richmond resident observed in 1851: 'No people are independent who are compelled to rely upon others for industry'[14].

The construction of railroads, the encouragement of direct trade, and the development of industry were grand plans to be sure. The urban leaders understood, however, that the increased economic activity generated by even a partial fulfilment of these programmes required rationalization in the city itself. In order for growth to be sustained, the city must be an efficient and attractive place in which to do business.

The plans for ordering the city typically emanated from the board of trade. At times, the planning process began and ended there. For more extensive projects, however, cooperation of the public sector was necessary, so leaders carefully guided their plans through that phase of the planning process. The primary function of the board was to ensure efficiency in the operation of the local economy. First the board regulated prices and established standards of quality for country produce. Competition was inefficient and often led to waste and conflict. By establishing prices and commission rates, the merchants protected themselves and eliminated price wars and corner-cutting that created chaos in the business community. By insisting on uniform inspection of produce to establish quality, the merchants protected their reputations in other cities. Cities that had established inspection systems were preferred by both domestic and foreign merchants. The board also functioned as a clearing house for information on markets and prices. The collection of accurate data, essential in any planning operation, affected business decisions. Domestic and foreign bond markets determined propitious moments to float bond issues for transportation systems. Commodity prices in other cities led to price modifications to remain competitive. Communities boasted high prices to the farmers and low prices to the hinterland merchants. If a city was outbid, it lost business. The adjustment in prices might trigger a change in freight, commission, and interest rates as well. All of these activities were dependent upon the receipt of accurate price data in a central location, accessible to the urban decision-makers[15].

The projection of a positive urban image was of great concern to board members. Visiting merchants and farmers often could not distinguish between a commodity and a stock exchange, but were impressed— favourably or unfavourably—by the conditions of the markets, the comfort of the hotels, and the general appearance of the city. The market place or square, where city and country met, was an important showcase for urban merchants. The Richmond Board of Trade, for example, successfully persuaded the city council to appropriate $3000 to refurbish market stalls in order 'to better accommodate buyers and sellers'[16]. Southern cities were proud of their hotels and hospitality. If produce deserved clean and modern accommodation, so did the people whose livelihood depended on the profitable exchange of produce. Visitors always compared accommodation in various cities. Travellers in Charleston admired the Mills House as 'a noble palace of an hotel', the 'best house' in the United States, and as 'much better ordered than Willard's at Washington'. Richmond's Exchange Hotel, remodelled in the 1840s to accommodate the city's renewed prosperity, was widely known for its well-appointed rooms, fine fare, and courteous service. Its French chandeliers and English broadlooms rivalled, according to contemporaries, New York's famous Astor House[17]. Yet, urban leaders were not content to point to the one magnificent hotel in their city. Savannah's elite boasted of the Screven House but regretted the absence of other comfortable accommodation. The Richmond Board of Trade, pleased with the reputation of the Exchange Hotel, was nonetheless unhappy with the city's other hotel facilities. In 1857, the members chartered a hotel company and raised $200,000 for the new building, 'so that our customers have the best accommodations that can be afforded'[18].

Southern urban leaders hoped to make the visitor's stay outside his hotel quarters equally as comfortable. As cities grew, leaders planned to systematize getting about the city. Directories appeared as a businessman's guide to other businessmen. In addition to names and addresses, city directories often displayed a list of the social and commercial organizations of the city as well as a list of hotels and newspapers—items that a visitor would find useful[19]. As a further aid, urban merchants led the movement to number the cities' houses and commercial establishments. The city familiar gave way to the city efficient.

Ordering the city was expensive. With the rapid increase in investment opportunities and the large capital outlays for hotels and market houses, private sources of capital were insufficient to implement all of the plans required to generate an efficient and attractive image. Local government, little more than a cipher early in the nineteenth century, came to exercise an increasing role in the planning process as urban leaders recognized its potential for collecting and disbursing revenues. The projects undertaken by local government invariably originated at board meetings—a fact which gave government policies a decided business orientation.

An array of urban services developed, initially planned by the board, but implemented by the city council. Gas lighting was one example of the close cooperation between the public and private sectors in planning for urban services. When Baltimore became the first American city to provide gas light for its streets in 1818, it did so by setting up a public utility. Funding came directly from council appropriations, and administrators of the gasworks received their instructions from the city council. The city connected gas outlets upon the request and prepayment of individuals desiring the service. New Orleans was more typical of southern cities when, in 1835, officials awarded a franchise to the New Orleans Gas Lighting and Banking Company headed by the theatre entrepreneur, James H. Caldwell, who later received a similar franchise for Mobile. The city usually erected and maintained lighting fixtures in the street at public expense. Whatever the arrangement adopted, gas lighting was as important as a fine hotel. 'The mere fact that a town is lit with gas', intoned the *Lynchburg Virginian*, 'is an assurance to a stranger that there is an intelligent, enterprising, and thrifty people, that understands and appreciates the blessings of a well-organized government ... It is a passport to public confidence and respect, a card to be admitted into the family of well-regulated cities'[20].

Passable thoroughfares were another requisite for entrance into 'the family of well-regulated cities'. The condition of most urban streets throughout the early nineteenth century was a frequent target of derision and disgust for foreign visitors. A popular story of the period told of a man neck-deep in mud who, when asked if he needed some help in negotiating the soggy terrain, replied 'No; but the horse I'm riding sure could'. Yet, streets were serious business to local planners, as one Alexandria journal noted: 'There are few things which operate against a city more than bad streets, and especially when they are the principal ones'[21]. Here again, the public and private sectors were partners in the planning process. The city charged private property-owners for paving streets, while the city provided the labour and materials. Alexandria, in paving its major thoroughfare, King Street, levied a special tax on property owners fronting the street at a rate of $1.25 to $1.30 per front foot depending on value and issued $8000 worth of corporate bonds. The total cost of the project was $13,000. For such major projects, cities expected abutting property owners to pay for only a portion of the paving cost[22].

An unpaved avenue was a visible problem with the remedy relatively simple, if somewhat expensive. Disease, however, was an unseen enemy whose cure baffled physicians in antebellum America. Preventive measures included quarantine and street cleaning, but these remedies were applied haphazardly because of their expense and because implementation did not guarantee health. Savannah officials, for example, spent $200,000 to drain marshy areas around the city, yet yellow fever frequented that city as often and with as much severity as in other southern cities that did not go through that trouble and expense. The only defence against epidemic disease that local leaders generally felt capable of mustering was to organize local government and the press (usually controlled by an urban leader) to issue denials of the presence of an epidemic and to reassure rural customers that their market city was indeed a healthy place. If word of an epidemic leaked out, official statements were quick to point out that the disease was confined to those individuals who were not acclimatized to the rigours of southern summers. This elaborate public relations campaign was essential because disease, in economic terms, took a frightful toll. New Orleans, for example, lost $45.4 million in commerce between 1846 and 1850 as the result of an epidemic[23].

Crime and fire were two other unpleasant consequences of urban growth that urban leaders confronted in the late antebellum years. Local government in southern cities gradually assumed greater control over fire regulations and firefighting. Wooden buildings were prohibited in crowded districts and the volunteer companies that often fought each other with more gusto than they battled fires were placed under the supervision of a city official, appointed by the city council for that purpose[24].

Crime, especially against property, advanced with prosperity. As with fire prevention, local government began to assume a greater role in law enforcement, though the individual citizen was very much the first line of defence. The haphazard night watch gave way to more systematized, uniformed personnel in Charleston and Richmond though a significant abatement of crime was not apparent. Local newspapers, for their part, adopted the same public relations technique that they had employed in connection with epidemics. A safe city was, by definition, an efficient and attractive environment[25].

The business orientation of the urban elite did not cause it to ignore some of the more aesthetic aspects of growth planning. The city beautiful in fact could enhance the urban image so assiduously cultivated by boosters. The southern city, after all, could not appear to be so devoted to business that the physical city would have no more charm than, say, an old brick exchange building. Besides, growth was overtaking the open spaces in southern cities. As the popularity of parks and other rural amenities manifested itself in the North, southern urban leaders developed plans to protect and enlarge their open spaces. A Norfolk newspaper registered a common concern when it observed:

> In Norfolk we have sadly neglected to promote those public improvements which take the shape of verdant interspaces in the midst of population ... The city would be wise to purchase appropriate areas like New York's Central Park or Boston's Common. A few years hence will see our places of recreation closed up by masses of brick and mortar.[26]

The planting and maintenance of trees was a typical first step in environmental planning. Savannah leaders enhanced what ordinarily would have been a monotonous gridiron street plan by lining its long streets with trees. On the widest streets, the city also planted trees down the middle of the thoroughfare. As early as 1807, the local government appointed a Superintendent of Trees and during the next three years appropriated more than $1000 for planting trees—but only in the public squares and along the two major streets. The city catered for pedestrian traffic by lacing the squares with walks and providing benches for tired strollers[27]. Eventually, the leaders completed their environmental plan by creating a park on the outskirts of the city. By the 1850s, the years of care had produced a lovely environment for the enjoyment of visitors: 'Savannah is a city of trees and gardens. It reminds me of what William Penn wished that his beloved Philadelphia might be—"a green garden town" '[28]. Other cities equally concerned with their appearance to visitors initiated tree-planting programmes and planned parks. Natchez underwrote a tree nursery from the beginning of the nineteenth century. In addition, the city urged residents to plant and to cultivate chinaberry trees in order to 'contribute as well to the health as to the beauty of the city'. Alexandria rejoiced in its efforts at tree planting by observing that 'strangers and visitors to our town notice the improved appearance of many of our streets in consequence of the beautiful shade trees that have ... been planted along the sidewalks'. Trees and parks, like hotels and market stalls, enhanced the urban image and made the city a more pleasant environment in which to do business[29].

The plans designed by southern urban leaders were comprehensive, ranging from inter-regional transportation systems to tree-planting campaigns. These programmes would stimulate, control, and sustain urban growth, while helping the southern region to a degree of economic and political independence. The success or failure of the plans, then, must be measured against these objectives.

Southern cities generally had reached a high point of prosperity by 1860. In terms of sheer population growth, some of the figures were impressive; older cities like New Orleans and Savannah had increased their populations by 45 per cent during the 1850s, while relatively new Memphis had registered a gain of 155 per cent. Fledgling cities like Atlanta and Houston promised great advances in the future urban South. All told, the urban population of the South increased by three and a half times the total southern population increase in the first half of the nineteenth century, compared with the northern urban growth rate of two and a half times the entire northern population[30]. But population statistics reveal only one aspect of urban growth in the Old South. Southern cities invested heavily in railroads. Virginia's effort was especially noteworthy. In 1847, the Old Dominion possessed six railroads and 270 miles of track, ranking her seventh in the nation in railroad mileage. By 1858 the number of railroad companies had increased to nineteen and the length of open track to 1321 miles, placing Virginia third in the country behind only New York and Pennsylvania[31].

There were also some successes in stimulating direct export trade and manufacturing. Savannah established a lucrative lumber commerce with several Caribbean islands. By 1860 Richmond exports to South American ports exceeded those of any other United States port, including New York. Richmond also had become, by that date, the South's most diversified industrial centre. The capital of Virginia manufactured more tobacco than any other city in the world by 1860 and was among the nation's leading flour-milling centres. In addition to the processing industries, the Tredegar and Belle Isle iron foundries established Richmond as the South's heavy industrial centre. Georgia cities, not to be outdone, invested in textile mills. By 1848 there were thirty-two mills in urban Georgia, with over one-third of the manufactured product finding markets outside the state. By the mid-1850s J. D. B. De Bow was referring to Georgia as the 'Empire State of the South'. Augusta was the state's foremost textile centre, though Columbus became a serious rival in the late 1840s. A new cotton factory erected in the latter city in 1845 caused one urban booster to exclaim: 'Columbus will, if not compare advantageously with Lowell, at least have begun the good work'. By 1851 citizens had invested nearly $1,000,000 in local textile industries[32].

All of this activity was bound to have a significant impact on the southern city itself, as the policies discussed earlier implied. In physical terms alone, the alteration was impressive. A visitor returning to a southern city after a ten-year absence would scarcely recognize the place. The open spaces, crevices, and even farms were gone. Venerable Richmond chronicler Samuel Mordecai observed in 1860 that 'a few years ago ... the city was all hills, valleys, and deep ravines'. Progress had removed most of these 'barriers to man and horse', and houses and stores had replaced the wilderness[33]. In addition to the new houses and stores, fine hotels, commodity exchanges, market houses, and railroad depots transformed land use in the central business district. In fact, for the first time an identifiable business district emerged as residences pushed outward toward the periphery. Suburbs appeared, mainly as the location of cheap housing[34]. The necessity of directories, house numbers, and the ward system of representation underscored this physical growth. In terms of urban services, southern cities advanced to modernity. To be without a water system or gas lighting was clearly an indication of 'old fogyism', in the vernacular of the times. Moreover, local government extended paved streets, and health, fire, and police services to their citizens. The southern city even attempted to maintain its leisurely ambience by initiating environmental planning.

Perhaps most important, southern cities developed an urban consciousness, a feeling that the city was a distinct environment with distinct needs. The plans for growth had broken the insularity of southern cities. The southern city was a part of the modern urban nation. Innovations in services or in commercial procedures originating in other cities were avidly duplicated by southern urban leaders. Information via the press and periodical literature flowed freely between cities regardless of region. Thus, a commonality of interests developed among cities which set them apart from their rural brethren. Though southern urban leaders carefully cultivated rural investment, customers, and produce, a growing intellectual estrangement was evident. Commodity exchanges dampened competition and therefore lessened the farmers' choices; urban leaders believed that a revised tax structure favouring merchants rather than farmers should be the cornerstone of state tax policy; and free trade became anathema to emerging southern industrialists, while it was an article of faith among agriculturalists. Stereotypes evolved reflecting the divergence between rural and urban. In 1851, the *Richmond Enquirer* noted 'a wide distinction between the people of Richmond and the people of the country'. Virginia farmer John Randolph Tucker pinpointed one element of distinction in a letter to an aspiring politician: 'If Politics be your object, flee a city, the most tainted and corrupted air for pure political aspirations'. The editor of a Richmond daily, himself a prominent member of that city's elite, retorted by agreeing that 'there is a great amount of vice in cities, but only because there is a great amount of humanity. The country is not without vice.

There's probably more scandal and gossipping in a small town in twenty-four hours than there has been in London or New York for the last one-hundred years'[35]. This banter demonstrates not only a sense of urban identity but of civic pride as well. Each day in the press or at board meetings, the city's image was an influence on policy. The physical improvements evident in the city were brick and mortar testimonials to this pride.

By all measures, quantitative or qualitative, it was apparent that the leaders' plans for growth had in fact produced growth. The costs involved, however, both monetary and social, were significant. As the list of urban services grew and the local government participation in these services increased accordingly, the expense of rationalizing urban growth became more onerous. In addition, the burdens of maintaining adequate service levels occurred at a time when city governments had plunged heavily into railroad investments. Of the $2,000,000 debt hanging over Richmond in 1857, $1,266,000 resulted from internal improvement expenditures[36]. Progress was one thing, but bankruptcy was quite another, so southern cities groped for solutions to a problem of urban modernity.

The solutions proposed by civic leaders revealed the planning theory behind all of their plans for urban growth: what benefited business, benefited the city. Not surprisingly, local government sought to lower the property tax while maintaining the level of services. In a time of economic distress this fiscal sleight of hand was accomplished through various means. Savannah officials proposed to close the resulting revenue gap by levying an income tax on its residents in 1841. The public outcry forced the council to repeal the tax. Alexandria officials were more successful as they lowered the property tax in 1855 while increasing the capitation tax on white male inhabitants. Irate citizens in Lynchburg, however, forced their government to retract its entire tax package—a package that reduced merchant's taxes by forty per cent and increased the income tax by one-half of one per cent[37].

The growing citizen unrest at their exclusion from the planning process extended beyond tax policy to the urban services themselves. Despite the leaders' extravagance with respect to railroads, a crude, but very strict cost-benefit formula guided expenditures for services. The benefits of a particular service to the city must exceed the costs to the leadership in terms of increased taxes. Since the leaders perceived their interests and the city's interests as identical it was evident that the implementation of some services would be selective. Street lighting, for example, rarely went beyond the business district and only the major thoroughfares of the community were paved and maintained. Because these services, in most southern cities, depended on the benefit assessment of property-holders, the poorer districts of the community went without them. Further, since few visitors ventured beyond the business district it was sufficient to present that area as a showcase while neglecting the rest of the city.

A similar logic pervaded the other urban services. The increased efficiency of fire protection was confined to the business district. It was unlikely that firemen would converge on a burning residence far removed from downtown. Local businessmen more than likely paid for fire equipment and refreshments, so the stimulus to protect business property was greater than for other structures. Similarly, police protection was generally absent in the poorer sections of town. Since the violent brawls that frequently characterized life in these parts rarely spilled over into 'better' areas, it seemed unnecessary to invest in a comprehensive, professional force. In terms of health planning, the cost-benefit calculation was even more obvious. Leaders viewed quarantine as a restraint on trade. Hence, the one preventive measure that might have resulted in some success was implemented only during times of severe public pressure. As one disgusted New Orleans health reformer complained in 1854: 'The leading idea has always been convenience for commerce'[38]. So it was with garbage collection. When the Alexandria city council instituted a garbage collection system in the 1850s it soon became evident that pick-ups were limited. One resident scoffed at this charade: 'What a humbug is the "Garbage Cart" law! In some parts of the city, the garbage cart never goes— never has gone'[39]. The southern city's performance on health was so spotty that residents in some cities successfully appealed to the state legislature to impose health planning on the city[40].

The financial and social inequities mitigated the successes of growth policy, though growth certainly occurred. Achieving the objective of regional independence, however, was an outright failure. The frustrating aspect of the failure was that the southern city had attained so much, yet it was more dependent on northern cities than ever before. Southern urban leaders, in bringing their cities into the national urban network, had, in effect, sealed their dependent status. The economic heart of that network was at New York. The more trade secured by southern cities, the greater the volume of traffic with northern cities. Southern railroads and shipping lanes became funnels to northern cities. The European direct trade connection remained elusive. As one southern entrepreneur lamented: 'We are mere way stations to Philadelphia, New York, and Boston'[41]. Even the mouth of the Mississippi 'practically and commercially [was] more at New York and Boston than at New Orleans'. New York's economic planners were earlier and more aggressive than the leaders of other cities. As the leader of the 'Business Revolution' New York contained the services, railroad connections, and organizations to outbid rivals. The city even had Central Park[42].

Southern urban leaders (and a number of northern boosters as well) were simply not fast enough. Even had they been at New York's heels, however, it is doubtful whether regional independence would have occurred. An interdependent national economy was emerging which drew all regions closer together. Isolation might have been achieved, but only by eschewing growth and therefore ensuring stagnation. It was no coincidence that the development of a national economy and the growth of southern cities occurred simultaneously.

CONCLUSIONS

The analysis of urban growth planning in the Old South began with a reference to the attempt of present-day American cities to reverse their decline through aggressive growth policies. Although historical analogy has limitations as an analytical tool, it is at least interesting, if not instructive, to relate the findings from this study to more contemporary urban planning endeavours.

The first principle that can be discerned from the analysis of southern urban growth planning is the dominance of the business viewpoint in planning theory and practice. This is not surprising considering the individuals who participated in the planning process—resident businessmen who were leaders of numerous community activities. The close connection between planning and business continued into the twentieth century and has been under serious attack for at least the last two decades. As planner Frances Fox Piven observed recently: 'Our past failures are due to the subservience of the planning profession to dominant economic and political interests'[43]. Southern urban leaders might have reminded her, however, that a good deal of their planning success rested on the principle of serving business interests. Indeed, there seems to be a reawakening interest in business as a planning partner in American cities today. Planners are tapping the resources of the financial community for neighbourhood redevelopment projects and are looking to downtown merchants to help restore a measure of vitality to the city's economic base. There is now, of course, no unitary interest between planner and businessman, though the former appreciates the financial resources and expertise of the latter. Business leaders, for their part, are forming merchants' associations, working through the chamber of commerce, and organizing their colleagues in much the same manner as their nineteenth-century forebears. Associations remain an effective mechanism for formulating, if not implementing, plans for growth[44].

The second principle, closely related to the first, involves the exclusive planning process in nineteenth-century southern cities. The process was confined to a tight-knit group of leaders. Plan implementation reflected their parochial interests, although they claimed to represent the entire community. Citizen participation is an essential part of contemporary planning efforts. Federal legislation has made citizen involvement mandatory in certain cases. Planners and decision-makers, however, continue to apply policies selectively. In the 1950s and 1960s local implementation of federal plans concentrated on the worst areas of the city, with mixed results at best. Since the passage of the federal Community Development Act in 1974, the selection process has shifted to more stable areas of the city. The watchword is now conservation rather than renewal. There seems to be a growing realization that planners cannot rebuild cities from the bottom up, but must concentrate on the more salvageable areas of the city. With the renewed emphasis on growth, urban downtowns and stable neighbourhoods are the target of local plans.

The contemporary situation is analogous to the selective application of urban services in the Old South. The civic leaders of that era felt that the extension of certain services beyond the business district and some of the more affluent residential areas was not remunerative. That is, such extensions would not lead to urban growth but would, on the other hand, increase the financial burden of the propertied. While few planners today would espouse such wholesale neglect, there is a temptation to abandon the perennial failures for newer, more showy, and more reliable projects that can increase the tax base and enhance the city's image. The current fascination with downtown shopping malls is an example of this trend.

A final principle of nineteenth-century growth planning relates to the interdependence of the southern city with its region and with the national urban system. The plans formulated by urban leaders were economically sound: an economic infrastructure designed to expand an export economy, and the creation of an efficient and attractive city. Predictably, growth occurred, but in a national context, the urban South became inextricably bound to northern urban centres as the price of its growth. In that sense, the southern city's economic achievements were and would be circumscribed by its secondary position within the national economy, regardless of local growth policies. The interdependence of cities and nation is as strong, if not stronger, today. Policies designed to stimulate urban growth can in consequence be submerged because of lack of regional or federal co-operation. Urban leaders in the Old South depended a great deal upon the investments, patronage, and good will of individuals living in the immediate hinterland. Improvement in regional relations today would not only ease urban burdens in such areas as housing and transportation, but would relieve, to some extent, increasingly strained suburban budgets. The national economy a century ago was a lopsided mechanism with economic power centred in New York. The federal government, at that time, lacked the precedent to ensure a more even distribution of national wealth. Today, ironically, the national economy, though more diffuse, increasingly gravitates to southern cities. The older cities of the Northeast and Midwest send more in taxes to Washington than they receive in federal expenditures. If these cities are to experience a renaissance, the federal government should modify its current disbursement programme.

Clearly, there are no easy solutions for American cities today. While southern cities grew, the benefits of this growth were not shared by the entire urban population. Further, a national economy limited and defined the extent and nature of southern urban growth. Planners in today's cities are seeking to stimulate economic growth with equity while urging federal law-makers to maintain an equilibrium in the national economy. The fulfilment of these three objectives—economic growth, equity, and a national economic equilibrium—simultaneously, appears unlikely. It is evident that priorities must be established. If disinvestment is 'the key problem of the city' according to one prominent planning educator, then economic growth should remain a high priority objective or else the city will become a repository for the 'useless and the hopeless', as Herbert Gans has warned. Without growth, in short, there can be no equity, nor will there be any need for equilibrium[45].

NOTES

1. Smiley, David L. (1972) The quest for a central theme in southern history. *Southern Atlantic Quarterly,* **62**, pp. 307–25.
2. *Richmond Enquirer,* February 27, 1854.
3. See Glazer, Walter S. (1972) Participation and power: voluntary association and the functional organization of Cincinnati in 1840. *Historical Methods Newsletter,* **5**, pp. 151–68; Griffen, Clyde (1972) Occupational mobility in nineteenth-century America. *Journal of Social History,* **5**, pp. 310–30; Pessen, Edward (1972) Who governed the nation's cities in the era of the common man? *Political Science Quarterly,* **87**, pp. 591–614.
4. Goldfield, David R. (1977) *Urban Growth in the Age of Sectionalism: Virginia, 1847–1861.* Baton Rouge: Louisiana State University Press, chapter 2.
5. Reed, Merl E. (1966) *New Orleans and the Railroads: The Struggle for Commercial Empire.* Baton Rouge: Louisiana State University Press, pp. 81–3; French, S. Bassett, 'Biographical sketches', MSS, 160, Virginia State Library.
6. Frisch, Michael H. (1972) *Town into City: Springfield, Massachusetts and the Meaning of Community, 1840–1880.* Cambridge, Mass.: Harvard University Press; Hoffecker, Carol E. (1974) *Wilmington, Delaware: Portrait of an Industrial City, 1830–1910.* Charlottesville: University Press of Virginia.
7. Goheen, Peter G. (1971) Industrialization and the growth of cities in nineteenth-century America. *American Studies,* **14**, pp. 49–65.
8. See Albion, Robert G. (1939) *The Rise of New York Port, 1815–1860.* New York: C. Scribner's Sons; Abbott, Carl (1976) Planning in the Old Northwest, presented at Southern Historical Association Convention, Atlanta, Georgia, November 12, 1976.
9. See Schmidt, Louis B. (1939) Internal commerce and the development of the national economy before 1860. *Journal of Political Economy,* **47**, pp. 798–822; Wheeler, Kenneth W. (1968) *To Wear a City's Crown: The Beginnings of Urban Growth in Texas.* Cambridge, Mass.: Harvard University Press; Goldfield, David R. (1977) *Urban Growth in the Age of Sectionalism: Virginia, 1847–1861.* Baton Rouge: Louisiana State University Press, chapter 6.

28   THE RISE OF MODERN URBAN PLANNING

10. Fitzhugh, George (1854) *Sociology for the South, or, The Failure of Free Society.* New York, pp. 141–2.
11. Burwell, William M. (1852) Virginia Commercial Convention. *De Bow's Review*, 12, p. 30.
12. Contests for the trade of the Mississippi Valley. *De Bow's Review*, 3, 1847, pp. 98–108.
13. Portsmouth (Va.) *Daily Pilot*, July 8, 1850; see also Foreign trade of Virginia and the South. *De Bow's Review*, 13, 1852, pp. 493–503.
14. Norfolk *Southern Argus*, September 20, 1851; *Mobile Register*, quoted in Miller, Randall (1972) Daniel Pratt's industrial urbanism: the cotton mill town in antebellum Alabama. *Alabama Historical Quarterly*, 34, p. 7; *Richmond Enquirer*, December 17, 1850.
15. See *Richmond Enquirer*, June 9, 1854; Wheeling *Daily Intelligencer*, March 2, 1860.
16. Richmond *Daily Dispatch*, June 15, 1855.
17. Quoted in Steen, Ivan D., Charleston in the 1850s: as described by British travellers. *South Carolina Historical Magazine*, 36; Irby, Richard, Recollection of men, places, and events, 1845–1900, Richard Irby MSS, Alderman Library, University of Virginia, n.p.
18. Richmond *Daily Dispatch*, March 18, 1857.
19. See Butters, James (1855) *Butters' Richmond Directory 1855*. Richmond; Montague, William L. (1852) *Richmond Directory and Business Advertiser for 1852*. Baltimore, introduction.
20. Eaton, Clement (1961) *The Growth of Southern Civilization, 1790–1860*. New York: Harper, pp. 257-8; *Lynchburg Virginian*, April 21, 1851.
21. *Alexandria Gazette*, January 26, 1858.
22. *Ibid.,* March 8, 1859.
23. Goldfield, David R. (1976) The business of health planning: disease prevention in the Old South. *Journal of Southern History*, 42, pp. 557–70.
24. See Mobile: its past and present. *De Bow's Review*, 28, 1860, p. 305; Commercial and industrial cities of the United States: Richmond, Virginia. *Hunt's Merchants Magazine and Commercial Review*, 40, 1859, pp. 61-2.
25. See *Alexandria Gazette*, June 8, 1854; December 5, 1854; March 29, 1855; March 11, 1858.
26. Norfolk *Southern Argus*, December 4, 1852.
27. The cities of Georgia—Savannah. *De Bow's Review*, 28, pp. 20–8; Teaford, Jon C. (1975) *The Municipal Revolution in America*. Chicago: Chicago University Press, p. 107.
28. Pyle, Curtis B. (1853) Letters from the South. By our Corresponding Editor. *Masonic Mirror and American Keystone*, 2, April 6–May 25, 1853, pp. 115, 125–6, 171, in Schwaab, Eugene L. (ed.),*Travels in the Old South*. Lexington: University Press of Kentucky, 1973, vol. 2, p. 527.
29. Quoted in James, D. Clayton (1968) *Antebellum Natchez*. Baton Rouge: Louisiana State University Press, p. 83; *Alexandria Gazette*, May 21, 1851.
30. Statistical references helpful to studies of the urban South include the U.S. Bureau of the Census, *Compendium of the Census* (1850 to 1870 for the antebellum era); Progress of the population in the United States. *Hunt's Merchants Magazine and Commercial Review*, 32, February 1855, pp. 191–5;

Dodd, Donald B. and Wynelle S. (1973) *Historical Statistics of the South, 1790–1970.* University: University of Alabama Press; Curry, Leonard P. (1974) Urbanization and urbanism in the Old South: a comparative view. *Journal of Southern History,* 40, pp. 43–60.
31. Railroads of the United States. *Hunt's Merchants Magazine and Commercial Review,* 28, January 1853, pp. 110–15.
32. Eisterhold, John A. (1973) Savannah: lumber centre of the South Atlantic. *Georgia Historical Quarterly,* 57, pp. 526–43; Exports of flour to South America. *Hunt's Merchants Magazine and Commercial Review,* 40, March 1859, p. 351; Griffen, Richard W. (1958) The origins of the Industrial Revolution in Georgia: cotton textiles, 1810–1865. *Georgia Historical Quarterly,* 42, pp. 355–75.
33. Mordecai, Samuel (1860) *Virginia, Especially Richmond in By-gone Days: Being Reminiscences and Last Words of an Old Citizen.* Richmond, pp. 76–7.
34. See *Alexandria Gazette,* September 14, 1860; Richmond *Daily Dispatch,* July 14, 1860.
35. *Richmond Enquirer,* August 25, 1851; John Randolph Tucker to Muscoe R. H. Garnett, July 24, 1848, in Charles F. Mercer MSS, Virginia State Library; Richmond *Daily Dispatch,* October 18, 1859.
36. Richmond *Daily Dispatch,* March 27, 1857.
37. Savannah *Daily Morning News,* January 19, 1850; *Alexandria Gazette,* April 12, 1855; May 22, 1855; June 14, 1856; *Lynchburg Virginian,* May 5, 1857.
38. Quoted in Barton, Edward H. (1857) *The Cause and Prevention of Yellow Fever at New Orleans and Other Cities in America.* New York, p. 12.
39. *Alexandria Gazette,* April 7, 1856.
40. James, D. Clayton (1968) *Antebellum Natchez.* Baton Rouge: Louisiana State University Press, p. 86.
41. Virginia Board of Public Works, *Annual Report, 1858.* Richmond, 1858, pp. 68–9.
42. Quoted in Schmidt, Louis B. (1939) Internal commerce and the development of the national economy before 1860. *Journal of Political Economy,* 47, p. 803; see also Cochran, Thomas C. (1974) The Business Revolution. *American Historical Review,* 79, pp. 1449–66.
43. Piven, Frances Fox (1975) Planning and class interests. *Journal of the American Institute of Planners,* 41, p. 303.
44. See Goldfield, David R. (1976) Historic planning and redevelopment in Minneapolis. *Journal of the American Institute of Planners,* 42, pp. 76–86.
45. Long, Norton E. (1975) Another view of responsible planning. *Journal of the American Institute of Planners,* 41, p. 313; Gans, Herbert, The future of American cities, speech delivered at Conference on the Urban South, Norfolk, Virginia, February 14, 1976.

3

The role of the competition
in the genesis
of urban planning:
Germany and Austria
in the nineteenth century

PETER BREITLING

The history of the competition as an element in urban planning remains largely unwritten. Indeed, competitions have been virtually ignored in urban and planning historiography, even though important conclusions can be drawn from them about prevailing relationships between the theory and the practice of planning. Many of the ideas and aspirations which inspired earlier generations of architects and planners can be detected in competition briefs, entries and adjudications, whereas they are scarcely expressed at all in other sources. In this respect, competitions may be regarded as a mirror both of planning ideals and of contemporary understanding of the planner's role. Also instructive are the longer-term effects of the competitions. The impact of winning entries on actual planning decisions helps reveal how the ideas of the leading practitioners of the day were adopted and reworked by the urban authorities to form part of a coherent local policy. The competition thus forms an important part of that obscure process, the generation of practical planning policies, which Gordon Cherry has urged us to investigate in detail[1].

The availability of source materials for nineteenth-century planning competitions varies greatly from case to case. Some of the very important

competitions were described in varying degrees of detail in special publications or in the relevant journals of the time. In other cases the original
plans submitted by the winning entrants have survived in the archives.
However, many competitions have left only patchy records, or are
completely undocumented. Consequently, this paper cannot pretend to
provide a full overview of the beginnings of the urban planning competition
in the German-speaking world. Instead, it concentrates on crucial
examples from the 1850s and the 1890s, competitions which exercised a key
influence not only on the development of town planning but on the general
evolution of the big-city phenomenon throughout Europe.

The terms *'Städtebau'* and *'Stadtplanung'*, the German equivalents of
'town planning' and 'urban planning', came into general use very late. Until
the end of the nineteenth century the most common expression was
'Stadterweiterung' (town extension). It was not until the early twentieth
century that it was fully displaced by *'Städtebau'*, the term popularized by
Camillo Sitte and Josef Stübben. Strictly speaking, therefore, the nineteenth-
century competitions were town-extension competitions rather than town-
planning competitions in the full sense of the term[2]. However,
as we shall soon see, the concept of 'town extension' came to incorporate a
very wide range of urban planning objectives.

THE COMPETITION IN THE MID-NINETEENTH CENTURY

Architectural competitions, and even competitions with an urban planning
element, were by no means an innovation of the mid-nineteenth century. As
early as 1748, for instance, the design of the Place de la Concorde in Paris
had been opened to a public competition, for which over sixty architects
entered[3]. In Germany and the Austrian empire similar competitions for the
design of individual elements of the townscape became common from
around 1840. Among them were the following[4]:

1838	flood-protection works along the Danube in Pest
1841	model arrangement for the main square of a large Italian city
1842	design of the railway-station district in Venice
1851, 1861	colonnades for Karlsbad
1858	project for a town hall with adjacent shops in Berlin
1863	shopping area on the Promenade in Baden
1865	baths in the spa of Kissingen

By the 1860s and 1870s the architectural competition had clearly reached
full maturity, as indicated by the appointment in 1869 of a committee to
draw up a standard set of rules for such contests. Moreover, the urban
planning competition had now come on the scene.

In 1763, shortly after her accession, Empress Catherine II of Russia had held an international competition for a building plan for St. Petersburg. This was the first time that a competition had been used to produce more than an isolated architectural project; a general scheme was sought for the regulation of the existing city linked with an ambitious extension of the built area.[5] However, this early example was not emulated for some time, and the tradition of the urban planning competition was not firmly established until 1847, when the City of Brussels held a competition for the development of the Rue Royale in association with an open square and a covered market. After 1850 a number of large cities held international planning competitions in order to produce schemes for big extension or reconstruction projects, or even guidelines for the development of the city as a whole. Among them were Vienna (1858), Brno (1861), Budapest (1871), Mannheim (1872), Dresden (1878), Aachen (1878), Cologne (1880), Kassel (1883), Zurich (1883), Dessau (1888), Hanover (1891), Munich (1893), and Vienna (1893). The importance of these competitions lay not only in the stimulus they gave to the emergence of town planning as an independent discipline, but in their contribution to the growth of public appreciation of the objectives of planning[6].

In the development of town planning in the German-speaking world the most important competitions were the Ringstrasse competition in Vienna in 1858, and the big city-extension competitions in Munich and Vienna in 1893. In view of their paradigmatic character, their influence on planning orthodoxy, and their impact on the development of Vienna and Munich, we shall concentrate in what follows on these three crucial events, referring more briefly to other competitions of the period.

The Ringstrasse Competition in Vienna

Werner Hegemann relates that during the revolutionary disturbances of 1848 one of the architects who had entered for the Brussels competition, Johann Georg Müller, made a speech at a meeting of the Vienna Architects' Association. In it he made a strong call for the adoption of the principle that the designs for public architectural and planning schemes should be selected by open competition. So convincing was his case that he obtained the support of many Viennese architects for a petition advocating the principle which he submitted to the Ministry of the Interior. After a brief delay Müller's proposal was accepted. He must have been surprised, for it was not yet generally appreciated to what extent the administration had accelerated its procedures under the impact of revolution. Even more unusual was the State's ready acceptance of an idea proposed by a private citizen[7].

The adoption of the competition principle was a timely one, for the city

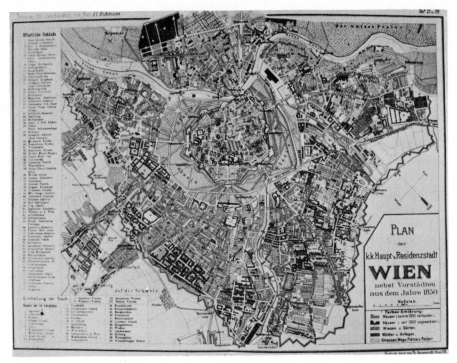

FIGURE 3.1. Vienna and its suburbs in 1850, a city divided by fortifications.

of Vienna was approaching an important turning-point in the history of its physical development. In the eighteenth and early nineteenth centuries the growth of the city had been unregulated, and much building had gone on in suburbs outside the walls. Already in 1777 and 1817 it had been seriously suggested that the fortifications should be removed and that houses should be built on the cleared land, for the general benefit of an increasingly congested city. There had also been numerous calls for administrative reforms to allow the city to expand freely into the surrounding areas. It was not however until 1848 that revolution created the necessary preconditions of these changes. The feudal system of landownership was abolished, and in 1850 a new administrative system freed the local authorities from the rigid control of the State. These reforms allowed the City of Vienna to annex its thirty-four previously independent suburban communities. This rationalization threw into relief the anachronistic physical arrangement of the city, which was dominated by its ring fortifications. In mid-century the Vienna urban area fell clearly into three parts: the old town (the area which now lies within the Ringstrasse), the intermediate suburbs *(Vorstädte)* between the bastions and the *Linienwall,* an outlying fortification line built in 1704 to keep out the marauding Kuruzze hordes, and the outer suburbs *(Vororte)* outside the *Linienwall.* This division, which had economic and social, as well as physical, effects, had long ceased to serve any real needs.

The key to the physical reorganization of the city was clearly the removal of the fortifications. Even before the official decision to demolish them was announced, numerous proposals were put forward by architects for the use of the extensive field of fire *(glacis)* which separated the old town from the intermediate suburbs. Many of these architects were later to take part in the Ringstrasse competition. Outstanding among them was Ludwig Förster, later to be placed equal first in the competition, who concentrated his efforts on the problem in the early 1850s. Underlying this enthusiasm was not only the obvious practical utility of the scheme, but its value as a symbol of the important political and social changes taking place in Austria.

According to Klaus Eggert, the most influential advocate of a planned extension of Vienna was Alexander Freiherr von Bach, the Minister of the Interior. The result of his efforts was the famous letter which he received from the Emperor Franz Joseph in 1856, giving the go-ahead for the redevelopment of the fortifications[8]. In this letter the emperor signified his agreement with his minister's view that the polyglot Austrian empire required for its capital a Greater Vienna which surpassed the cities of provincial Austria not only in size but also in the grandeur of its buildings. Although the key passages of the letter have often been cited, we must quote from it again here in order to establish the context in which the Ringstrasse competition was held:

> Dear Freiherr von Bach!
>
> It is my will that the extension of the inner city of Vienna should be undertaken as soon as possible, with a view to establishing appropriate links with the suburbs. Attention shall at the same time be given to the regularization and embellishment of my seat and capital city. To this end I cede the ramparts and fortifications of the inner city, together with the ditch which lies outside them.
>
> Such land as is gained by the cession of these areas, including the field of fire, and which is not designated by the plan for other uses, is to be made available for private building. Monies generated by the sale of sites are to constitute a building fund to help defray costs falling on the Treasury as a result of the scheme, and in particular to finance the construction of public buildings and the reconstruction of such military installations as continue to be needed.[9]

The official brief for the extension-plan competition was published on 31 January 1858. By the end of February, 426 enquiries had been received from all over the advanced world. Public interest in the course of the competition and in the resulting entries was intense. This atmosphere generated a host of subsidiary suggestions and proposals from both professional and lay circles during and after the competition. For instance, a politician suggested that, as Vienna was the metropolis of a multinational empire, each district of the city should be allocated to a particular nationality and built in the appropriate style in order to remind immigrants of their former homeland.

In the end, eighty-five entries were submitted. The problem then arose of evaluating them and converting them into practical plans, a difficulty which has attended the planning competition until today. The jury soon recognized that three prizes would be insufficient to reward all the entries which contained valuable proposals; on the other hand, no single scheme was capable of being put into effect without modification. In its judgment, announced on 31 December 1858, the jury declined to rank the leading entries in a clear order of preference. It gave three equal-first prizes to Professor Ludwig Förster, to the partnership of Professor Eduard van der Nüll and Siccard von Siccardsburg, and to the court architect of Prince Kinski, Friedrich Stache. Three equal-second prizes were awarded to Martin Kink, provincial engineer *(Landesbaudirektor)* of Styria, to Peter Josef Lenné, general director of parks and gardens at the Prussian royal court, and to a private architect, Eduard Strache. Finally, the jury commended as 'noteworthy' two schemes submitted through the Ministry of the Interior by government officials. These were by the section-heads Moriz von Löhr and Vincenz Streffleur, and by the engineer, Ludwig Zettl.

Ludwig Förster wanted to reorganize the whole of the city of Vienna. He combined plans for new quays, boulevards and parks in the extension zone with proposals for the redevelopment of the old town, the regulation of the Danube and the creation of a river-port in the Kaiserwasser. He wanted to construct a ring railway line round the outer suburbs, and to build a central station in front of the Invalidenhaus. All these proposed developments were set within a comprehensive system of street-traffic routes. Van der Nüll and Siccardsburg concentrated much more closely on the development of the fortification zone itself, for which they proposed boulevards and an aesthetically pleasing arrangement of public buildings. The centre-point of their scheme was the imperial Hofburg. Stache, like Förster, took a broad view and proposed a traffic system of radial and ring streets.

Among the second prizes, Lenné, true to his special interests, made numerous proposals for the setting of monumental buildings in parks and walks. Kink's entry contained many useful ideas for the control of the annual floods and ice-jams on the Danube, and for the use of land reclaimed by the regulation of the river between Nussdorf and Albern. Löhr and Zettl, finally, had naturally concentrated on questions which currently pre-occupied the State administration. Zettl wanted to lay out boulevards directly outside the old town, and build an underground horse-drawn tramway in the Stadtgraben. He also proposed a central station near the Stubentorbrücke and the rerouting of heavy traffic onto the Esplanaden-strasse[10].

Although Ludwig Förster's entry was particularly close to the ideas of the jury, and in many respects provided the basis for later decisions,

FIGURE 3.2. Ludwig Förster's equal first prize entry to the 1858 Ringstrasse competition.

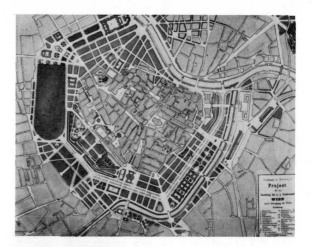

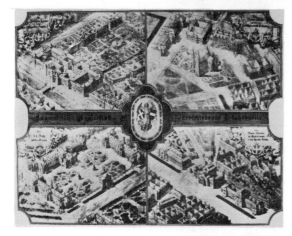

FIGURE 3.3. A detail sheet from the equal first prize entry of Eduard van der Null and Siccard von Siccardsburg.

FIGURE 3.4. The equal second prize entry of Josef Peter Lenné.

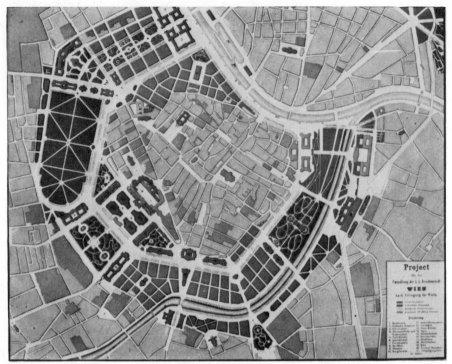

FIGURE 3.5. Official extension plan for central Vienna elaborated by the special committee for the evaluation of the results of the Ringstrasse competition.

Förster was given no further part in the elaboration of the scheme. The evaluation of the results of the competition was entrusted to a new committee which incorporated the best proposals in an official extension plan. This plan was approved by the emperor on 1 September 1859 and in its essentials it remained in force throughout the whole of the construction of the Ringstrasse area. The only changes made were in the siting of individual public buildings, which continued to be debated into the 1870s. All the prize-winning competition entrants were rewarded with design commissions for these monumental buildings, and soon forgot their disappointment at their exclusion from the general planning process.

The exceptional atmosphere in which the competition took place generated some exaggerated hopes. In their book, *Das bürgerliche Wohnhaus und das Wiener Zinshaus* (The middle-class house and the Viennese tenement block), Eitelberger and Ferstel had called for the building of single-family houses on the field of fire and had opposed the sale of building sites at inner-city prices:

> The sale of these building sites should be undertaken with the interests of the community in mind, and not as a purely speculative operation. The objective should be public welfare, and not short-term gains.[11]

These proposals, and an opposing statement by the architect, Ferdinand Fellner[12], triggered off a long public controversy about housing and land policy, the only concrete result of which was a thirty-year tax reduction on buildings in the Ringstrasse area. The idea of building single-family houses on English lines scarcely took root in Vienna. In 1872 Heinrich Ferstel managed to found a 'Cottage Association' which developed a residential district of about 300 homes in Währing, but the *Zinsburg* (rental castle) continued to dominate the Viennese housing stock, as it still does today.

The execution of the town-extension plan produced sharp exchanges between the central government and the City of Vienna. The municipality maintained that under the local-government law of 1850 it should have the right to play a major part in the direction of the enterprise. In particular, it argued that the State had no right to dispose of the former field of fire. It also felt that the huge tax reductions conceded to builders were unfair to other taxpayers. The biggest blow of all was the new Viennese building code of 23 September 1859. This enactment subjected all important issues to the authority of a building committee of the Ministry of the Interior, thus virtually re-establishing the pre-1850 arrangement under which building matters in Vienna had been dominated by the imperial building council *(Hofbaurat)*. However, the municipality's counter-proposals for the development of the Ringstrasse area were rejected by the Ministry of the Interior in 1860, with the emperor's support. The City's protests achieved only one minor success; the Minister of the Interior gave a vague undertaking to consider rescinding part of the tax reductions if the municipality did what was expected of it, and gave the extension scheme its full support.

After this reverse for the municipality, the development of the Ringstrasse area came, in effect, under the exclusive control of the central government's City-Extension Commission. Money flooded in from the sale of sites and it proved possible to finance nearly all the new public buildings from this source. A surplus was even available to finance part of the cost of street building and underground works, but the municipality nevertheless had to pay 3 million of the 4.7 million gilders spent on them.

Contemporary comments on, and reactions to, the big changes in the Ringstrasse district are strongly reminiscent of the debate on conservation and modernization in our own day. For example, we can read in a publication commemorating Franz Joseph I's jubilee in 1888:

> On 29 March 1858 the first bricks were thrown down from the Rotenturm bastion. A large crowd of onlookers had gathered; some were delighted to see their long-cherished wishes and hopes at last coming true, while others were sad to see the historic character of their city, and the pretty walks along the bastions and through the field of fire, thus desecrated.[13]

The Ringstrasse competition can best be understood as an amalgam of traditional and forward-looking elements. It was a fortuitous event rather than the inevitable result of fundamental changes taking place in Austria. K.E.O. Fritsch, who wrote that 'in Prussia the State authorities would never have held such a competition, for fear that it would give the impression that they had no ideas of their own', over-estimated the extent to which revolutionary events in the 1840s and 1850s had undermined the strength of the Austrian bureaucracy as far as Vienna was concerned[14]. The old, autocratic tradition was reflected in the emperor's initial hand-written letter which started the whole scheme, and in the subordination of the municipality to the State authorities. The influence of the army survived the fall of the fortifications. The competition brief itself required the retention of the barracks to the south of the old town and the planning of new ones in the north. Communications between these two military strongpoints had to be laid out on a generous scale to permit rapid troop movements[15]. Moreover, the influence of the State bureaucracy made itself felt in the competition, as for instance the jury revealed when it accepted two entries by government officials and included them in its final adjudication. The author of one of these projects, Moriz Ritter von Löhr, later served as government representative on technical and administrative matters in the City-Extension Commission which carried out the scheme[16]. On the other hand, the decision to hold an international architectural competition betokened the strength of liberal ideas. Liberal principles also governed the organization of building operations, in that development companies were allowed to participate in the division of the land into plots, and tax incentives were used to encourage construction[17]. Certainly, contemporaries regarded the competition as an indication of the beginning of a systematic approach to urban extension and the whole event caused a sensation. Although it principally affected a district within the built-up area of Vienna, it was, in effect, Austria's first town-extension competition and perhaps the first worthy of that name to be held in Europe, outside Russia. Werner Hegemann hailed the Ringstrasse development as the nineteenth century's greatest urban planning achievement after Haussmann's reconstruction of Paris. He even suggested that the Viennese extension of 1857 began the movement which matured in Germany years later under the name of Städtebau[18].

Much more could be said than space here permits. The Ringstrasse development is one of the best-documented urban projects of the nineteenth century. The Fritz-Thyssen Foundation has sponsored a massive Ringstrasse research project in art and architectural history, the first results of which have been appearing since the early 1970s in a richly illustrated series of publications[19]. The architectural side of the Ringstrasse is particularly interesting, but even a brief discussion here would overstep the limits of our theme. Suffice it to say that the great interest which the Ringstrasse stimulated in architectural circles in the mid- and late-nineteenth century was by no means unconnected with its planning, for the basic scheme allowed buildings in a variety of eclectic styles to combine in a total artistic unity, thus establishing the distinctive merit of historicism as an approach to artistic creation[20].

THE WIDER IMPACT OF THE RINGSTRASSE AND THE COLOGNE COMPETITION OF 1880

Vienna was just one of many continental cities which converted its obsolete fortifications to new uses during the nineteenth century. However, until the revolutions of 1848 it had been customary to lay out spacious parks and green belts on the land previously occupied by earthworks or fields of fire. Bremen, Frankfurt, Brunswick and Münster, for instance, had taken such a course during the first half of the century. The great Vienna competition marked the end of an era, and in a sense ushered in the new urban age of the second half of the nineteenth century in which massive urban growth and the adoption of a liberal, market-oriented land policy were to prevent the allocation of valuable inner-city land to open space. By the end of the century Josef Stübben could write in his great textbook of town planning:

> When disused fortifications are redeveloped nowadays, it is unfortunately impossible to devote as much attention to landscape aspects by the laying out of parks and walks as once used to be the case. Today economic considerations almost always require that the land be put to productive building use, which means that natural features are entirely subordinated.[21]

This change was already apparent in the Cologne town-extension competition of 1880, the next important milestone after the Vienna contest. Indeed, it had much in common with the Ringstrasse competition.

In 1880 the City of Cologne had acquired the ring fortification zone, which the Prussian military authorities no longer required. In the same year a competition brief was drawn up for the development of the area. The first prize was awarded to the entry submitted by Karl Henrici and Josef Stübben, of Aachen. Shortly afterwards, Stübben was invited to come to Cologne to direct the extension work, which had already been started on the basis of his scheme. Viennese and also Parisian influences are apparent in the main feature of the scheme, a six-kilometre long Ringstrasse, mostly forty metres in width but rising to 128 metres on the broadest section. As in Vienna, the competition provided an opportunity and a focus for consideration of the shaping of the whole traffic system. When the extension scheme was adopted it was also decided to reconstruct the central station next to the cathedral, to build an elevated railway system, and to move the goods station. However, the competition did not lead to a general development plan or transport strategy for the city as a whole. In fact, these results were not achieved until after the First World War, when the outer

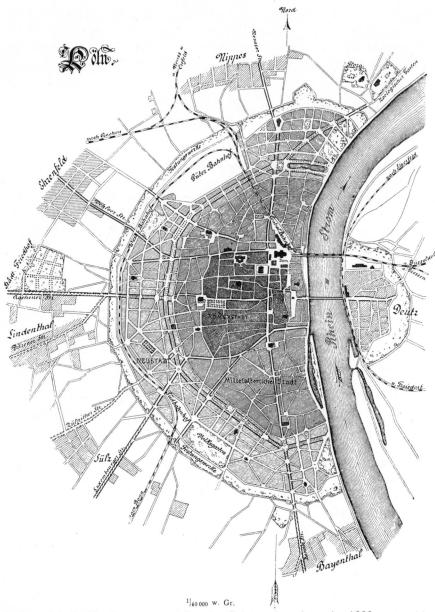

FIGURE 3.6. Stübben's extension plan for Cologne based on the 1880 competition results.

fortification ring was handed over to the municipal authorities. Fritz Schumacher, winner of a restricted-entry competition, was invited to Cologne for a three-year period as city planner and presided over the preparation of a general development plan for the city[22].

THE VIENNA CITY-EXTENSION COMPETITION OF 1892/93

During the development of the Ringstrasse area from the late 1850s Vienna's inner suburbs had been linked both functionally and legally to the inner city. However, the numerous suburbs outside the *Linienwall* had retained their independence, tackling their technical and planning problems from a purely local standpoint. They paid no attention whatever to the needs of Greater Vienna, which from a functional point of view was already in existence. The only exception to this pattern of small-minded, piecemeal development was the cottage settlement started by Heinrich Ferstel in Währing in 1872. However, some stimulus to consideration of the urban area as a whole was provided by a scheme for a ring road, roughly on the line of the old *Linienwall,* which was finally agreed in 1883.

The creation of Greater Vienna, like the annexation of the inner suburbs, was begun by an initiative of the emperor. This time, however, four years elapsed between his proclamation of the new administrative arrangements and the organization of the associated competition. In 1888 Franz Joseph I gave a speech at the opening of a park on the new ring road. He chose this occasion to announce the reform of the government of the Vienna area: 'I dearly wish that as this new garden flourishes and blooms, so will the suburbs continue to grow and prosper with, as far as is possible, no physical barriers between them and their parent city'[23]. On 19 December 1890 the outer suburbs were officially annexed by the City of Vienna, the area of which increased more than threefold, from 5500 to 17,800 hectares. The number of inhabitants rose by about sixty-four per cent, from 800,000 to 1,300,000. This step was accompanied by other important measures. The ring road was completed, and the building code of 1883 was extended. A total of 1263 houses, altered or reconstructed in connection with roadworks, were exempted from taxation for eighteen years. A preliminary building-zone plan was drawn up. Most important of all, the whole area was properly mapped for the first time to replace the antiquated cadastral plans which, despite their multiplicity of scales and various inaccuracies, had previously served. To provide the basis for an eventual 'general city map' the available cadastral plans were redrawn to a scale of 1 : 2880, brought up to date, and comple-mented by the addition of street-names, ages of buildings, and contours.

All these preparations led up to the competition for a general regulating plan for the whole urban area of Vienna, announced on 27 October 1892. Entrants were required to respect public-works schemes which had already been approved, including the metropolitan railway and collector sewer networks, the regulation of the River Wien, and the conversion of the Danube canal into a sheltered winter port. Indeed, decisions to regulate the River Wien and to demolish the Franz-Joseph Barracks lay behind a subsidiary competition, for the planning of the area around the Stubenring, which was announced in November 1892. The winners of this second competition were the Mayreder brothers (first prize), Heinrich Goldemund, later planning director of Vienna (second prize), and A. Streit (third prize).

Meanwhile, the main competition had aroused great interest and by the closing date, on 3 November 1893, fifteen entries had been received. Two first prizes of 20,000 crowns each went to Josef Stübben of Cologne and Otto Wagner of Vienna. Three second prizes of 10,000 crowns were awarded to the Mayreder brothers, to the partnership of Reinhold, Simony and Bach, and to Eugen Fassbender, the architect. Three third prizes went to Alfred Frühwirt from Plauen, Ludwig Baumann from Vienna, and the Munich architects, Lasne and Heindl. Outstanding among the honourable mentions were the entry of Lehnert, the Berlin architect, and an anonymous project bearing the motto 'I.R.A.'. To extract the best from the winning entries a special office was set up under the immediate control of the city's director of planning. This arrangement worked well, for it established direct contact between all the city's technical and aesthetic departments and thus prevented inter-departmental disagreements from holding up the planning process. The only setback for the new office occurred in its dealings with the wily and influential Otto Wagner. Wagner had not received a prize for his entry in the Stubenring competition but he nevertheless managed to have his scheme adopted against the better judgment of the technical experts, and to include in it his own design for a post-office savings bank, later recognized as one of his outstanding works.

The biggest contribution to the planning development of Vienna was made by Eugen Fassbender's scheme which, like Stache's entry in the Ringstrasse competition, bore the motto 'A.E.I.O.U.' *(Austria erit in orbe ultima)*[24]. In recent years Rudolf Wurzer has carried out extensive researches into Fassbender's proposals and their long-term influence[25]. Fassbender proposed a functionally articulated urban structure with local centres and a *Volksring,* as he called it. This latter feature was subsequently adopted by the authorities as the *'Wald und Wiesengürtel'* (wood and meadow belt)[26]. In Wurzer's opinion, Fassbender's competition entry constitutes the second theoretical urban model to emerge in the recent history of town planning (the first being Arturo Soria y Mata's linear city of 1882). He sees it as superior to the later models of Theodor Fritsch and Ebenezer Howard in that it related to an existing metropolis rather than a green-field site.[27]

THE MUNICH CITY-EXTENSION COMPETITION OF 1893

At about the same time as Vienna, the city authorities of the Bavarian royal capital of Munich decided to organize a competition for an extension plan. As in Vienna, great excitement was aroused. In Munich, too, there had been earlier competitions; for instance, in 1851 entrants for a competition for the design of an institution of higher education had been required to make proposals for the planning of the nearby Maximilianstrasse. However, this was not primarily a planning competition in that King Maximilian II's main aim in organizing it was to discover a specifically 'German style' of architecture[28]. The 1893 competition, on the other hand, was a genuine effort to seek urban planning proposals in the full sense of the term. In the 1880s Munich had grown at an astonishing rate, and in one five-year period its population had increased by twenty-five per cent. This rate of increase was surpassed in Germany only by Magdeburg, if we exclude towns which registered population increases by annexing their suburbs. Since the end of the 1880s it had been agreed in specialist circles that a general strategy must be developed for the extension of the city and the regulation of the existing built-up area[29]. The idea of a competition was much favoured, for the city authorities were considered to be incompetent to produce such a plan. In any case, they revealed no ambition to undertake the work. Because the city had no existing growth-plan at all, and none of the technical options had been excluded, the terms of reference of the competition were extremely broad. Certainly, entrants were allowed much greater freedom than in Vienna or in the Dessau and Hanover competitions of 1888 and 1891. It is not therefore surprising that the entries should have differed so widely from one another, or that some of the proposals should have been based on unrealistic assumptions. For instance, the Munich architect, Otto Lasne, predicted that the population of the city, some 380,000 in 1893, would have passed the million mark by 1918[30].

The competition was, for the Munich of those days, sumptuously mounted. The jury was staffed by the leading planners of the time: Reinhard Baumeister, the author of the first German planning manual, Camillo Sitte, Josef Stübben, and Paul Wallot, the designer of the Reichstag in Berlin[31]. Prizes of 6000, 4000, 3000 and 2000 marks were offered; these were very generous amounts indeed by the standards of the time. However, these attractions failed to generate more than thirteen entries. As was customary, each was identified by a motto, and the list makes interesting reading: *Parzival, Bayerns Hauptstadt, Endlich, Munihha, Bavaria, 1253–1893, Realist, Ländlich-Sittlich, Licht und Luft, München im 20. Jahrhundert, Meinem lieben München,* and *Nicht für Heute*[32]. The degree of elaboration and the standard of presentation varied greatly, but most of the participants had put a great deal of effort into this massive project, for which a survey plan (1 : 10,000) and thirty-one detailed sheets (1 : 5000) were required. The most thorough entry was Karl Henrici's *'Realist'.* His explanatory text was in the highly original form of a platonic dialogue between a 'Voice of Time' and the 'Realist', with the former raising objections to Henrici's scheme and the latter defending it.

The jury could not agree on a clear order and gave four equal-first prizes to Gerhard Aengeneyndt (*Bayerns Hauptstadt*), Alfred Frühwirt (*Munihha*), Johannes Lehnert (*Bavaria*), and Karl Henrici. Henrici's was singled out as

FIGURE 3.7. Henrici's *'Realist'* project for the Munich city extension competition.   FIGURE 3.8. A detail from Henrici's *'Realist'* project.

the best scheme from an artistic point of view, though the adjudication mentioned as a 'shortcoming' of his proposals that having divided the city into distinct districts *(Baubezirke)*, he had failed to give enough attention to providing an organic network of traffic routes[33]. This comment suggests a split in the jury. Henrici had indeed under-emphasized traffic links while concentrating on the physical design of his individual districts and especially of their central squares. This emphasis must have appealed to Camillo Sitte, who prepared the report on Henrici's scheme, and no doubt backed it for the first prize. However, Sitte had attacked Baumeister on aesthetic grounds in his book, *Der Städtebau nach seinen künstlerischen Grundsätzen,* and the competition result suggests that Baumeister prevented Sitte from having entirely his own way[34]. The impression of internal disagreements is reinforced by the wording of the adjudication, which strongly suggests that the jury knew who some of the entrants were, despite the standard efforts to preserve anonymity[35]. The picture was further complicated by the separate award of two prizes by the City of Munich to entries submitted by local architects, and by the jury's special mention of Georg Josef Hauberisser's *'Meinem lieben Munchen'* which had ignored the brief by submitting only a single survey plan and no detailed plans. Hauberisser was, however, the architect of the new Munich town hall.

FIGURE 3.9. View of XV
SW II market square
from Henrici's *Realist*
project.

The most influential entry was Henrici's, in its effect both on the general evolution of planning thought and on the development of Munich. Henrici had included numerous detailed designs for his beloved squares. They were enhanced by some finely-drawn perspectives by his pupil, Pützer. After the competition he published his commentary and Pützer's drawings in a book which kept the debate about the competition alive for some time[36]. The preface to his commentary is so representative of late-nineteenth-century planning debates that it is worth quoting at length:

> It is being recognized more and more clearly that the beautiful architectural views of our traditional German towns are not the product of mere chance. Their basic features are the product of artistic attention... Our sharpest encounter with artistic beauty of this type occurs in towns and villages which have remained unaltered over the years and have retained their original character. It would however be wrong to assume that those who built these ancient towns had only a fortunate, instinctive sense of aesthetics which made them obey the correct laws of beauty unconsciously. Camillo Sitte has recently rediscovered the artistic principles which guided our predecessors, particularly in the design of squares, and has published them in a clear, convincing and readily applicable form. His book, *Der Städtebau nach seinen künstlerischen Grundsätzen,* may fairly be regarded as a turning-point in the history of modern urban planning. In my project for the extension of Munich I have tried to apply (as I did in my earlier entries for the Dessau and Hanover competitions) those artistic principles to the very different needs of large towns in our day. I hope that the perspective drawings, which I owe to the artistic talents of my pupil, Friedrich Pützer, will prove the practicality of such an approach.
>   It emerged in the preparation of these drawings that it was often necessary to modify the lines of streets and squares, and to change the positions of the

featured buildings *(Turmgebäude)* in order to produce a satisfying visual effect. This experience entirely convinces me that it is wrong to leave artistic details to chance. Their basis, or framework, must be incorporated into the plan itself . . .

I hope that my exposition shows that aspirations of variety, complexity and picturesque richness do not conflict with conscientious attention to the proper needs of traffic and public health. Indeed, I am convinced that truly satisfying urban beauty can arise only from the full satisfaction of practical requirements. This is in fact why beautiful old townscapes impress us so much; when reflecting, as we often do, that not a single detail is out of place, we are in fact acknowledging that they bear the stamp of functional appropriateness.

In publishing this work my dearest wish is that it will stimulate my colleagues, the architects of Germany, to join in greater numbers than they previously have in the work of reforming our modern urban planning. We must conquer a new, fertile field for our work, snatching it from the claws of the shameless speculator and freeing it from the chains of banality forged by slavish obedience to the building line. I hope furthermore that the planning authorities will recognize that traffic is only one of the factors affecting the design of streets and squares, and that their main task should be to satisfy the need for public buildings and other communal facilities. In their planning they should lay down as much as wise foresight will permit. In this work the central and local authorities should work closely together.

Finally, I hope that the layman will welcome this chance to see how planning works, and will learn from it that in the effort to produce a comfortable urban environment, hopes and aspirations as well as purely practical considerations have to be thrown into the scales. May this book, in sum, allow that solidly based idealism which is a feature of our national character to bloom and flourish in the field of town planning.

In Munich, as in Vienna, a special department, the *Stadterweiterungsbüro* (town-extension office), was set up to distil a practicable planning scheme from the various entries. Henrici's ideas were outstandingly influential. The first director of the department was Theodor Fischer, an architect. In the 1890s it was still normal for planning departments to be headed by engineers, and Fischer's appointment was very much a novelty. An admirer of Camillo Sitte, Fischer tried to put into effect Henrici's intentions, notably by creating local centres in individual districts of the city and enhancing them with specially designed public buildings and squares. He was attacked from many sides, sometimes maliciously[37]. However, during his period as director he managed not only to complete an extension plan for Munich (known as the *Staffelbauplan)*[38], but also with the help of sympathetic architects like Bertsch and Lasne, to convert some of Henrici's ideas into reality in certain districts of the city[39]. In the residential districts which Fischer planned for the Neu-Westend Development Company, church and school buildings were designed and located exactly as Henrici's scheme had proposed. In these areas Henrici's, and ultimately Camillo

Sitte's, ideas were realized to an extent scarcely surpassed elsewhere, and
Munich thus marks the final transition from the period of Parisian
influence on German planning to the new Sittesque era[40]. The
Staffelbauplan (building zone plan) was particularly significant in that it
was one of the first general town-development plans to include detailed
prescriptions for the type and intensity of site use. In fact, it will continue to
guide development control decisions in Munich until 1980[41].

PLANNING COMPETITIONS AFTER THE TURN OF THE CENTURY

Although the effects of the great competitions of the 1890s on the development of planning in general and of the institution of the competition in
particular still await thorough investigation, they definitely contributed
to the reinforcement of town planning as an independent discipline. They
also confirmed the value of the competition as a means of securing high-
quality planning ideas, and contests continued to be organized in great
numbers down to the First World War. The whole phenomenon was
encouraged by *Der Städtebau,* the specialized planning journal launched by
Camillo Sitte and Theodor Goecke in 1904, which devoted much space to
the announcement of competitions and to comment on their results. The
presentation of competition entries also improved greatly, in response to
standards set in the 1890s. A particularly beautiful example was the entry
submitted by the Mayreder brothers for the Karlsbad competition in 1908.
Rewarded with a second prize, it showed just how well architects had
mastered the technique of conveying their vision of a future built environment to both judges and public[42].

It was, however, in Berlin that the planning competition reached its
pre-war apotheosis. In the Prussian capital the call for a competition for a
general development plan had first been heard in the 1850s. However, the
police-president, who at that time was responsible for the planning of the
city, had entrusted the task to an official, the engineer James Hobrecht.
Although Hobrecht's plan was heavily criticized in specialist circles in the
1860s and 1870s[43], it was not until nearly fifty years after its completion
that a competition was held for a development plan for Greater Berlin[44]. In
this competition, too, one entry aroused special interest even though it was
not awarded the first prize. This was the project submitted by the team of
Rudolf Eberstadt, Bruno Möhring and Richard Petersen. Their proposals
suggested that the vanguard of German planners was already moving a step
beyond the 'planning according to artistic principles' which Sitte had
advocated. As Henrici had done in Munich, they issued their own statement
in 1910 under the title, *Gross-Berlin: ein Programm für die Planung der
neuzeitlichen Grosstadt.*

Eberstadt, Möhring and Petersen put their main stress, not on aesthetics,

FIGURE 3.10. The Mayreder brothers 1908 Karlsbad competition entry, *'Colonnae'*, showing the perfection of rendering in pre-First World War competitions.

but on the housing environment. The friendly critique of their scheme by Theodor Goecke, once the close associate of the now departed Camillo Sitte, reveals how planning orthodoxy continued to evolve in Germany:

> These principles show us new ways of escaping from the unhealthy urban condition in which we are currently trapped, a condition which is beyond the capacity of any of our public-utility building companies to relieve... We need a real urban planning policy, and a recognition that planning does not simply mean planning streets, but planning houses—houses, above all, for people of limited means ... That a street be wide or narrow, straight or crooked, becomes very much a matter of secondary importance. It is a technical question, a matter of artistic detail. First of all we need an all-embracing, social concept of the city. Only when we have a socially satisfactory housing environment—and we are a long way from it at the moment—will we be able to produce an art of town planning which will truly reflect the urban Culture of our age![45]

Of course, planning theory and practice would have developed in the German-speaking world without the competition. The competition, however, offered many advantages which would have been more difficult to secure in other ways. The lure of instantaneous success, of overnight fame, attracted many able, young designers. Public interest was assured; even the air of mystery which surrounded the anonymous entries with their curious mottos contributed to the excitement. The judges, many of whom were also active planners, were stimulated both by their contact with the entries and by their discussions among themselves. Idealism and thinking on a large scale were encouraged, but because a winning scheme was rarely applied without reworking by the authorities, there was no serious danger of a town being saddled with a superficially impressive but impracticable project. Although a direct causal link is impossible to prove, it is surely no coincidence that the German-speaking countries, the main home of the planning competition, had acquired a position of unquestioned world pre-eminence in urban planning before the First World War.

NOTES

1. See Cherry, G. E. (1980) The place of Neville Chamberlain in British town planning, in Cherry (ed.), *Shaping an Urban World: Planning in the Twentieth Century*. London: Mansell. Although they still await concerted, comparative study, individual competitions have long attracted the interest of scholars. See, for example, Mayer, Wolfgang (1972) Gebietsänderungen im Raume Wien 1850–1910 und die Debatten um das Entstehen eines Generalregulier-ungsplanes von Wien. Unpublished dissertation, Vienna.

2. The term 'town extension' is prominent in the first general study of the technical aspects of town planning to be published in German: Baumeister, R. (1876) *Stadterweiterungen in technischer, baupolizeilicher und wirtschaftlicher Beziehung*. Berlin: Verlag Ernst und Korn. Baumeister, who came from Hamburg, was Professor of Engineering at Karlsruhe Polytechnic. His book remained without a rival for more than a decade. Even after *'Städtebau'* came into general use, the term *'Stadterweiterung'* survived for a long time in both practice and the literature. In 1921, for instance, the term *'innere Stadter-weiterung'* was used to describe urban renewal in Schilling, Otto (1921) *Innere Stadterweiterung*. Berlin: Der Zirkel Architekturverlag. The impli-cations of the changes in usage are discussed in Albers, Gerd (1975) *Entwick-lungslinien im Städtebau*. Dusseldorf: Bertelsmann Fachverlag.

3. See *Monuments érigés en France à la gloire Louis XV*. Paris, 1775, and the supplement, *Choix des principaux projets qui ont été proposés pour placer la statue du Roi dans les différents quartiers de Paris.*These are discussed in Hegemann, W. (1913) *Der Städtebau nach den Ergebnissen der allgemeinen Städtebau Ausstellung in Berlin*, vol. 2. Berlin: Verlag Ernst Wasmuth, p. 206.

4. These and subsequent examples of competitions have been taken from the following periodicals: *Allgemeine Bauzeitung*. Vienna: Ludwig Försters Verlag, 1836, monthly; *Deutsche Bauzeitung*. Stuttgart: Deutsche Verlagsanstalt, 1866, monthly; *Zeitschrift des Allgemeinen Architekten und Ingenieurvereins Hannover*. Wiesbaden: C. W. Kreidels Verlag, 1904.

5. *Mémoires sur les objets les plus importants de l'architecture*. Paris, 1772, pp. 63ff.

6. Wurzer, R. (1974) Die Gestaltung der deutschen Stadt im 19. Jahrhundert, in Grote, L. (ed.), *Die deutsche Stadt im 19. Jahrhundert.* Munich: Prestel Verlag, pp. 9–32.
7. See Hegemann, W. (1913) *Der Städtebau nach den Ergebnissen, der allgemeinen Städtebau Ausstellung in Berlin,* vol. 2. Berlin: Verlag Ernst Wasmuth, p. 50.
8. Eggert, Klaus (1971) Die Ringstrasse, in Pötscher, P. (ed.), *Wiener Geschichtsbücher,* vol. 7. Wiesbaden: Franz Steiner Verlag, p. 22.
9. Habsburg, Franz Joseph I, Handschreiben an Innenminister Freiherr von Bach, printed in *Wiener Zeitung,* no. 296, 25 December 1856 (quoted in *Wien 1848–1888.* Vienna: Gemeinderath der Stadt Wien, 1888).
10. The results of the competition were the subject of a special publication: Eitelberger, Rudolf von (1859) *Die preisgekrönten Entwürfe zur Erweiterung der inneren Stadt Wien.* Vienna: Kaiserlich-königliche Staatsdruckerei. Friedrich Stache published his own entry, which bore the motto 'A.E.I.O.U.', as *Das künftige Wien: ein Beitrag zur Enstehungsgeschichte desselben: Denkschrift zu den Plänen für die Erweiterung und Verschönung Wiens . . .* (1857).
11. Eitelberger, R. von, and Ferstel, H. (1860) *Das bürgerliche Wohnhaus und das Wiener Zinshaus.* Vienna: author.
12. Fellner, Ferdinand (1860) *Wie Wien bauen soll! Zur Beleuchtung des bürgerlichen Wohnhauses . . .* Vienna: Druck und Verlag der typographisch und literarisch-artistischen Anstalt.
13. Weiss, Karl (1888) Die bauliche Neugestaltung der Stadt, in *Wien 1848-1888,* vol. 1. Vienna: Gemeinderath der Stadt Wien, p. 252.
14. Fritsch, K. E. O. (1911) Kritik am Berliner Bebauungsplan, quoted in Hegemann, W. (1913) *Der Städtebau nach den Ergebnissen der allgemeinen Städtebau Ausstellung in Berlin,* vol. 1. Berlin: Verlag Ernst Wasmuth, p. 131.
15. Wagner, Walter (1961) Die Stellungnahmen der Wiener Militärbehörden zur Wiener Stadterweiterung in den Jahren 1848–1957. *Jahrbuch des Vereins für Geschichte der Stadt Wien,* 17-18, p. 216.
16. *Wien 1848–1888,* vol. 1. Vienna: Gemeinderath der Stadt Wien, 1888, p. 257.
17. For the political and social background of the Ringstrasse competition, see Lichtenberger, Elisabeth (1970) Wirtschaftsfunktion und Sozialstruktur der Wiener Ringstrasse, in Wagner-Rieger, Renate (ed.), *Die Wiener Ringstrasse: Bild einer Epoche,* vol. 6. Vienna: Hermann Böhlaus Nachlolger, pp. 17–26.
18. Quoted in Goldemund, Heinrich (1935) Der Städtebauliche Werdegang Wiens, in *Hundert Jahre Wiener Stadtbauamt.* Vienna: Technikerschaft des Wiener Stadtbauamtes und der grossen Technischen Unternehmungen der Stadt Wien.
19. Wagner-Rieger, Renate (ed.) (1969–) *Die Wiener Ringstrasse: Bild einer Epoche: die Erweiterung der inneren Stadt Wien unter Kaiser Franz Joseph.* Eleven volumes are planned in the series.
20. Eggert, Klaus (1971) Die Ringstrasse, in Pötscher, P. (ed.), *Wiener Geschichtsbücher,* vol. 7. Weisbaden: Franz Steiner Verlag, p. 7.
21. Stübben, Josef (1907) *Der Städtebau* (2nd ed.) Stuttgart: Alfred Kröner Verlag, p. 322.
22. Ockert, Erich (1950) *Fritz Schumacher: sein Schaffen als Städtebauer und Landesplaner.* Tübingen: Ernst Wasmuth Verlag, p. 71.
23. Quoted in *Hundert Jahre Wiener Stadtbauamt.* Vienna: Technikerschaft des

THE ROLE OF THE COMPETITION

Wiener Stadtbauamtes und der grossen Technischen Unternehmungen der Stadt Wien, 1935, p. 71.

24. Fassbender, E. G. B. (1893) *'Austria erit in orbe ultima': Erläuterung zum Entwurf eines Generalregulierungsplanes über das gesamte Gemeindegebiet von Wien.* Vienna: Verlag des Magistrates der Stadt Wien. Other entrants also published commentaries on their proposals, as follow: Wagner, Otto (1894) *'Artis sola domina necessitas'.* Vienna: author; Bach, T., Reinhold, A., and Simony, L. (1893) *Bemerkungen zu dem Entwurfe für einen Generalregulierungsplan über das gesamte Gemeindegebiet von Wien.* Vienna: authors; Anon. (1894) *Erläuterungsbericht zu dem Generalregulierungsplan—Entwurf mit dem Motto 'Es gibt nur a Kaiserstadt, es gibt nur a Wien'.* Vienna: Verlag des Magistrates der Stadt Wien; Anon. (1893) *Erläuterungsbericht zum Entwurf 'Wean bleibt Wean' für einen Generalregulierungsplan über das Gemeindegebiet von Wien.* Vienna: author.

25. See Wurzer, Rudolf (1970) Eugen G. B. Fassbender, in *Handbuch der Raumforschung und Raumordnung.* Hamburg: Gebrüder Jänecke Verlag, cols. 684ff.

26. Fassbender, E. G. B. (1898) *Ein Volksring für Wien.* Vienna: R. Lechner Verlag.

27. See Wurzer, Rudolf (1970) Eugen G. B. Fassbender, in *Handbuch der Raumforschung und Raumordnung.* Hamburg: Gebrüder Jänecke Verlag, cols. 684ff. Wurzer acknowledges that a case might be made for recognizing Cerdá's Barcelona *ensanche* (extension) of 1859 as an even earlier theoretical model than the *Ciudad Lineal.*

28. Hahn, August (1952) Der Maximilianstil, in Gollwitzer, Heinz (ed.), *Hundert Jahre Maximilaneum, 1852–1952.* Munich: Technische Universität, p. 77.

29. Weber, C. (1894) *München und seine Stadterweiterung* (2nd ed.). Munich: Bayerische Baugewerks—Anzeiger und Technische Rundschau, p. 2.

30. *Ibid.,* p. 4.

31. Wallot originally agreed to join the jury but failed to take part in the adjudication.

32. Munihha was the name of the monastic estate, first documented in 1035, from which the city of Munich grew. It means 'belonging to the monks'.

33. Hegemann, W. (1913) *Der Städtebau nach den Ergebnissen der allgemeinen Städtebau Austellung in Berlin,* vol. 2. Berlin: Verlag Ernst Wasmuth, p. 265.

34. Sitte, Camillo (1889) *Der Städtebau nach seinen künstlerischen Grundsätzen.* Vienna, pp. 93–4.

35. I base this opinion on detailed study of the manuscript reports of the jury, now held in the architectural collection of the Technische Universität, Munich.

36. Henrici, Karl (1893) *Preisgekrönter Konkurrenzentwurf zu der Stadterweiterung Münchens.* Munich: C. Werner.

37. Breitling, Peter (1978) Die grossstädtische Entwicklung Münchens im 19. Jahrhundert, in Jäger, H. (ed.), *Probleme des Städtewesens im industriellen Zeitalter.* Cologne/Vienna: Böhlau Verlag.

38. See *Wasmuths Lexikon der Baukunst,* vol. 4. Berlin: Verlag Ernst Wasmuth, 1932, p. 433.

39. Blössner, A. (1949) Verhandlungen und Planungen zur städtebaulichen Entwicklung der Stadt München von 1871 bis 1933. Unpublished typescript,

p. 50. Little else has been published on Fischer's work in Munich but the occasional reference to it is made in the journal, *Der Städtebau.*

40. Hegemann, W. (1913) *Der Städtebau nach den Ergebnissen der allgemeinen Städtebau Austellung in Berlin,* vol. 2. Berlin: Verlag Ernst Wasmuth, p. 271.

41. Under the German planning act *(Bundesbaugesetz)* of 1960, older plans can remain in force until 1980 if they affect the type and intensity of site usage and local streets and paths.

42. Mayreder, Karl and Julius (1908) Zweiter Preis 'Collonnae': Wettbewerb für die Verbindung der Marktbrunn- und Schlossbrunn-Kollonade in Karlsbad, in Scheurembrandt, Hermann (ed.), *Architektur-Konkurrenzen,* vol. 3. Leipzig/ Berlin: Verlag Ernst Wasmuth, pp. 9ff.

43. The best-known criticism of the Hobrecht plan is Bruch, Ernst (1870) Die bauliche Zukunft Berlins und der Bebauungsplan. *Deutsche Bauzeitung,* 4, pp. 71–9.

44. See *Wettbewerb Gross-Berlin 1910: die preisgekrönten Entwürfe mit Erläuterungsberichten.* Berlin: Senat für das Bauwesen, 1911.

45. Goecke, Theodor (1910) Besprechung der Schrift 'Gross-Berlin' von Möhring, Eberstadt, Petersen. *Der Städtebau,* 7 (2).

4

The genesis and special characteristics of town-planning instruments in Italy, 1880-1914

DONATELLA CALABI

In the years 1880–1914 we can identify, more easily than in other periods, some of the distinctive characteristics of Italian town planning. The development of the discipline in Italy differs from the general pattern for Western capitalist countries. In particular, the sequence 'industrialization —urbanization—birth of modern town planning', which is so often suggested as the basis of a new 'urban science' in industrialized countries, is of doubtful applicability to Italy.

The 1880s saw a radical shift in international economic life, with crises, the Great Depression, and the creation of new alliances. In Italy too they were momentous years. The capitalist economic system decisively entered a phase of systemization and consolidation, as the monetary system was stabilized and new economic production relationships emerged. This development was reinforced by the major intervention of the State, and of local authorities under the control of the State, in a variety of sectors. Public intervention occurred in the following areas:

(a) Finance. Here, a successful effort was made to liberate Italy progressively from financial dependence on foreign countries, particularly Germany. Instrumental here was the growth of a national credit system on the basis of the popular credit banks, customs reforms, and protectionism.

(b) Administration. The franchise was widened in 1882, while executive power was strengthened in order to dominate domestic affairs. The view here, which was especially strongly held in the early 1900s, was that executive power could be made more efficient by strengthening the State, and that the administration could, and should, be considered as an instrument of political action. As a result, new 'centralist' tendencies emerged; a number of government departments were set up to deal with specific technical areas, supervisory departments were created, and new powers were given to the *Giunta Provinciale Amministrativa,* while the powers of prefects and sub-prefects were extended in relation to public assistance, public works, building commissions (*commissione edilizia*), and the corps of sanitary engineers.

(c) Social reform. A new national sanitary code, in the shape of the Crispi law of 1888, acted as an instrument of social control, and new legislation was passed on labour matters (child labour, industrial accidents) and on public assistance (friendly societies).

(d) Public expenditure. An extraordinary expansion occurred here at both State and municipal levels to counter the effects of depressions and to increase demand in an otherwise depressed market, with frequent recourse to subsidies, interest-free loans, capital grants (with special laws for the South), and premiums. In addition, a system of granting franchises to private interests, especially in the service sector, was used to produce developments in land reclamation, reafforestation, public health, education, infrastructure and transport.

These were the processes which gave Italian town planning its special characteristics. Although the 1880s saw a marked development of the urbanization process and of the physical growth of towns as capital flowed into building[1], town planning was much more the product of the expansion of public administration outlined above[2]. It took the form of a set of institutions rather than of a true scientific discipline. It was an administrative activity rather than urban planning in the sense in which it is now generally understood.

This divergence of the Italian experience from the general model may be emphasized as follows. First, no simple or direct link can be established between the physical and demographic growth of towns and the industrialization process. This is because in many regions of Italy industrial take-off was delayed or discontinuous. Certainly, an urban network was present and certain changes occurred in it during the later nineteenth century, but it was the product of very much earlier periods[3]. Secondly, legislative powers for public works were passed in 1865 as just one part (Addendum F) of the law of administrative unification (General Law no. 2248), while town-planning powers were merely one part (Chs. VI and VII) of the compulsory purchase law of 1865. As such, they were included in subsequent legislation, such as the Naples law of 1885, the Luzzatti law of 1903, and the building sites taxation bill of 1904. However, they were not codified or separately enacted until the town-planning law was passed in 1942[4].

For all their limitations, the 1865 powers permitted, for the first time in Italy, the creation of specific instruments for the control of urban changes. These instruments were marked throughout the later nineteenth century and beyond by the following characteristics:

(a) Two different instruments of intervention were available: *regulating plans (piani regolatori edilizi)* for the reconstruction or improvement of existing centres, and *extension plans (piani di ampliamento urbano)*. Both were applicable only at the level of the individual local-authority area, where they were used for limited interventions designed to satisfy current needs. They had no broader frame of reference and they did not aim to exercise comprehensive control over development as a whole. There was no echo here of the ideas of the German planning theorist, Reinhard Baumeister, nor of the comprehensive planning resolutions of the Berlin or Mannheim architects' associations in the late nineteenth and early twentieth centuries[5]. In Italy, considerations of public health were uppermost, and one of the main objectives of 'planning' was to prevent the overcrowding of major centres. This was a far cry from the development plans exhibited by major German cities at the International City Exhibition in Dresden in 1903.

(b) The powers were applicable only to towns of more than 10,000 inhabitants.

(c) The adoption of the powers was purely voluntary, even for large towns.

(d) The legislation failed completely to make any reference to the content of the plans. The separation of different functions was not mentioned and there was no reference to anything comparable to the idea of zoning, already delineated in Germany by Baumeister as early as 1876.

These distinctive characteristics can be explained by reference to the objectives of early Italian town-planning legislation, objectives which seem to be somewhat different from those which underlay early legislation in other European countries, such as Germany and Britain. These first legislative measures were closely linked to the State's need to get a public-works policy underway, and they formed part of the procedure for the execution of public works. The compulsory purchase powers provided were designed to permit the execution of specific public works; they were not part of a general programme for the public ownership of land, and they did not even allow compulsory purchase for the rearrangement of building sites. They were not designed to set up a tutelage over private property and the ruling class associated with it, as the relevant parliamentary debates reveal only too clearly; they were merely intended to allow the authorities to intervene on the ground by acquiring such areas of land as were necessary for specific schemes of public utility.

Of course, urban plans were not completely absent in Italy in the years after the unification. Though few in number, they are well known, including as they do Florence, Rome, Milan and Naples. None of them, however, can be seen as routine applications of widely-used powers; they were special measures, sometimes supported by special legislation, intended to deal with temporary problems, emergencies, or 'extraordinary and exceptional circumstances', predominantly in very large cities. Indeed, the 'town planning' paragraphs of the 1865 law were voted more to allow the capital to be moved from Turin to Florence, in response to the demands of domestic restructuring, than to meet a general need for an overall rationalization of urban development as perceived by a bourgeoisie with interests in urban property. Thus we find Florence, which 'as the new capital faced a problem of space, time and money'[6], undertaking between 1864 and 1867 a series of municipal schemes involving compulsory purchase, the leasing of sites, the floating of loans, and the use of building companies, as part of Giuseppe Poggi's extension plan. Subsequently, between 1885 and 1895, we see the execution there of the works included in the reconstruction plan for the town centre[7]. Even the Rome regulating plan of 1873, which differed somewhat from the national picture because of the special character of the Roman ruling class and the unusually strong influence of owners of landed and house property on the city[8], was principally motivated by the transfer of the capital from Florence to Rome on 1 July 1871.

The Naples law, which followed in 1885, redefined and perfected the procedure for compulsory purchase. Yet it too made no claims to general applicability, and was openly presented as an emergency response to the extraordinary situation created by a cholera epidemic. To this end, it restated the compulsory purchase procedure, and accelerated it, in the form of a 'declaration of public utility' for the acquisition, demolition, and reconstruction of whole districts, which had the effect of encouraging heavy investment in the slum areas of the centre. The law rested on exceptional State financial aid, which was to be applied to the execution of a plan drawn up by the municipality and approved by the Ministry of the Interior. In this case, building policy was dictated by the technical and hygienic need for an efficient sewerage system. Consequently, the main features of the resulting scheme were the sewer system, the levels of the streets, a number of indications about industrial location which followed from the extension of the port, and, finally, the extension of building development to the east. The executive plan drawn up by the City Council in 1888 was more a division of the plan area into a number of different concessions (the works were let out in individual contracts to a series of companies, owing to the risks involved)[9], than a 'scheme which orders and organizes the subdivision of the land destined for urban development . . . a plan design which includes full indications for the division of urban building land with the lines of the streets, public spaces, and transport routes . . . an exercise in the division of

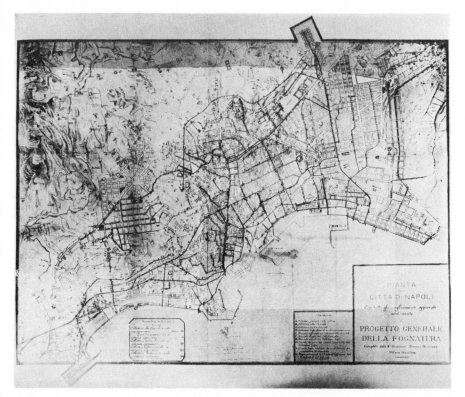

FIGURE 4.1. Naples. General sewer plan, drawn up in 1889 by the municipal water department to incorporate a number of schemes for the extension of the system included in approved *progetti di ampliamento*. Note the extensive area of planned streets to the north and south of the town.

land into specific sites', in Rudolf Eberstadt's classic definition of a town-planning scheme[10].

On the basis of the Naples law, other Italian cities, including Turin, Bologna, and Venice, adopted a slum-clearance plan (*piano di risanamento*). Yet, to confirm the assertions made above about the absence of a comprehensive view in Italian town-planning measures, it will suffice to quote from the agenda for the meeting of the commission appointed by the Ministry of Public Instruction which, on 24 June 1891, approved the Venice plan:

> the slum clearance plan and the regulating plan take the form of a limited number of schemes of limited importance, and projects for partial transformations, which correspond perhaps to certain general principles, but which are not mutually connected and interdependent. Each of them can stand on its own.[11]

Like Venice, many small and medium-sized Italian cities, while changing little in size, experienced big functional changes, the reconstruction

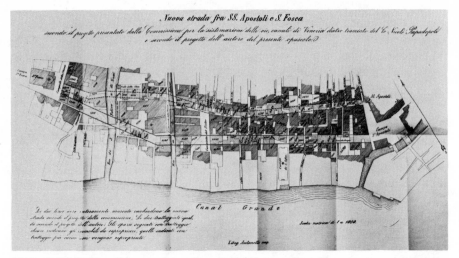

FIGURE 4.2. Venice. Schemes for a direct link between the railway station and the city centre—the Papadopoli and Fani routes for the proposed new street from Santi Apostoli to Santa Fosca, in 1868.

of certain districts, and the public and private building of service networks. They constituted the basic urban network of a country which had urbanized in the pre-industrial period in a relatively homogeneous fashion, and consequently they are, for the purposes of this discussion, a more important source than some of the large cities. In conformity with the changes which they experienced, their 'town-planning powers' developed principally in the form of interventions by the municipal authorities to allow the appropriate operations—a series of partial projects, resolutions about specific changes, and approvals of public-works schemes, public service networks, and transport services. They were measures of administration and urban management rather than of general planning.

By the end of the nineteenth century, then, a distinctive context for planning activity had emerged in Italy. Its towns, like those of other European countries, were passing through a dynamic phase of physical change. The changes, however, had their own special characteristics which were further influenced by the desire of the State, the executive and the ruling class to strengthen their position. As a result, urban intervention took place largely on an *ad hoc* basis. Use was made of a variety of specific powers but they were hardly ever systematized into general rules. Indeed, not all of them were capable of incorporation into a recognizable discipline of town planning. They were more appropriate to the resolution of specific problems and, at the same time, to general city government, than to the control, or the attempted control, of the overall shape of the town and its more obvious contradictions.

The implications of this distinctive context are best investigated by analysing the interaction of the emerging economic forces, the decision mechanisms, and the policies adopted, not in the big cities, but in a number of 'ordinary' towns. As a starting-point, we shall concentrate on those initiatives, examples of which are to be found almost everywhere, which implied a comprehensive transformation of the town through its adaptation to functional needs, the improvement of service networks, or changes in its surrounding areas, and which had the effect of turning certain parts of the town into marginal and/or degraded areas. As our sample we shall take the towns of the Veneto: Treviso, Padua, Vicenza and Verona[12]. They were quite close to one another, between thirty and eighty kilometres apart. They experienced rapid but balanced economic growth, yet remained distinct from the major industrial concentrations of the north. Their populations in the later nineteenth century varied from 10,000 (Treviso) to 45,000 (Verona). Their built-up areas varied between 120 and 430 hectares. They experienced no visible growth in population or area until the first decade of the twentieth century. The major urban changes of the period were in the field of the isolated or overall improvement of *services*, particularly in the following areas:

 (a) The *building of railway lines,* depots and stations outside the town in mid-century. In the following decades the municipal authorities linked them with a rectilinear thoroughfare, lined by a series of building blocks, to an existing main street, and thus connected them functionally to the rest of the town. This did not involve the creation of a new street system, and at most a breach was made in the town wall (Treviso) or a gate was demolished (Padua). Then, in the early twentieth century, we find that the main street and the new station road were *regulated* by the establishment of standard building lines and heights. These works often constituted the major capital effort of the town councils in the 1880s and 1890s. In addition, streets outside the walls, whose course was largely determined by the line of the walls themselves, were linked up during the nineteenth century by a circumvallatory road. But this, once again, was not part of a general plan; it was the product of individual municipal decisions about the building of short stretches of new streets.

 (b) The *alteration of existing buildings* (such as convents or palaces), and/or their conversion to new uses, or the alteration of specific parts of the town. These modifications were to meet the needs of public and private bodies, civil institutions, administrative departments, commerce, and services. They were much more common than the construction of new buildings. They involved a number of modifications in the immediate vicinity, such as the opening of new streets, the culverting of watercourses, and demolitions. They were the product of municipal decisions, and often involved agreements between the municipal authorities and private interests. The related financial decisions were part of the ordinary municipal budget. They were governed in the early years by the town's 'building and embellishment regulations', and later by the 'building

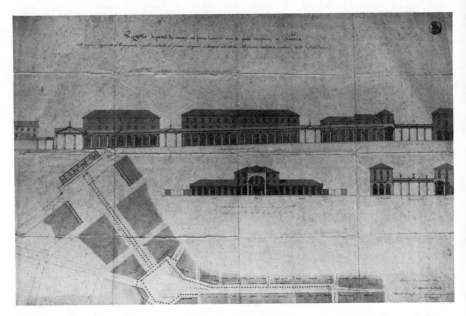

FIGURE 4.3. Novara. P. A. Antonelli's scheme for porticoes to line the Corso di Porta Sempione, a new thoroughfare linking the town centre to the railway station. The scheme was approved by the town council in 1857 as part of its extension plan (*piano di ampliamento*).

regulations' and 'public health regulations', which covered street widenings and building lines. Such new building as was undertaken lay outside the town, on the edge of the built-up area when no unified fortification system existed (Vicenza), and otherwise outside the walls (Padua, Treviso, Verona). Breaches were opened for a number of new streets, or gates were demolished or isolated. Such new building mainly took the form of individual installations, such as barracks, hospitals, lunatic asylums, cemeteries, and industrial stores. Residential building formed only a part of this development, and most of it was the product of individual operations of very limited scope. It conformed to the existing street network (including the circumvallatory road), and lay outside such comprehensive, large-scale regulating plans as some of the towns eventually drew up.

(c) The creation of public service networks from mid-century (though not at the same time in each town). Most of the work was carried out by private companies on the basis of leases agreed with the town council, and the new installations were laid along the town's existing streets. Further extensions were carried out progressively by the same companies, without altering the overall pattern. A gas system for public lighting was the first to be set up (1845) in all the towns, by the Lyons Gas Company. Water and electricity networks were set up in Padua, Vicenza and Verona in the second half of the nineteenth century, where they were limited to the formerly fortified central areas, and took the form of aerial or underground systems following the line of the streets. The first public transport lines appeared around the turn of the century; in all the towns a line ran from the station across the centre and out to the other side. The sewerage system did not appear until much later, and the first plans date only from the 1930s. From the end of the nineteenth century the town councils began to pass resolutions about the municipalization of these services, as part of a national debate about municipalization and in anticipation of legal reforms in this area. When the leases expired, many of these services were taken over by the municipal authorities, with Padua consciously following the example of Glasgow in this respect.

None of these improvements can be found in any municipal 'plan'. 'Town-planning' regulations did not extend beyond the 'building and embellishment regulations', which were brought up to date, but no more, in the 1870s and 1880s, and the first regulating plans. The improvements have to be traced in the records of the municipal administrations and the proceedings of the town councils[13]. These include technical information on the scheduling and financial aspects of the works. They generally include a budget, which indicates possible sources of finance and establishes the basis of negotiations with private interests. From all points of view these projects lay within the public sphere; they were *public works* in the full sense of the term, rather than mere building operations. There are a number of variations, of course, but none of the schemes fell outside the control of the public administration. However, this public activity does not appear to have extended to the division of virgin land in order to give it a potential development value.

In a similar way, schemes for the municipal control of public service networks were studied and debated, and came to occupy an important place in urban administration. This prominence was the product of the municipalities' particular concern with *services,* which included poor relief and education as well as the main service networks. One of the arguments most frequently used around the turn of the century to support the municipalization of public services (gas, water, electricity, transport) was that they could be run just as cheaply as by private interests, while avoiding the drawbacks of monopolies (antiquated equipment, irregular services, poor services on outer routes, and defective timetables). In addition, however, there was a desire to create a new source of local revenue separate from the tax system, and consequently to permit tax reforms. These discussions did not always lead to municipalization, but, at the very least, the independence of the private franchise-holders was normally constrained.

These debates, which can be found in the proceedings of all the town councils from the late 1880s, formed part of a wider discussion about the financing of local government[14]. This discussion laid part at least of the foundation for the law of 1903 on the direct municipal management of public services[15]. The discussion, together with the internal contradictions of the 1903 law, are very indicative of the role which public administration was tending to assume in Italy around the turn of the century. Clearly, public authority could not yet take the place of private enterprise; for instance, it was not permitted to act as a house-building agency, even in an emergency, as the Naples experience had shown. However, it could cooperate with private enterprise, and take profit considerations into account, through the negotiation of contracts (franchises and conventions) which established reciprocal rights and duties. On this basis—that of good government measured in terms of profit or at least of a balanced budget—public administration defined both its own sphere of activity and that of the private interests with which it cooperated in urban matters.

However, when we look for a regulating plan in the full sense of the term—a town-planning instrument designed to rationalize the growth of the town as a whole, and a statement of the local authority's land and building policy in the face of private interests—we find that none of the towns adopted one. Particularly instructive here is the example of Padua, which in 1872 drew up a 'regulating plan', the only town in the Veneto to do so until the 1920s. Thirty years later, in 1902, the town council dismissed this effort in the following terms:

> But it was a collection of more or less practicable proposals for physical improvements. It was stimulated, more than anything else, by the need to widen a large number of our streets. To be made comprehensive it would have required further detailed study and a financial strategy which the municipal authorities nevertheless felt unable to undertake. This was because the schemes included in the plan would have involved an expenditure of many millions, without perhaps improving proportionately the general well-being of the town ... Between 1871 and 1876, on the contrary, the authorities' only action was to remove from the Regulating Plan the thoroughfare from the Piazza Vittorio Emanuele II to the Porta Codalunga. Instead, it improved the street by a number of small widenings, but never managed to finish the widening of the whole street ... gradually, the Regulating Plan fell into obscurity as new needs emerged ... Overall, the studies carried out for the Plan, despite certain obvious merits, suffered from the almost complete failure to consider the growth of the town. This aspect should have been studied before attention was given to street improvements, whether large or small.

Significantly, the council went on in 1902 to formulate 'proposals for works relating to public health, streets, building, the lighting of the suburbs, and the moral, industrial and commercial development of Padua'[16], but it did not include them in a general town plan.

Italy's failure to follow the example of many other Western countries during these years by consolidating the various 'planning instruments' into

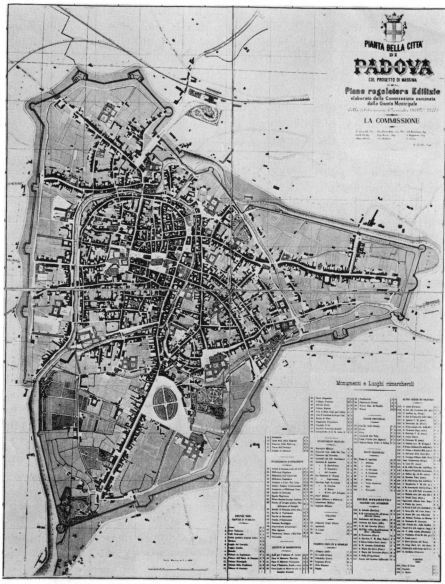

FIGURE 4.4. Padua. Regulating plan (*piano regolatore edilizio*) of 1872. Note the absence of signs of growth.

a coherent disciplinary corpus is further underlined by the lack of theoretical work. There were no specialist journals, in contrast to Germany and England, and the 'planning' articles which appeared first in the *Giornale dell'Ingegnere-Architetto ed Agronomo*[17] and later in *Il Politecnico*[18] dealt mainly with very isolated technical matters (comments or notes about schemes carried out), and frequently with questions of regional infrastructure (land reclamation, canals, and railways). The question of the definition of the discipline was discussed on the basis of a developing division of labour and specialization. The issue of the engineer's role was discussed in *Il Politecnico* in the context of the creation of a modern and efficient State which would incorporate its consideration of technical schemes into a general philosophy of public enterprise. Other journals, which we cannot include among the 'planning' publications, such as *La Critica Sociale* or the *Giornale degli Economisti,* systematically considered those problems of urban government, local finance, the direct or indirect management of public services, and the negotiation of franchises which were so important in Italian town planning.

No essays or treatises dealing specifically with town planning were published. The publisher Hoepli did however issue a number of popular handbooks which, although they referred to the work of Baumeister, Stübben, Eberstadt and Gurlitt, themselves were quite different in terms of their scope, features, and authors. The only general textbook, Aristide Caccia's *Costruzione, transformazione e ampliamento delle città* of 1915[19], turns out to be a rewrite, twenty-five years after its original appearance, of Stübben's *Der Städtebau.* Although Caccia greatly adapted it to correspond to Italian conditions, it is considerably shortened and highly schematic, and it uses Stübben's division of the material, chapter plan, and content. Similarly, textbooks on residential building, workers' housing, and self-help building, quite a large number of which appeared between 1880 and 1915[20], include references to the situation abroad, particularly in Germany and England[21]. These are not presented merely as successful examples to be followed, but affect the whole structure of the textbooks and their contents. Even so, none of them, not even Marc'Aurelio Boldi's well-organized effort[22], is comparable to Eberstadt in the precise description of the building process in large cities, and the explanation of the links between urban growth, rising ground rents, the purchase and development of land, credit facilities and the formation of property companies, and the sale or renting of the resulting dwellings.

To conclude, we can see that the Italian failure to use codified town-planning instruments, and the lack of interest in the creation of a systematic, theoretical discipline, was the result by the turn of the century of:

(*a*) the limited growth of Italian towns;
(*b*) the absence in many of them of explosive contradictions resulting from a rapid rise in land values;
(*c*) the limited role of big landlords (and of land rent) as a ruling class in the towns during the consolidation period of the post-unification capitalist State. Instead, small and medium-sized towns like those of the Veneto are dominated by the old class of rural property owners,

while large cities are controlled by the new entrepreneurial bourgeoisie[23].

Nevertheless, this did not mean that central and local government authorities were not interested in urban changes, nor that no *instruments of management* were adopted for the towns.

On the basis of these conjectures, we can discern a dual reason for beginning to study the special character of the 'Italian approach' to town planning. On the one hand, we have a specific opportunity to remedy the complete lack of studies of decision-making processes and policies applied to control urban changes in a unified Italy; of studies of institutions, new management mechanisms, and relations between public and private enterprise in urban physical restructuring; of studies of the role of the new technique of 'town planning' (distinct from that of the architect and the engineer, but also definitely different from the technique of town planning as understood in Germany). This gap in our historiography survives despite the extraordinary richness of recent historical studies of social, economic, political and cultural matters, and the existence of a number of tentative essays in urban history[24]. On the other hand, we have a more general opportunity to confirm, even if only negatively, a number of hypotheses put forward in recent studies about the generic characteristics of the general regulating plan as a means of controlling income from land, and about the links between efforts to rationalize or redistribute the advantages which derive from the ownership of urban land and from membership of the landowning class, and the birth of the discipline of town planning and of the instruments appropriate to these ends[25].

NOTES

1. In the period under consideration, there were two peaks of capital investment in residential building, approximately in 1896 and 1907; see Secchi, Bernardo (1976) Il settore edilizio e fondiario in una prospettiva storica, in Mioni, Alberto (ed.), *Sulla crescita urbana in Italia*. Milan: Angeli, p. 121.
2. Described, in a detailed way, in many works about the history of Italy after unification, particularly: Caracciolo, Alberto (1969) *Stato e società civile*. Turin: Einaudi; Castronovo, Valerio (1975) *La storia economica*. Turin: Einaudi; Zanni Rosiello, Isabella (ed.) (1976) *Gli apparati statali dall'unità al fascismo*. Bologna: Il Mulino; Farina, Francesco (1976) Modelli interpretativi e caratteri del capitalismo italiano. *Quaderni storici*, **32**, p. 487.
3. Gambi, Lucio (1974) Il reticolo urbano in Italia nei primi vent'anni dopo l'unificazione. *Quaderni storici,* **27**, p. 735.
4. Antonini, Ezio (1976) Le regole del gioco della crescita urbana in Italia: la normativa urbanistica dal 1865 al 1942, in Mioni, Alberto (ed.), *Sulla crescita urbana in Italia*. Milan: Angeli, p. 145.
5. *Beraten der deutschen Architekten und Ingenieur Vereine,* Berlin 1874, Mannheim 1906, in Stübben, Joseph (1924) *Der Städtebau* (3rd edition). Darmstadt, appendix, pp. 699, 700.

6. Guerroni, Giuseppe (1871) Firenze rinnovata. *Nuova Antologia,* 16 (4), p. 765.
7. Michelucci, Giovanni, and Migliorini, Ermanno (1953) Lo sviluppo della città nell' '800. *Urbanistica,* 12, p. 16.
8. Giovanni Giolitti underlines this difference in his paper included in the bill, 'Provvedimenti per la città di Roma', in *Atti Parlamentari,* Camera dei Deputati, Sess. 1902–1904, Docum. vol. 12; doc. no. 561.
9. Società per il Risanamento di Napoli nel Settantesimo della sua Fondazione (1950) *Napoli: contributi allo studio della città,* vol. 2. Naples; Russo, G., *Il Risanamento e l'ampliamento della città di Napoli* (contains an extensive bibliography); Alisio, Giancarlo, Aspetti della cultura dell'800 a Napoli: il risanamento e l'ampliamento della città. *L'Architettura. Cronache e Storia,* 255.
10. Eberstadt, Rudolf (1909) *Handbuch des Wohnungswesens und der Wohnungsfrage.* Jena: Fischer, part 2, para. 29.
11. Commissione del Ministero delle Pubblica Istruzione (1891) *Ordine del giorno di approvazione del Piano di Risanamento di Venezia, votato il 24 giugno 1891,* in *Il commune di Venezia.* Venice.
12. Folin, Marino (1971) Ricerca CNR/Città del Veneto. Typed paper and bibliography, Venice: IUAV.
13. The proceedings of the Padua, Vicenza, Verona, and Treviso city councils of these years.
14. Raddi, A. (1894) Dati e note sull'esercizio dei pubblici servizi comunali. *Il Giornale degli Economisti,* 2nd series, 5, p. 323; Caldara, E. (1899) Teoria e pratica dei servizi pubblici communali. *La Critica Sociale,* 8, p. 314; Brioschi, L. (1900) L'eloquenza delle cifre nelle municipalizzacioni. *Il Giornale degli Economisti,* 2nd series, 21, p. 593; Labriola, A. (1900) Le imprese municipali debonno dare un profitto? *La Critica Sociale,* 10, pp. 170, 349; these last articles began a great debate in the same journal during the whole year, particularly: Municipalis (pseud.), Il regime finanziario delle imprese municipali. p. 255; Negro, L., Ancora il profitto nelle imprese municipali. p. 377; Leone, L. (1902) Il progetto della municipalizzazione. *La Critica Sociale,* 12, p. 61; Bonomi, I. (1902) Il problema finanziario nella municipalizzazione dei pubblici servizi. *La Critica Sociale,* 12, p. 362; Montemartini, G. (1907) La politica municipale dei grandi centri urbani. *Il Giornale degli Economisti,* 2nd series, 18, p. 1149.
15. Law No. 103, March 29, 1903, modifying article 39 of Law No. 561, December 27, 1896.
16. Municipio di Padova (1903) *Proposte della Giunta Municipale al Consiglio Comunale su vari lavori.* Padua: Soc. Coop. Tip., p. 4.
17. *Giornale dell'Ingegnere-Architetto ed Agronomo,* journal kept alive until 1867, later annexed to *Il Politecnico, Giornale dell'Ingegnere-Architetto civile ed industriale.* The editorial staff was formed by: F. Brioschi, G. Colombo, A. Cottrau; and E. Lombardini and L. Tatti, engineers.
18. *Il Politecnico,* founded in 1839 by Carlo Cattaneo, ceased publication between 1845 and 1859; it was published again after the unification by different editors until 1869, when it merged with *Il Giornale dell'Ingegnere-Architetto ed Agronomo,* changing its title (see note 17).
19. Caccia, Aristide (1915) *Costruzione, trasformazione e ampliamento delle città.* Milan: Hoepli. The subtitle is: '(compilato sulla traccia del *Der Städtebau* di J.

Stübben) ad uso degli ingegneri, architetti, uffici tecnici e amministrazioni municipali' (edited following *Der Städtebau* by Stübben, to be used by engineers, architects, technical offices and local authorities).

20. Sacchi, Archimede (1886) *Le abitazioni.* Milan: Hoepli; Landi, G. (1900) *L'abitazione moderna.* Modena: Soc. Tip; Casalini, Giulio (1902) *Un grande problema sociale: le abitazioni a buon mercato.* Milan: Uffici della 'Critica Sociale'; Bassi, Ercole (1902) *Il problema delle case popolari e i mezzi per risolverlo.* Milan: Agnelli; Pedrini, Antonio (1910) *La casa dell'avvenire.* Milan: Hoepli.

21. Castronovo, Valerio (1976) Soggetti pubblici della crescita urbana: gli enti per l'edilizia popolare, 1900–1950, in Mioni, Alberto (ed.) *Sulla crescita urbana in Italia.* Milan: Angeli, p. 155.

22. Boldi, Marc'Aurelio (1910) *Le case popolari: monografia completa technico-economico-sociale.* Milan: Hoepli.

23. Caracciolo, Alberto (1975) *Storia sociale.* Turin: Einaudi.

24. For instance the new journals *Storia urbana,* Milan: Angeli, 1977– and *Storia della città,* Rome: Electa, 1977–. However, town planning problems (connected with the birth of the subject, or the role of the intellectual or technician town-planner), and institutional aspects (public boards for the control of urban and rural changes) are hardly represented here.

25. Calabi, Donatella and Folin, Marino (eds.) (1975), *Werner Hegemann, Catalogo delle Esposizioni Internazionali di Urbanistica di Berlino e Düsseldorf, 1910–12.* Milan: Il Saggiatore.

5

Housing reform and the emergence of town planning in Britain before 1914

JOHN NELSON TARN

The picture of Raymond Unwin pacing out the site at Letchworth in 1903, visualizing the kind of physical development he would like to see in the first garden city[1], illustrates very well the gulf which exists between the ideas of that first generation of planners, who saw their task as an extension of architecture, and the modern planner, who frequently regards the physical aspects of planning as a quite separate job to be carried through when the main work of forecasting and structure-planning has been completed. Even wider, however, was the gulf that stretched between the early planners and the average citizen of 1830 or 1840, when few people regarded the town as a physical or social entity capable of being grasped in its entirety.

THE INDUSTRIAL TOWN: IMAGE AND REALITY

The bewilderment of the early Victorian was very largely the product of the emergence of a completely new phenomenon, the industrial town. Brushing aside a weak tradition of urban design which had bloomed in somewhat uncertain fashion in the eighteenth and early nineteenth centuries, it threw up a number of unprecedented characteristics. Not the least of these was the contrast between the rich man's suburb on the periphery and the inner tangle of housing and industry. The one was a corollary of the other and both must have seemed equally necessary and logical at the time—at least to the rich—since all major British towns which grew up in the last century present the same basic image. The relationship of working-class housing to industry, so inextricable in the middle of the last century, yet so irritating to us today, was the outcome of a society organized entirely differently from our own.

Industry gravitated to logical, convenient places, usually related closely to the availability of raw materials and the practicality of easy transport. The constant tendency for mills and factories to increase in scale simply served to underline the problem of growth and siting in an unplanned age. Following the industrial development came the housing. In the early industrial society, people were obliged to live near to their work because of the conditions of labour; there was not time for the worker to ask environmental questions and his employer did not yet consider them to be a problem. For the first time in history, because of the nature of many factory processes, working-class ghettos were created. But the owners and managers fled from what they clearly recognized as unpleasant surroundings and set up new suburbs, up-wind from the sources of their wealth and employment. The sector of the community which had choice about how it lived, made that choice quite decisively. The labourer took what the market forces offered him by way of a home; new or converted it was likely to be overcrowded and basic in the extreme. He had no choice.

The villas and mansions which went up for the newly affluent were constructed in suburbs which, at their best, were strikingly low-density developments, often heavily landscaped and romantic both in detail design and in concept. These suburbs were clearly recognizable and usually different by nature even from the reasonably well-built semi-villas and terraces of the artisan and trading classes which provided the buffer, physically as well as socially, between rich and poor. Often, like The Park at Nottingham[2], Victoria Park at Manchester[3], or Cressington Park in Liverpool[4], they were private estates approached through gates and segregated from the surrounding neighbourhood.

When working at this level of investment the builders always took advantage of the sensible natural amenities like aspect or prospect, which the later planners were to outline as basic housing requirements for everybody. The development of the south-facing slopes of Sharrow and Broomhall at Sheffield is a good example of this preference and it is still possible to see the change in quality and class of housing as you move from side to side of the valley: the less desirable northern slopes covered with housing in grid-iron terraces, the southern slopes gently laid out with villas on curving roads eased along the contours[5]. Here indeed is the Victorian garden suburb, but it was a restricted development for a favoured few.

A second contrast lay in the town centre. Here, the physical separation of conflicting elements was impossible, for industry and working-class housing usually edged perilously close to the very heart of the town. The solution adopted in nearly every substantial Victorian city was therefore to create an illusion of civic grandeur and cultural elegance which would hide the real squalor underlying the new-found wealth.

Civic elegance took several forms. First, the corporate image of the city was summed up in its town hall and other public assembly places. Town halls are an essential part of the image or the memory of the urban community in Leeds, Manchester and Birmingham, for example, amongst the cities, in Halifax and Rochdale in the group of smaller towns. Blatant imitation was not uncommon; the town hall in Morley is clearly a miniature version of Leeds. Town halls seem to have been built at the point when a city felt it had finally 'arrived' and had a new consciousness of its place in the world. The great steel city of Sheffield built its town hall in the late 1890s while Liverpool, which was a port of considerable wealth when most of the other towns were mere villages, built one in the mid-eighteenth century and added St. George's Hall, a fine public place of assembly combined with law courts, in the 1840s[6].

Secondly, individual commercial firms, banks and insurance companies, the family shops which grew into new department stores, and the railway companies with their stations and hotels, whose scale was more in keeping with the new system of transport than the old coaching inn, all strove for an image which epitomized pride in achievement, individuality and personal success, and a sense of stability which the great piles of stone, brick and terracotta seemed to symbolize. For them architects scoured ancient Rome and the medieval world as well as their own fantastic imaginations for artistic languages which would adequately express the stature of the newly-rich merchants and bankers of Victorian Britain; men who were intensely proud but not a little insecure, who sought to create the right impression through the acquisition of tangible riches; men who desperately patronized the fashionable artists of the new age from the pre-Raphaelites onwards, and founded art collections which are the pride of many a northern city art gallery to which they were very often bequeathed.

Fine new streets were built through the tangle of medieval towns and in that piecemeal and informal way which is so English, Liverpool, Manchester and Birmingham were built or built anew on a scale of increasing magnificence. Rarely, as in Newcastle upon Tyne[7], is there a consistency of development due to unique circumstances; more often the pattern of land ownership produced a picturesque effect with a Grecian bank, a Renaissance palazzo office or a Jacobean style hotel jostling one another, and on occasion Gothic design for good measure.

This amazing fertility of ideas was in part the product of affluence and supreme confidence, but behind the ostentatious display of wealth and success is a wistfulness, a longing for an environment rescued from the past and vaguely considered more attractive. There was an uneasiness about the new towns, suggesting that the architects were creating scenery, to obscure what lay behind, to give the illusion which was thought necessary if the visitor was to enjoy his stay and complete his business.

So the several aspects of the British Victorian town are slowly delineated. The places which so many still come to see are just those parts which their builders wanted us to see. If it was some kind of imaginary theatre for acting out a civilizing ritual, then it was also a direct and real expression of a fraction of the lifestyle of the period. The civic city and the affluent suburbs were in stark contrast to the serried ranks of terraced houses for the rest eddying around the huge smoking chimneys of the factories, like some unwilling lover fatally attracted to what in his heart he knew to be repulsive. The city-centre buildings served a necessary function, even if their clothes were rather like those of Cinderella. The rich language of the period was very much in keeping with the different social dynamics which inspired the various new building types[8].

It is also perhaps worth remembering that building during this period was entirely the responsibility of private enterprise; there were no artificial and levelling yardsticks or standardized cost-per-square-metre with which to contend. The relationship between function and cost was one of effectiveness and pride, so money was spent in rather different ways from what we would accept today. And, just as architects were happily occupied in this branch of building to the exclusion of all the socially responsible areas such as housing, schools, hospitals, and social facilities with which they are now involved, so too the scale and richness of this limited amount of building might be seen as a squandering of too much on too little for the benefit of the few. But that would also be simplistic and historically a crude judgement, although it does serve to highlight the gap between the majority of building—particularly housing—and the realm of high design. The workhouses, schools, and hospitals all became semi-public commissions between 1834 and 1870, and several famous architects were involved in their design. Gilbert Scott, indeed, launched his practice with a posse of workhouses.

THE HOUSING OF THE WORKERS

One wonders whether the old, the infirm and the destitute would have been gladdened by the reflection, on passing through the gates of the workhouse, that probably for the first time in their lives they were to sleep in architect-designed accommodation. The houses from which they had come, far from being the work of architects, were rather the product of the operation of a series of negative rules. The houses themselves were built as a direct response to public demand, which in its turn was dictated by broad economic circumstances and the decisions and policies of local industrialists. Where a factory or a mill was built on virgin ground the speculative builder followed and, except in rare cases like Titus Salt's decision to move his mill to a new position well outside Bradford where he felt obliged to organize more than just his mill enterprises, the growth of whole towns was motivated by the interaction of industrialist and speculative builder.

The housing was clearly related to known need and carefully pitched at the appropriate level of the market. All the evidence suggests that it was pitched at the minimum level, because there was no offer of choice. The increasing demand for accommodation within older towns led to the over-occupancy of existing housing stock, which had declined rapidly in desirability, and to all kinds of back-land development, most of it very unhealthy to live in because it lacked elementary amenities and seemed to defy control. The standard form of new housing was the terrace or row, which once had been the only known language for building urban homes, but which now was so debased in character and increased in quantity that it took on an entirely new appearance. The siting of the terraces was as dense as possible, and their construction was full of short cuts and bad building practice.

However, consistency and pattern were not features of this early industrial housing. It was not even consistently defective. The fragmented, small-scale building and land-development industry often worked slowly. Beresford has shown how in Leeds it could take several decades for a street of houses to be completed. Dyos's study of Camberwell revealed the ways in which builders responded to events and changing circumstances, creating eventually a series of housing developments which have no relationship to one another and no better reasons for existing than their initial saleability[9]. Other variations sprang from the intermittent and imperfect intervention of public authority. In most towns during the first half of the century there were no effective building regulations, and the modern public services, draignage, water supply, street lighting and scavenging were in private hands. This situation prevailed until after mid-century in most places and even in towns where there were attempts to produce building legislation it usually only applied to virgin land development and not to the redevelopment of existing streets. So all sorts of malpractices are clearly evident over all the country usually until after 1875, although there was a gradual growth of responsibility and a slow move towards municipal involvement in services such as drainage and water supply after the passing of the Public Health Act in 1848. Even after 1875, unscrupulous builders could continue to evade; in London, for instance, there are examples of builders who flouted the spirit of the law quite late in the century because they were technically outside the limits where the London Building Act applied[10].

On the other hand, in certain important respects this housing reflected strengths and virtues within the local communities. A number of large towns generated distinctive forms of housing which often spread to their regional satellites. The clearest examples, perhaps, are the large tracts of back-to-back housing which form the main working-class districts in Leeds, which Maurice Beresford has researched[11], the cottage flats of Tyneside[12], the tenement blocks of Glasgow[13], and the courtyard housing of Birmingham[14], Liverpool[15] and Nottingham[16]. These were, in their way, quite local traditions of building, differing in nature but not often in layout. Some of them were well built for artisans—even the back-to-backs—and apart from their visual monotony, by the latter part of the century, they were sanitary and acceptable. Moreover, even the poorest districts contained more than just houses. Churches and chapels of all denominations were usually built soon after the housing and they became the focus of more than just spiritual life as the vast Sunday School buildings of many a Nonconformist chapel will still demonstrate. They were often the only visual interruption in the sea of regular terraces of houses and factory chimneys rising above the huge mass of the mill or factory. They were usually the only buildings, with the possible exception of the mill itself, where an architect had taken a hand in the design. The day-to-day needs of the community, such as shopping or the provision of the public house, were gradually infiltrated into the existing housing layout and clear patterns emerge of corner shops and pubs all originally started by enterprising individuals. Only open space was completely lacking; the need for it did not occur to most developers at the cheaper end of the market. The corporate garden of the kind often found in the classical town, alternating with the terraces of houses, would have been a luxury; the private garden was inessential and the backyard with its privy was thought to be quite adequate for the needs of most people.

The resulting residential structure does not, of course, represent any attempt to plan in an orderly way; it simply reflects the upsurge of private initiatives and the resilience of local residents, demonstrating to us the retrospective needs of a community. Whether the facilities occurred in the 'right' places or not, in any planned sense, is difficult to tell because our social pattern has changed. The corner shop has given way to the supermarket, the television set has replaced a whole host of other forms of entertainment, the church and chapel are less relevant and private transport has become a social force. The street and the road junction are that much more dangerous today. It is extremely difficult for us to judge the effectiveness of the original development. All we can say is that it did not prevent a process of adaptation in which facilities responding to popular demand were inserted into the original pattern of development. From this point of view, the terraced housing of the nineteenth-century industrial town can be regarded as the product of deep-seated preferences among its occupants; that the Scottish and continental tenement block was kept at bay may in part have been a victory for the consumer rather than merely the result of poor organization in the building industry.

The Origins of Town Planning

Whatever virtues we may ultimately detect in the building process of working-class districts, it cannot be regarded as 'planned' development in any acceptable sense of the term. In this respect it ran counter to the practice of formal, classical planning which had achieved a foothold in Britain between the mid-seventeenth and early nineteenth centuries. This had, however, always been a weak and uncertain tradition. The British had shown less enthusiasm for it than had, for instance, the French. London rejected Wren's classical plan after the Great Fire in 1666. With the notable exceptions of Bath and the New Town of Edinburgh, most classical schemes were tiny fragments added to existing towns. The British attitude to their towns in the seventeenth and eighteenth centuries shows a clear leaning towards a picturesque rather than a baroque sense of design, towards the semi-formal rather than the formal, to such an extent as to suggest a national characteristic of deliberately underplaying one's architectural hand. Indeed, underlying this tendency to understatement we may well discover, once again, the fundamental inclination towards terraced houses rather than flatted blocks.

Exceptional or flawed though it may have been, the classical mode of urban design achieved physical expression in a sufficient number of towns in Britain to constitute a clear alternative to the uncoordinated growth of the industrial town. Moreover, Bath, Edinburgh, most of western London up to and including Regent's Park and Regent Street, and a host of more modest examples of town expansion elsewhere in Britain were organized in some of the ways we would term 'planning' today. They were all positive, conscious statements about, and reflections of, ways in which it was considered that people should live. When we examine the classical, pre-industrial town several qualities stand out which are still seen as important ingredients of successful design. The architects and builders of these towns were concerned with three factors: housing, the urban landscape, and prestigious public buildings[17]. Their ideas were shaped to a large extent by the people who would occupy the houses and enjoy the various amenities and therefore they were motivated by private speculative interest. There was logic in the organization of such building ventures and there was style in their execution. Nevertheless, they were of their time and for their time; they neither looked back nor forward. They did not provide a convenient solution to the organizational problems of the industrial town and after 1840 they ceased to be emulated almost everywhere.

When planning became self-conscious and began to be regarded as a special organizational skill in the early years of the twentieth century, the embryo-planners of Britain looked once again at those 'planned' towns of the classical age for one type of inspiration. However, for another type they looked at medieval, romantic towns, and often produced a compromise, an amalgam of the two which was the mark, for instance, of Raymond Unwin's work[18]. The main roots of British town planning cannot be sought in the classical town.

By 1840 it could well have appeared that there was now no such thing as a commonly-held attitude to town design, even if there had been one a century earlier, and certainly little serious thought was given to the problems of urban growth or to their implications. For those who by 1900 were trying to think of the town as some kind of balanced but evolutionary organism there was little to grasp by way of recent urban theory. But just as the threads of architectural design had become diffuse during Victoria's reign, making it impossible to see clearly which ones were significant for the future, so too in the development of planning there were a number of conflicting views to draw upon and it would be quite wrong to discuss the years between 1830 and 1900 as entirely negative even though there was no movement readily discernible as town planning in the sense that Howard or Unwin used the phrase.

MODEL COMMUNITIES, PHILANTHROPY, AND PUBLIC REGULATION

The reaction against classical architecture, the traditional language of the town, which became such an important facet of Victorian taste, to some extent resulted from the rapid decline in the quality of the urban environment while the industrial city developed. Eighteenth-century towns were so constricted in size that the problem of monotony hardly merited consideration; the contrast of town and country enhanced each in its turn. The working-class ghetto, the single-class suburb, rarely existed. Most towns were small and sufficiently slow-growing to have withstood the hazards which their *laisser-faire* evolution inevitably created for human health. One of the great problems with the new industrial city was the speed with which it grew, over-balancing the whole problem of human resistance to disease and taxing the existing resources of the community to the extreme. It required more dynamic organization to provide street cleaning and lighting as well as scavenging, water supply and drainage, than any industrial community was then capable of providing. It perhaps is not until the advent of men like Joseph Chamberlain at Birmingham[19] that we see the power of the community fully in action for the first time. By then frustration with the industrial town and the way in which it was managed was extreme.

Intervention by municipal authority was so hesitant and partial that for much of the century the only clear alternative to the mass of unregulated, speculative workers' housing was provided by a small group of 'model' communities. However, to many people these places have a highly organized and rather harsh appearance. Saltaire, for instance, begun in 1850, was a completely new mill town but the streets of cheaper housing are frankly mean and unattractive, relieved only by the unusually large number

FIGURE 5.1. Houses at Saltaire, near Bradford. Designed by the Bradford architectural partnership of Lockwood and Mawson, and built between 1850 and 1863 by the
textile manufacturer, Sir Titus Salt, Saltaire was the most ambitious of the model
villages of mid-nineteenth century Britain.

of public benefactions—chapel, almshouses, institute, even a park—made
by Salt himself[20]. Later in the century, the small development that Hartley
built outside his jam factory at Aintree in Liverpool illustrates how modest
was the environmental and design progress made during nearly four
decades[21]. Apart from the delightful and rather open layout of
Bromborough Village, built by Price's Patent Candle Co. on the Wirral in the
1850s[22], there seems to be no evidence of English working-class housing,
built paternalistically or philanthropically, which demonstrated that the
pattern of detail development might conveniently or usefully be varied from
the standard layout technique adopted by the speculative builder[23].

If these model villages followed the housing layout already established
by the speculative sector and thus add little to the physical idea of the town,
it is nevertheless important to recognize that the comprehension of a
'community' which is demonstrated by them, perhaps most clearly at
Saltaire, but which can also be seen in a number of other early villages like
Bromborough, is a 'planned' dimension not seen elsewhere. Detailed

studies of both these places[24] show how the industrialists tried to create a balanced community with shops, churches, schools, village institutes, libraries and recreational facilities. In part they were obliged to do more than the speculator, because the villages were isolated and the residents could not use existing facilities, particularly shops or markets. The level of paternalism, of course, was high and the need to attract labour produced a more thoughtful view of what constituted a community than was considered necessary in an existing town. But it would be wrong to read more into that than a natural desire on the part of the industrialist to make his new venture successful. The provision of amenities should be seen as a step towards a concept for a planned community even if the motivation was quite often rather selfish. For instance, when a school was provided its location and facilities were naturally related to what amounted to a catchment area. This lesson could not be learned in existing towns until after the Education Act of 1870, when the board school began to appear as a normal part of the urban structure, forming an important and familiar social and physical focus of many a new suburb.

Most of the industrialists, of course, built on isolated sites; this indeed was very often the reason why they had to provide houses for their workers. From mid-century, however, they were joined by a new building agency, the philanthropic organization, which provided housing in towns. Most such work was in London, but there were sporadic examples in other towns, large and small.

Philanthropic organizations are rather more difficult to incorporate into the development of a Victorian planning theory because much of their work was so heavily influenced by economic pressures that its physical nature was almost an accidental by-product. Apart from the early experimenters of the late 1840s and 1850s the main evidence has to be gleaned from the years after 1860 when Waterlow's Improved Industrial Dwellings Company and the Peabody Trust were at work[25]. They sought to build within the existing urban confines of London, and to add to the housing stock as well as to improve upon its quality. They pursued quite different policies, but they both elected to build tenement blocks of walk-up flats, not more than five floors in height. The height and the density were a result of economic as well as social pressures. Peabody, being the better financed, bought up plots of land, demolished the existing poor-quality housing and built standardized tenement blocks around a hard-surfaced open space. The whole development was enclosed by railings and it was very carefully managed. The design of the blocks was arrived at by experiment, but it changed little over three decades and its appearance was characteristically stark and forbidding. Waterlow's company would buy up a short stretch of cottages and replace them with a single tall block, but one which looked slightly more humane than the Peabody variety, not so much by positive choice one suspects as by accident, since they had no architect. It is

FIGURE 5.2. Sandringham Buildings, Charing Cross Road, built in connection with a street-improvement scheme by the Improved Industrial Dwellings Company in 1884. Such huge blocks, which national clearance legislation and high land values in central London combined to make necessary, were already arousing criticism on both social and economic grounds.

interesting that even when they could afford a larger tract of land, on the Bethnal Green Estate, they operated in a similar way and the street pattern did not change, only the height of the building increased.

Other philanthropic organizations, up to the end of the century, followed a similar pattern, with but one exception, the Artizans', Labourers' and General Dwellings Company. Their three cottage estates in Battersea, Kilburn and Wood Green[26], particularly the two earlier ones begun in the 1870s, would pass for better-quality bye-law street developments by any good builder. On closer inspection it is clear that the standard of layout and the quality of building was better than usual for those years, but it is a fine distinction of degree rather than of essence.

So the evidence builds up to support an argument that model dwellings were by nature either a repetition of part of the existing housing patterns or else rather gaunt tenement blocks. The emphasis was upon good construction to safeguard health and good management to make up for popular ignorance of sanitation. In the public mind model housing was a rarity and, even if you could accept its paternalism, it was a depressing place in which to live and most people remained suspicious about the long-term health issues in high-density developments, despite the growing evidence that their fears were ill-founded. Nevertheless model tenements were usually a stabilizing influence on those who lived in them and the evidence was that tenants both prospered and were healthy.

The problems which faced the urban housing reformer were greater than those of out-of-town developers and model village builders, and the products of the philanthropic organizations never earned more than grudging respect. They were able to prove that proper attention to sanitary and constructional matters could make even high-density developments perfectly healthy, but this achievement was not readily acknowledged. Instead, many sanitary reformers continued to distrust high densities until the end of the nineteenth century and into the twentieth. And, as high densities seemed inescapable for the great mass of the urban population, the main thrust of legislation was directed towards correcting problems which were considered to be detrimental to health. Its connection with planning may therefore appear to be tenuous; however, the battles over health legislation formed part of the whole debate about the relationship between private liberty and the rights of the community or the State. In this respect, the development of health legislation led not only to the social principles of the Welfare State, but to the whole concept of planning as a social process.

The steps by which the present British position was reached were inevitably slow and it is difficult now to appreciate the way in which public-health legislation gradually provided the controlling framework for new development. Of the two great nineteenth-century Public Health Acts of 1848 and 1875, the latter is the more important for the urban historian, because it is as a result of this Act that the model bye-law code was produced. It is important to realize that building bye-laws were, from that point onwards, interpreted in terms primarily of public-health legislation. There had, of course, been a whole stream of building legislation going back even before the nineteenth century. The sequence of eighteenth-century Building Acts in London, for example, were initially concerned with fire precautions[27]. It is then interesting to find that during the early nineteenth century it was in towns like Liverpool and Glasgow, which had the worst housing problems in the British Isles, due largely to the influx of poor Irish people, that private legislation was first obtained to regulate new building and its external space standards. London followed with a series of Acts, the first in 1844, the second in 1855, which remained in force until the codifying Act of 1894. These Acts were complicated, their provisions varied and there was no clearly discernible pattern, except that they all attempted to regulate the width of streets, the width of back lanes and the open-space provision at the rear of buildings. Private Acts of Parliament later became a means of avoiding the implications of national, health-orientated, legislation; and the so-called 'model-clauses' Acts of the 1840s, which set out to provide standard clauses properly drafted for inclusion in local Acts, had little real impact on the country as a whole. It was probably not until the 1880s, when most responsible local authorities began to adopt the model code, that any uniformity began to emerge. By that time, of course, the anomaly was London itself, still operating under the Act of 1855 which was by the 1880s much less stringent than the model code.

In London, the first regulations controlling the height of buildings in relation to space between buildings at both front and rear were made necessary in 1894 because of unique pressures for high building. Whilst the Acts themselves make an interesting study and one can clearly see the attempt which was made through them to wrestle with the problem of minimum standards of space, much of the early legislation applied only to virgin land, within certain boundaries laid out after the passing of the relevant Act, rather than to the redevelopment of old sites within existing towns. Moreover, the operation of the Acts until some point late in the century was clearly arbitrary and patchy, depending to a great extent upon the quality of local government and the desire of a town to improve itself. In many towns there was little wish for strict building or public-health controls because of the problems which might accrue, particularly in a financial way, to the ratepayers and until the direct elections of 1888 it is difficult to find consistent and well-applied building regulations. Indeed, until the newly-formed London County Council began to set an example by lobbying for new powers after its creation in 1888, it was normal for local authorities to wait until they were required to take action by Parliament[28]. Nevertheless, by the end of the century some kind of building code was in force in most urban areas. These building Acts and bye-laws dealt with other issues as well as space about buildings, but it is these provisions which are most relevant to the development of town planning because it was the interpretation in physical terms of their rules which created the new districts of the towns themselves.

The second series of Acts which play a significant part in the development of urban policy were concerned with slum clearances—the Torrens Act of 1868 and particularly the Cross Act of 1875. These represent the first attempts to put right the insanitary areas within existing cities and the complex provisions which were written into them attempted to safeguard the interest of the individual, whilst pressing the claims of the State. Like the building code, the practical operation of the slum clearance Acts was difficult and often almost impossible[29]. They resulted in the desperate kind of high-density housing whose appearance few people enjoyed, but which proved fairly conclusively that high-density housing need not be unhealthy. The layout of the slum-cleared sites took the form of five- or six-floor blocks of tenements, arranged in various patterns according to the organization who built them, but until the 1890s little attention was paid to their appearance or to their impact as part of the town[30]. However, the London County Council then broke new ground by setting up the first local-authority architects' department, and this was the first organization to employ a team of young, qualified, architects to design housing[31]. The influence of this departure was considerable.

The earlier trusts and companies had very rarely used competent designers. Their work was carried out by builders, sometimes by surveyors and occasionally by architects whose interest in built form seems to have been negligible. One can well understand, however, why organizations like the Peabody Trust proceeded in the way they did. Economic issues made it necessary to have a simple building formula. Despite all their marked social successes their principal failure seems to have been in exacerbating the environmental issues associated with urban living, and intensifying the atmosphere of urban gloom.

Most legislation for health, building or slum clearance can be seen as either a response to an existing, even a deteriorating, situation or an attempt to cure an existing ill. Epidemics of cholera, which were no respecters of either rich or poor, can be seen to have motivated legislation faster than any other factor in the 1840s but few were willing to create permanent mandatory powers in less dangerous times. None of the new legislation was comprehensive, none of it sought to do more than control and contain an existing situation with the minimum amount of interference. The building code sought to avoid new situations developing where unhealthy conditions could prevail and epidemics rage; the slum-clearance code sought to rehouse as many people as had been displaced in order to avoid exacerbating the overcrowding problem. Both were fundamental issues; both taxed the Victorian conscience as well as the legislature and it is possible to argue that the appearance of towns and the broader environmental framework which we associate with the town-planning schemes were refinements that could not possibly have consideration until later in the development of this movement. None of the legislation attempted to formulate a policy for town expansion and growth; it merely set out to stop it being worse than what had been built earlier.

SUBURBS

One form of reaction to this debilitating environment was to provide a public park[32]. In many towns, however, the creation of a park, rather like the construction of model dwellings, served merely to accentuate the contrast between it and the huge areas of unredeemed urban housing.

Because housing was a speculative business, it was assumed that any provision of open space was the responsibility of others. But who were these other people and by what standard were these public amenities to be provided? To us such a vague attitude seems deplorable but for most rate-payers and councillors such things were a needless expense and much of the impetus for open space and formal parks lay with philanthropists and the early preservation societies.

We can trace the development of the public park from that famous early example at Birkenhead, created between 1843 and 1847[33], right through the century both as civic activity and private munificence. All of this was evidence that various people appreciated the problem and the hazard of living in cities, but there is no evidence that the picturesque quality of the park, perhaps with a fringe of villas, represents a shift in attitude to the nature of town development. It was a welcome incident, no more. If open space were to be provided on a revolutionary scale in the nineteenth-century town, it could only be through the pursuit, not of communal interest, but of self-interest. The product of that self-interest was the suburb.

The worst examples of suburban developments date from the first half of the century when building control was weak, house-building standards were low, and the need for accommodation was often dramatically high. During the second half there was no sudden improvement, but a slow drift towards better building standards keeping pace to some extent with the growth of a more stable artisan class. In a city as large as London there were many differing opinions about how best to resolve the overcrowding problem and the shortage of housing. The influence of the railways, for example, was itself a mixed blessing. On the one hand the companies often encouraged suburban development[34], on the other hand they could exacerbate the problem of overcrowding as they bought up land to extend their lines further into the heart of cities like London, very often by demolishing housing occupied by the poor.

The different brands of housing for the artisan and the various parts of the middle class produced a range of housing which, after 1875, could certainly be regarded as substantial in construction and reasonable in quality. As the century wore on, the growing expectancy of higher living standards amongst the artisans, coupled with an increasing sense of mobility encouraged by the suburban railway[35], created a wider market and most speculatively-built houses appeared with gardens both back and front, and with ornamental details and a variety of minor refinements. Adequate drainage, the supply of water and the provision of the basic public utilities ceased to be contentious issues and their provision became part of normal building practice. So the public-health issue declined in importance; yet because it had been dominant for so long it remained a positive factor in the popular view of housing long after it ceased to be a serious threat. The popular belief that high-density living was unhealthy disappeared very slowly and, from the future planners' point of view, the equally popular association of urban living conditions with the sheer physical ugliness of many buildings on slum-cleared sites made the whole idea of 'anti-town' a natural alternative. The early planners were to respond to this popular wish to escape from the symbolic urbanism of the town by creating the notion of the garden city.

For the time being, however, even when the quality of building had improved and when private open space in the form of gardens and street planting had become normal practice, the layouts in most cases still conformed to the pattern prescribed by the bye-laws and before them by the building Acts. Whilst to the historian the model bye-law code is a landmark of progress, in common parlance the term 'bye-law street' is one of abuse. The aerial photographs of innumerable cities, showing the regular grid of streets built after 1875 and stretching without interruption for mile after mile, may well suggest an improvement on earlier, tighter layouts which in turn can be distinguished from the pattern of back-to-back or courtyard developments which preceded them. But the tangle of houses and industry which form the centre of the industrial cities, built in any of these three phases, are different only by degree and not by nature; none of the housing seems to give any hint of identity or the shaping of humane communities within the total city. For most people this sort of housing continued to foster the concept of the monotonous Victorian town; certainly for the artisan and the lower middle class, whose housing remained of a very basic kind, the atmosphere must always have been rather depressing even when it was no longer dangerous to health. As building standards rose and building layout measured itself to the post-1875 code, many cities outside London were also beginning to experience the debilitating problems associated with sheer physical size.

It is possible, however, by studying the housing developments for the rich, to trace a sequence of almost romantic suburbs which do not coincide with the bye-law pattern, but rely rather upon landscape design and picturesque effects. These suggest that one branch of the urban tradition withered away and was replaced by a wilful expression of individuality, the like of which had not been seen since Elizabethan times. The architectural historian usually traces this back to the picturesque movement in landscape design late in the eighteenth century[36] and to the work of architects like John Nash. Within a basically urban framework it is particularly well illustrated by Nash's capacity not only to handle the Roman grandeur of the terraces in Regent's Park, but also the seemingly whimsical designs for Park Village East and Park Village West which form an integral part of his development[37]. It is true that many people were bored with Classicism and that this boredom can be traced back much further into the eighteenth century to the revival of Rococo gothic which was considered to be amusing rather than a serious alternative style. The gothic thread can also be traced through to the industrial town where it became the language of escapism; romantic villas with medieval decoration were an obvious antidote to the rhythmical, mechanistic qualities of multi-floored mills and endless ribbons of terraces. But in many ways these were merely architectural posturings for a series of mixed motives and the Victorian suburbs in places like North Oxford have social, even political, foundations as well as ones associated with the history of urban 'planning'[38].

These suburbs are, however, an important expression of the taste of one influential sector of the community and its desire to express individuality rather than cohesiveness. The social upheavals of the period threw up a class of person who built vulgar houses, independent villas which seemed to seek idiosyncracy for its own sake. They do not necessarily represent all that Pugin suggested in *Contrasts*. Their medievalism is not spiritual and based on the nobility of craft skills, but a more earthy reaction to the reality of industrial society elsewhere in the town. They are, when put together as a group, the precursors of the physical aspects of planned developments at the end of the century. What the rich could aspire to in the 1830s and 1840s would ultimately and inexorably percolate down through the English class system.

The semi-villas of the middle class began by emulating the styles of the rich. But then came the wind of change; the new socialist view of architecture propounded by William Morris and Philip Webb[39]. The villas of North Oxford, which developed out of the curious mixture of architectural and social thinking propounded by John Ruskin, represent this thread too, and out of it all emerged very clearly the middle-class architectural and planning landmark, Bedford Park[40]. Bedford Park is a miniature version of an upper-class romantic suburb of a particular kind. It is compressed but it is complete. It represents the new architectural image of the 1870s and while the young men at the L.C.C. would later regard Norman Shaw, who was its architect, as a member of the establishment, nevertheless there is a stylistic thread which moves from Bedford Park to the marvellous cottage estates of the London County Council at the beginning of the twentieth century.

There is also, of course, a paradox. It is that the cottage estates of the London County Council represent a physical reinterpretation of the bye-law street layout pattern. Until Old Oak at Acton[41] there is not a curve in an L.C.C. layout[42]. They were built at high density with many minimum-frontage houses, yet they appear very different from the streets we have seen previously and it is in appearance that the change is first measured. Design, layout, the handling of detail, and the space between buildings are all ingredients of the urban scene both in terms of building regulations and of early town planning.

Here, then, is the beginning of the common ground. But few would call

FIGURE 5.3. Foliot Street, on the London County Council's Old Oak Estate, Acton. A product of the Council's deliberate switch to the building of suburban, cottage estates at the turn of the century, Old Oak was the last such scheme to be undertaken before the First World War. It exhibits many of the refinements, including the varied road layout, which had made the L.C.C. Architects' Office the best-known municipal design team in the country by the early 1900s.

the early L.C.C. estates town planning in the accepted sense of the word. They were an experiment, the result of a new policy belonging to the dynamic era which developed at the end of the century following the urban transport revolutions of the 1880s and 1890s. They were a logical extension of existing housing policies and an alternative to slum clearance.

GARDEN SUBURBS AND NEW CONCEPTS OF PLANNED COMMUNITIES

We may now turn to Port Sunlight, built from 1892 by the first Lord Leverhulme, and to Bournville, started by George Cadbury outside Birmingham in 1895. Bournville is the more important socially and Port Sunlight the more significant architecturally. Bournville represents a serious, sober, attempt to build a new kind of environment while measuring up to contemporary economic problems. It was not a tied community and it offered an example for others to follow. Its layout techniques gradually introduced the curve, not so much for its own sake but in a steady dialogue between topography and the designer's understanding of micro-climate. Harvey, who was the first architect for Bournville, considered first the detail design of the house, its aspect and prospect; only then did he proceed from the individual unit to its setting and, within the total architectural climate in which he operated, he began to produce a concept of housing which broke the whole bye-law development[43].

Port Sunlight was very different. It was almost the architectural dream child of its creator. It was a philanthropic village. It was the only means of profit sharing of which Lever approved[44]. The original layout was to a large extent his own, dictated by the pattern of creeks which penetrate the site from the Mersey. For it he produced what we would now call the concept of a super-block, housing built around the periphery of an open area[45]. What most people do not notice is that at the rear of the housing there is a simple backyard and a back lane before you reach the large area of open ground which forms the central communal allotments, the equivalent of private gardens in a more traditional layout. At the front all is shared open space maintained by the company; there are no private gardens and there is an attention to architectural detail which is unique. Lever not only lavished on his development precise architectural care and variety of a high order, much of which was romantic and amounted to personal whimsy rather than a recreation of traditional building styles, but, in addition, he added resources and amenities which were quite out of proportion to a modest housing estate. It seduces by its physical beauty and, while the Cadbury family were munificent to Bournville, their gifts were more in keeping with the objectives they had in mind. Perhaps their Quaker conscience worked in a more appropriate way, too, than did Lever's idiosyncratic view, despite the fact that he was also a Nonconformist (although of a different persuasion). The Cadbury's, the Rowntrees at York who founded New Earswick, the Reckitts at Hull, and the Colemans at Norwich were all Nonconformists of one sort or another, but while they exchanged ideas, Lever seems always to have remained aloof, the individualist who did everything in his own way.

The layout for Bournville was the least organized of the whole group; it grew as the village gained in momentum and its form probably is best described as a deft and sensitive weaving of roads and house plots onto a piece of gently moulded and contoured open countryside. If it has some of the new spirit of the 1890s it certainly lacks any self-conscious or precocious qualities. Port Sunlight in its original form was a highly personal statement of its owner, very much in the spirit of the informal layouts of the rest of the group although arrived at by different means. But its layout was reorganized after a competition held in 1910. It is possible to overstress the City Beautiful character of the organizational plan which was laid over the partially developed village through Sir Charles Reilly's American connections, but Port Sunlight is now a mixture of formalized planning, woven around a layout based on a picturesque sense of general siting, the superblock idea and a respect for existing topography. Nevertheless it has a formality which is achieved only in landscape terms rather than created by buildings and this, too, is a typical English compromise both in technique and in impact. New Earswick, by contrast, shows Parker and Unwin in a much gentler light: a planned village of 1902 which attempted to draw on the traditional experience of village design and to gain as much individuality as possible from the clues given by the site itself[46]. It is informal and truly picturesque; it relates to the new architecture movement as well as the historic study of spatial relationships which formed Unwin's basis for planning and it attempted to create a community. It also begins to illustrate the application of planning ideas to layout techniques which show a grasp of issues beyond just the siting of houses. Port Sunlight also achieves this, of course, but by very extravagant means. In summary, then, the grasp of housing design in the broader structure of an environmental and planning framework is the new dimension which lifts house design out of the world of mere aesthetic change into that of town planning.

TOWARDS A DEFINITION OF PLANNING

These schemes brought designers into the field of housing by a different route but in a similar way to the architects of the London County Council. Their authors were, however, moved by much more than the desire to create healthy, comfortable housing; they were reflecting the emergence of a new and more coherent view of a desirable quality of life. This view had first found its expression in the romantic contrasts of medieval society and that of the nineteenth century made by Pugin[47], then, in the gradual shift to a theory of human aesthetics with growing social and political overtones in the influential writings of John Ruskin[48], the more explicitly political writings of Carlyle[49] and Morris[50], and the architectural response which this theory elicited from an architect like Philip Webb[51]. Raymond Unwin and his partner Barry Parker were clearly influenced by the mixture of political reform and romantic artistic simplicity which Morris distilled; so too were the early architects at the London County Council after 1890. Ebenezer Howard is, therefore, in this context merely the catalyst who pieced together and gave point to sentiments which were rapidly gaining currency and credence, both here and in America, for a new quasi-rural life style. His Garden City was a direct reaction to the minimum standards of the bye-law legislation and an expression of distaste for the quality of environment which private enterprise had thought suitable for ordinary folk. It also hinted at a sense of community and a planning structure which did not exist anywhere else at that time except perhaps in the model industrial villages.

We may add the other major works of Raymond Unwin now; first his initial plan for Letchworth in 1903 and the clearly delineated compromises with Ebenezer Howard's diagram for the garden city. The compromises

FIGURE 5.4. Broadway, Letchworth. This was the main axis of Parker and Unwin's original master plan for the first garden city. Laid out from 1904, it was many years before it acquired the mature landscape which alone could fully justify the original concept.

are made and are seen to be made, the reality of Letchworth acknowledges the topography and other existing factors yet the outcome shows an attitude to site planning and to house design which stands clearly in the political and aesthetic line which comes from Morris and Webb. Unwin's writings provide a guide to much of his inspiration. His discussion of the individual house, its design with the use of simple and natural materials, as well as his attitude to 'cottage' furnishings, clearly indicate a very elementary 'craft' approach which has its root in the freestyle. His study of town planning[52], which looks so clearly to historical precedent and to an analysis of towns and spaces in a way which we would describe as romantic and essentially physical, with wide-ranging examples and particular reference to the German tradition of town design, makes very clear the way in which the early planners, of which he was the leader, were seeking to develop their inspiration. To our way of thinking he devotes perhaps undue attention to the grouping of buildings, to the concept of the village green and the collection of houses around it[53]. His sense of community is a romantic one too. It is based upon a designer's idea of physical enclosure; it comes from his historic study of the space between buildings and his early

FIGURE 5.5. Woodlands, Adwick-le-Street, near Doncaster. Designed by the Chesterfield architect, Percy B. Houfton, in 1907, Woodlands was the most ambitious mining village of its day. Its curving layout, architecture, and low densities deliberately emulated the new residential style of the early twentieth century, previously applied mainly to middle-class housing.

training in architecture. While he was to develop far beyond this and to comprehend the nature of planning as a discipline separate from architecture, at the point where this account stops he is still a convinced romantic and, even if we include the development of Hampstead Garden Suburb, planned in 1905 and perhaps the apotheosis of the whole early planning movement, we have here, again, a great and predominant sense of architectural organization, aided and abetted by Lutyens. A private Act was needed to evade the bye-laws and this, in its turn, paved the way for the first Town Planning Act in 1909 which made possible the regular creation of planning schemes. We are not witnessing so much the overthrow of public health legislation as the return of the architect to the position of urban designer he had occupied in the days of John Wood at Bath and John Nash in London.

It is perhaps worth remembering that Britain was the pioneer industrial society, experiencing the whole gamut of problems associated with rapid growth and change ahead of other European countries. The process of industrial growth, its diversity and the speed with which it gathered momentum, are not uniform throughout Europe and the varying pattern of events as well as the length of the main growth period in each country all appear to have a significant effect on the way towns developed. But although the British were often the innovators, their traditional life-style survived and found a new, although rather debased, expression in the bye-law street. Other countries frequently looked to Britain for some sort of precedent although often they were more interested in the means rather than the ends. It is worth remembering that Hermann Muthesius, who was in England from 1896 to 1903, took a particular interest in recent English housing design because it appeared to have useful lessons for his own nation and yet, within a decade, the British were seemingly overtaken, particularly in the design of working-class housing, and delegations were off to Germany to find out what progress beyond their own had taken place in the wake of the rapid industrial expansion of the late nineteenth century[54]. What they all probably failed to grasp was the fundamental difference in life-style between the two nations, let alone the existence of a wide range of 'industrial vernacular styles' of building within this country. Perhaps when more work has been done to compare housing and planning policies amongst the European countries, the implications of industrial development will be seen to have as many facets as that of any other period, in an architectural as well as a social and economic sense.

In this discussion we have begged the question of whether the early idea of planning in Britain is synonymous with the idea of the garden suburb. Clearly, it contains other elements, among them being street improvements, traffic planning, and civic centres. If, however, we can accept that the British mode of planning was dominated by the suburb, we can go on to see that developments between the death of Nash and the incorporation of Bedford Park, Port Sunlight and Bournville into the national vocabulary as a recognizable setting for a new life-style were all essentially elements of the history of housing. Much of the search both for policies and examples must lie in the study of housing not just for one particular class, but for the whole range of social groups, simply because housing was the main artifact of the industrial town. It is of fundamental importance that, despite all the pressures of the industrial age, the British remained a nation who lived in houses rather than flats, even though much of the experimental work which attempted to resolve the problem of how to house the poor was concerned with flats and multi-storey living. It is important, too, to understand the structure of the building industry, the way house-building was financed, the problems which bad housing caused socially and the machinery set up by government to improve the standard of housing. Although there was little that was enforceable at first, late in the century the advent of more positive policies and a growing desire for action and improvement, together with new laws about housing, brought about a more creative, forward-looking view which paved the way for planning. The artifacts of housing are, in fact, all that we possess by way of serious evidence for the urban historian during much of the nineteenth century.

The British concept of town design, as it was beginning to emerge in the first few years of this century, was neither the City Beautiful nor the Futurist vision of a mechanistic Valhalla. It was not what Muthesius imagined either: it was a curious distillation of English characteristics, particularly the love of the house and its garden. It was rooted also in that equally curious mish-mash of politico-aesthetic reasoning propounded by Ruskin and Morris. Morris's vision of the city in *News from Nowhere*, Howard's concept of Garden City, and the freestyle architects' view of house design are all in their way expressions of frustration about society and the futility of the machine as a means of expressing human aspiration. The dignity of work and the right to live decently, the growing of flowers and vegetables and the application of vegetable dyes to simple hand-made fabrics, are all part of this new-found, if confusedly romantic, vision. The articulate found words to express what they believed to be the fundamental sickness of their society. The great mass of people saw it more simply; they wanted a better life in healthier surroundings. Because they were British— or more particularly English—their vision was of a house rather than a flat. But then the house was the unit of accommodation for the majority even throughout the nineteenth century. It was debased but it was not destroyed. The nature of its setting, the whole arrangement of space between buildings and the new-found scale of the town were its principal drawbacks and the nature of planning in this country might best be described as an attempt to grasp the idea of community structure and to seek out a new language for expressing the idea of the home. To the British a house was not and never will be by choice a machine for living in.

NOTES

1. See Jackson, F. (1976) Raymond Unwin. Unpublished Ph.D. thesis, Nottingham University.
2. See Edward, K. C. (1977) The Park Estate, Nottingham, in Simpson, M. A. and Lloyd, T. H. (eds.), *Middle Class Housing in Britain*. Newton Abbot: David and Charles.
3. Spiers, M. (1976) *Victoria Park, Manchester. A Nineteenth-Century Suburb in Its Social and Administrative Context*. Manchester: Manchester University Press.
4. This, like a series of other small estates in Liverpool, including Fulwood Park and Grassendale Park, has not yet been written up fully.
5. Tarn, J. N. (1977) Sheffield, in Simpson, M. A. and Lloyd, T. H. (eds.), *Middle Class Housing in Britain*. Newton Abbot: David and Charles.
6. Hughes, J. Q. (1964) *Seaport: Architecture and Townscape in Liverpool*. London: Lund Humphries.

7. Middlebrook, S. (1950) *Newcastle upon Tyne: Its Growth and Achievement.* Newcastle: Newcastle Chronicle and Journal; Wilkes, L. and Dodds, G. (1964) *Tyneside Classical: The Newcastle of Grainger, Dobson and Clayton.* London: John Murray.

8. One of the best illustrations of this sort of social striving is still Asa Briggs's (1968) account of the building of Leeds Town Hall in his *Victorian Cities.* Harmondsworth: Penguin, pp. 139ff.

9. Beresford, M. W. (1971) The back-to-back houses of Leeds, 1787-1937, in Chapman, S. D. (ed.), *The History of Working Class Housing.* Newton Abbot: David and Charles; Dyos, H. J. (1961) *Victorian Suburb: A Study of the Growth of Camberwell.* Leicester: Leicester University Press.

10. See for example the development of a site at Hackney Wick, London, as late as 1873, in *The Builder,* **31,** 6 December 1873, p. 969.

11. Beresford, M. W. (1971) The back-to-back houses of Leeds, 1787-1937, in Chapman, S. D. (ed.), *The History of Working Class Housing.* Newton Abbot: David and Charles.

12. Little has been written about these but see figures 1.4 and 1.5 in Tarn, J. N. (1973) *Five Per Cent Philanthropy.* Cambridge: Cambridge University Press.

13. Butt, J. (1971) Working-class housing in Glasgow, 1851–1914, in Chapman, S. D. (ed.), *The History of Working Class Housing.* Newton Abbot: David and Charles.

14. Chapman, S. D., and Bartlett, J. N. (1971) The contribution of building clubs and freehold land societies to working-class housing in Birmingham, in Chapman, S. D. (ed.), *The History of Working Class Housing.* Newton Abbot: David and Charles.

15. Chapman, S. D. (1971) Working-class housing in Nottingham during the Industrial Revolution, in Chapman, S. D. (ed.), *The History of Working Class Housing.* Newton Abbot: David and Charles.

16. This is not a comprehensive list of recent publications in this area; mention should also be made of studies by J. D. Marshall of Lancaster University on Lancashire working-class housing, and J. B. Lowe's *Iron Industry Housing Papers,* published as occasional papers by the Welsh School of Architecture, Cardiff.

17. Chalklin, C. W. (1974) *The Provincial Towns of Georgian England* (London: Edward Arnold) bridges many of the gaps and Saunders, A. (1969) *Regent's Park* (Newton Abbot: David and Charles) adds to the general background given by Summerson, J. (1945) *Georgian London.* London: Pleiades Books.

18. See Unwin's book, *Town Planning in Practice.* London: T. F. Unwin, 1909. Unwin drew extensively on world-wide examples and although he starts to work towards a theory of planning in this book his approach is pragmatic, an English compromise. At the other extreme see Lynch, K. (1960) *The Image of the City.* Cambridge, Mass.: M.I.T. Press, and other works by the same author.

19. See Briggs, A. (1952) *History of Birmingham,* vol. 2. Oxford: Oxford University Press.

20. Creese, W. L. (1966) *The Search for Environment.* New Haven: Yale University Press, chapter 2.

21. Tarn, J. N. (1973) *Five Per Cent Philanthropy.* Cambridge: Cambridge University Press, p. 161.

22. Tarn, J. N. (1965) The model village of Bromborough Pool. *Town Planning Review*, 35 (4), p. 329.
23. Mills, D. R. (ed.) (1973) *English Rural Communities*. London: Macmillan, gathers together a number of useful accounts of some rural ventures which add to the more usual urban literature.
24. Creese, W. L. (1966) *The Search for Environment*. New Haven: Yale University Press, and Tarn, J. N. (1973) *Five Per Cent Philanthropy*. Cambridge: Cambridge University Press; see also Richards, J. M. (1936) Sir Titus Salt. *Architectural Review*, 80, p. 216.
25. The Improved Industrial Dwellings Company was founded by Sidney Waterlow in 1863; see Tarn, J. N. (1968) The Improved Industrial Dwellings Company. *Transactions of the London and Middlesex Archaeological Society*, 22, p. 43. The Peabody Trust was set up in 1862; see Tarn, J. N. (1966) The Peabody Donation Fund. *Victorian Studies*, 10, p. 7.
26. Tarn, J. N. (1973) *Five Per Cent Philanthropy*. Cambridge: Cambridge University Press, p. 57.
27. See Summerson, J. (1945) *Georgian London*. London: Pleiades Books, chapter 5.
28. London County Council (1900) *The Housing Question in London* deals with the activities around 1890 quite fully. The whole subject of the growth of building legislation has been fully explored by Harper, R. H. (1978) The evolution of the English building regulations. Unpublished Ph.D. thesis, Sheffield University.
29. I have dealt with this in detail in chapter 5 of *Five Per Cent Philanthropy*. Cambridge: Cambridge University Press.
30. They are all described in detail in London County Council (1900) *The Housing Question in London*.
31. Not a great deal of work has been done on this interesting office, but see Jones, D. G. (1954) Some early works of the L.C.C. architects. *Architectural Association Journal*, 70, p. 95, and Hall, S. (1977) Radical housing: the L.C.C. contribution, 1889–1914. Unpublished B.Arch. thesis, Liverpool University.
32. Birkenhead was the first British town to have a public park; see Chadwick, G. F. (1966) *The Park and the Town*. New York: Praeger, p. 68.
33. *Ibid.*
34. See Dyos, H. J. (1961) *Victorian Suburb: A Study of the Growth of Camberwell*. Leicester: Leicester University Press.
35. See Barker, T. C., and Robbins, M. (1963) *A History of London Transport, I: The Nineteenth Century*. London: Allen and Unwin.
36. Willis, P., and Hunt, J. D. (eds.) (1975) *The Genius of Place: The English Landscape Garden, 1620–1820*. London: Elek.
37. Davis, T. (1973) *John Nash: The Prince Regent's Architect*. Newton Abbot: David and Charles, p. 63.
38. See Andrew Saint's account in Pevsner, N. (1974) *Oxfordshire* (Buildings of England series). Harmondsworth: Penguin, p. 317.
39. Brandon-Jones, P. (1963) Philip Webb, in Ferriday, P. (ed.) *Victorian Architecture*. London: Jonathan Cape, p. 247.
40. Saint, A. (1976) *Richard Norman Shaw*. New Haven: Yale University Press, p. 201.

41. For Old Oak, see London County Council (1913) *Housing of the Working Classes, 1855-1912,* p. 82, and London County Council (1937) *London Housing,* p. 135.
42. Except of course for the radial layout at Boundary Street, but that is hardly picturesque.
43. Harvey, W. A. (1906) *The Model Village and Its Cottages: Bournville.* London: B. T. Batsford.
44. See Wilson, C. (1954) *The History of Unilever,* vol. 1. London: Cassell, p. 36.
45. Reynolds, J. (1948) The model village of Port Sunlight. *Architects' Journal,* 107, p. 492, and Creese, W. L. (1966) *The Search for Environment.* New Haven: Yale University Press, p. 108.
46. Creese, W. L. (1966) *The Search for Environment.* New Haven: Yale University Press, p. 191; see also *One Man's Vision: The Story of the Joseph Rowntree Village Trust.* London: Allen and Unwin, 1954.
47. Pugin, A. W. N. (1836) *Contrasts.*
48. See particularly *The Stones of Venice* (1853), and *Unto This Last* (1860).
49. Carlyle, T. (1843) *Past and Present.*
50. For example, *Art and People* (1883), and *News From Nowhere* (1890).
51. See Lethaby, W. (1935) *Philip Webb and His Work.* Oxford: Oxford University Press.
52. Unwin, T. F. (1909) *Town Planning in Practice.*
53. Unwin, R. (1901) *The Art of Building a Home.* London: Longmans, Green and Company.
54. *Garden City,* 1 (6), July 1911.

6

Planning as environmental improvement: slum clearance in Victorian Edinburgh

P. J. SMITH

The belief in environmental improvement is one of the wellsprings of the urban planning idea, perhaps, even, its greatest ideological constant. Most pertinently, in the context of this paper, the improvement ethic has given coherence to attempts to explain the rise of the planning movement, by allowing it to be seen as a broadly-based advance from the beachheads of sanitary reform. To date, however, this evolutionary interpretation has not been well-grounded in empirical research, at the scale of the individual city[1]. The link between local planning practice and the larger horizons of planning thought is essentially unexplored.

If this gap is to be filled, the city of Edinburgh is a most appropriate starting point. Not only was it the scene of one of the earliest applications of a physical planning technique—the improvement scheme—as an instrument of sanitary reform, but Edinburgh's example was to have considerable influence in the subsequent development of national legislation and the codification of urban renewal practice[2]. At the local level, too, much was learned, particularly from the initial projects. Vital insights were obtained and new planning concepts began to emerge, again presaging the next shift of emphasis at the national level, as the problems of urban renewal and urban expansion were bracketed in the Housing, Town Planning, Etc. Act of 1909. At the same time, the Edinburgh experience illustrates the danger of accounting for the evolution of planning ideas in a neatly progressive model. Although the first slum clearance projects can be said to have evolved from earlier applications of the improvement scheme approach, they were nonetheless cast in institutional and physical forms which owed more to the past than to visions of the future. Entrenched images of the city and society, class prejudices and stereotypes, customary ways of doing things—all served to circumscribe the development of planning thought, and even to distort it. Attitudes were certainly modified in the light of further experience, but only to give way to new images and conventions which, in their time, were to be as circumscribing as anything that had gone before.

This apparent paradox can be approached in another way. The general British literature on the history of planning offers a progressive interpretation; the limited ends and conceptions of the sanitary reform movement, and the first cautious intervention by government in the urban environment, are seen to yield, step by step, to an ever-larger social vision and ever-more comprehensive expressions of collective purpose[3]. At least one scholar, however, views the sequence differently. To Benevolo, the planning institutions which were established in the nineteenth century were narrow technical instruments of a conservative ideology, and a betrayal of the revolutionary impulse of those utopian pioneers, Robert Owen and Charles Fourier. Rather than an enlightened broadening of social purpose and political will, Benevolo sees planning in the late nineteenth century as a simple extension of sanitary reform[4]. The planning tools of the day, such as the slum clearance scheme and building and zoning codes, were technically more advanced than the early sanitary legislation, but their ends were identical. Environmental improvement was still couched in limited physical terms.

The applications of the improvement scheme concept in Edinburgh, between 1860 and 1900, suggest that there is truth in both these interpretations. On the one hand, there were signs that planning's social welfare purpose was better understood, and that the physical problems of Edinburgh's slums were being seen in a larger perspective. Simultaneously, though, there was a narrowing of perspective, as local planning practice was depoliticized. The tension between social and sanitary reform, which was a marked characteristic of environmental improvement philosophy from the outset, was moderated at the practical level by reducing the improvement scheme to a device for getting rid of unhealthy houses.

THE IMPROVEMENT SCHEME CONCEPT IN HISTORICAL AND CRITICAL CONTEXT

As it began to evolve in England and Scotland in the eighteenth century, the improvement scheme took on two distinctive characteristics. In the first place, it was a legal instrument, sanctioned by Parliament through a long succession of private legislation. The general intent, always, was to permit some publicly incorporated authority—such as a land development company or a municipal corporation or an improvement commission—to usurp private property rights in the name of some larger collective interest. A power of expropriation was being granted, and Parliament's task was to define the conditions under which it could be exercised. The improvement scheme can thus be set firmly in the vanguard of the long process by which urban planning became a legal institution, since it established the basic principle that collective will is superior to individual rights in the urban environment.

The second characteristic concerns the improvement scheme as a physical planning concept. Its central powers, always, were clearance powers; the right of property acquisition was also a right of demolition and, along with that, a right of redevelopment. The objectives of the redevelopment exercises varied greatly, but the general intent, quite obviously, was to introduce new buildings, new streets and new open spaces into an urban fabric which was judged to be outmoded. Above all, throughout the nineteenth century, it was the street improvement which dominated in planning thought, embodying the concept which Baron Haussmann was to typify as *regularization*[5]. By this he meant the adaptation of urban form to the underlying functional order—the *new* order which was being imposed on the city by economic and technological changes, and which required that the street system be modified to create effective links among new traffic-generating nodes, such as railway stations or business clusters.

Inevitably, the early improvement schemes were concentrated in the central districts of the rapidly growing cities, where the processes of slum formation were also at their most active. Equally inevitably, the promoters of improvement schemes were quick to capitalize on this fact. In late Georgian London, slum clearance was commonly presented as a subsidiary benefit of major street improvements and, over the next few decades, any improvement proposal which could also be justified as a slum removal scheme was virtually assured of success[6]. Similarly, one of Haussmann's four planning goals in the reconstruction of central Paris, as enunciated in the 1850s, was 'the amelioration of the state of health of the town through the systematic destruction of infected alleyways and centers of epidemics'[7].

The logical next step, which was pioneered by the city corporations of Edinburgh and Glasgow in the 1860s, was to design improvement schemes which had slum clearance as their first objective. Other types of improvement schemes were still promoted, of course, but a major new variant had been invented[8]. The critical step had been taken, by which the modern planning movement was rendered one with the sanitary reform movement, though the physical planning concepts continued to be modelled on past experience. In effect, the relationship between street improvements and slum clearance was reversed, the slum clearance scheme gaining in persuasiveness if it could also be presented as a street improvement. The Glasgow Improvement Act of 1866, for instance, enabled the authority to open thirty-nine new streets[9], and later projects in London and Birmingham were to show a similar orientation[10]. New streets also tended to be equated with potential commercial development, and when this was combined with the expropriation costs of slum land, and the high site values which were created in the clearance areas[11], it was difficult for planners to envisage redevelopment which was substantially different from the earlier street improvement schemes. In the Glasgow case, much of the cleared land was used for shops, warehouses and artisans' tenements[12], while the Birmingham scheme of 1875 provided Joseph Chamberlain with a celebrated opportunity to reconstruct the city's business core[13]. In London, until well into the 1880s, slum clearance sites lay vacant, snarled in controversy, because they could not be sold cheaply enough to make them attractive even to the philanthropic builders of working-class dwellings[14]. And when they were eventually sold, at a heavy loss, the planning argument shifted to the ways in which high residential densities could be restored under redevelopment[15]. Even when the necessity of huge public subsidies was acknowledged and accepted, profitability was still the first consideration in the redevelopment plan.

As long as the planning emphasis centred on the physical consequences of redevelopment, or the vision of foul congestion and chaos giving way to orderly streets and handsome buildings, any sense of social purpose was inevitably obscured. From the outset, though, in the Glasgow and Edinburgh improvement schemes of the 1860s, social objectives were at least implied, in a paternalistic way[16]. At a minimum, slum clearance was supposed to lead to an improved standard of health and housing for the working classes; at best, it was believed that the slum population would be uplifted, socially and morally. The practical reality, according to contemporary and latter-day critics alike, was much crueller. 'The policy of sweeping clearances', thundered Patrick Geddes in 1915, 'is one of the most disastrous and pernicious blunders in the chequered history of sanitation'[17]. In particular, he condemned the street improvement approach—'this dreary and conventional plan'—because of its totally destructive impact on the slum community[18]. Homes were lost, social ties were torn asunder, demolition was indiscriminate; everything along the routes of the new streets had, willy-nilly, to be cleared. Affordable new housing was an economic impossibility for the displaced families, who were left with no alternative but to redraw the map of the slums, competing fiercely for the tighter and tighter supply of cheap housing which filtered down to them. As a method of relieving congestion, said Geddes, the improvement scheme was spurious. Its chief beneficiaries were the rack-renting landlords; its social costs were borne by the poor, for whom it brought nothing but hardship and grief.

The theme was to become a familiar one in the scanty literature on the improvement schemes[19], but Geddes's criticisms have a special edge, being based on thirty years' close observation of the urban renewal process in Edinburgh, backed by an enviable record of personal involvement in a variety of redevelopment and rehabilitation projects[20]. To cap it all, Geddes was also the leading planning theoretician of the day, so no one was better qualified to offer the definitive judgment on slum clearance policy.

Such criticisms, in turn, leave the impression that the improvement scheme concept was both ill-conceived and misbegotten—ill-conceived because it was a product of middle-class minds, imposing their images and shibboleths on the slum population; misbegotten because its overall effect was not to reduce the slums but rather to shift them around. At the same time, there was unmistakable evidence that health and housing conditions were improving in British cities, and in Glasgow and Edinburgh, at least, the improvement schemes were given the chief credit[21]. To the official mind, the need for further slum clearance had been amply demonstrated and, in Edinburgh alone, the initial scheme of 1867 was followed by three more between 1893 and 1900, a further seven in the 1920s and more than twenty smaller-scale ones in the 1930s. A notable planning convention had come into being.

INSTITUTIONAL FRAMEWORKS FOR ENVIRONMENTAL PLANNING IN EDINBURGH

The case study of Victorian experience which now follows is based on five improvement schemes undertaken by the town councils of Edinburgh and of Leith, the port of Edinburgh which was municipally independent until 1920. These schemes have been selected for two reasons: they cover the full range of local activity prior to the 1909 Act, and they illustrate the development of planning practice as a legal and administrative institution. The first step, represented by the Edinburgh improvement scheme of 1867, was taken entirely on local initiative and had to receive Parliament's special and unique sanction. In the next case, the Leith improvement scheme of 1880, local initiative was still essential but authority was drawn from a general public statute. Finally, in the Edinburgh schemes of 1893, 1898 and 1900, slum clearance was carried out as a statutory obligation imposed by central authority on the local officials.

THE LEGISLATIVE BASES OF THE IMPROVEMENT SCHEMES

Through the 1850s, as the corporations of Edinburgh and Leith became increasingly involved in sanitary reform activities, a growing sense of frustration is apparent from the civic records. Despite a great deal of pertinent legislation, little real progress was being made. There was talk of amending the general statute, the Police and Improvement (Scotland) Act of 1850, but Parliament was said to be unwilling to grant powers which were 'too broad'[22]. No firm initiatives were taken until William Lindsay, who was elected provost of Leith in 1860, mounted a strong reform campaign amongst the Scottish burghs. The result, in 1862, was the so-called Lindsay Act, which included, amongst its many clauses, the first attempt in Scotland to express the notion of slum clearance as a tool of sanitary improvement[23]. Lindsay, himself, planned to implement a clearance scheme in central Leith but, late in 1865, near the end of his term, he confessed to failure[24]. In fact, his Act was ineffective at any scale larger than the individual property; the notion of clearance *areas* had been expressed too vaguely.

This point is underlined by the concurrent experience in Edinburgh. When the Town Council decided to embark on its first slum clearance scheme, it did not use the Lindsay Act but secured private authorization through the Edinburgh Improvement Act of 1867[25]. In part, this can be explained by Edinburgh's traditional independence, and its steadfast preference for private legislation over the general statutes[26], but independence cannot be the full explanation in this instance. The Lindsay Act was well received in Edinburgh, and numerous sections were adopted as supplements to the city's own sanitary legislation[27]. Even more revealingly, at the same time that the Improvement Act was being promoted, the Town Council was promoting a provisional order for a miscellany of small improvement projects under the Lindsay Act[28]. The two instruments were seen as complementary rather than overlapping.

Edinburgh also took one other action under the 1862 Act in the appointment of Dr. Henry Littlejohn as the city's first medical officer of health[29], a position which he filled until 1908. In retrospect, one of Lindsay's greatest contributions was to define the sanitary powers and responsibilities of medical officers, and Littlejohn responded immediately. In 1865 he completed his *Report on the Sanitary Condition of Edinburgh,* a devastating analysis of the city's public health problems in which he advanced many recommendations for improvement, including the redevelopment of the worst of the slums. The Improvement Act which followed was a powerful piece of legislation. It specified, in all the detail of metes and bounds description, the properties that the Corporation was authorized to acquire and clear, embracing, in total, about 3250 dwellings and various other types of property spread over thirty-four separate clearance areas. The Corporation was also authorized to use some of the cleared land for opening new streets, or widening existing ones, but the remaining land could be disposed of as it saw fit. The Corporation was not required to redevelop the cleared sites with housing, and had no obligations to the displaced population, other than to phase the demolition programme so as to limit the number of people who would be evicted at any given time.

It was precisely this last point that Parliament felt obliged to clarify when the improvement scheme concept finally passed into general legislation in the Cross Acts—the Artizans and Labourers Dwellings Improvement Acts of 1875 and 1880. Cross's central principle was that the total working-class housing supply should not be diminished, so no local authority was permitted to embark on an improvement scheme without providing assurance that substitute dwellings would be available[30]. At first, under the 1875 Act, this requirement was to be satisfied on the clearance site or in its immediate vicinity, but the 1880 Act offered a broader alternative; except in London, substitute housing could be provided anywhere, as long as it was affordable, convenient and sanitary. More generally, though, the purpose of the Cross Acts was to allow all urban governments the right to take the kind of improvement action that Edinburgh had secured for itself in 1867. In brief, the powers which they could already apply against individual insanitary dwellings were now extended to insanitary areas. The chief legislative concern was to set out the procedures by which these powers could be exercised, with due protection for private property rights. And the pattern which was established then was to endure through many reworkings of the housing legislation, including, in particular, the Housing Act of 1890, which provided the enabling legislation for the Edinburgh improvement schemes of the succeeding decade.

THE ENVIRONMENTAL PLANNING SYSTEM

Neither the Lindsay Act nor the Edinburgh Improvement Act gave clear guidance on the preparation and implementation of redevelopment plans. It was therefore necessary for the Corporation of Edinburgh to construct its own planning system, step by step, as the sequence of events unfolded (figure 6.1). Without describing the process in detail, three points stand out.

(i) At all stages before implementation, the action shifted sequentially from the technical arena to the political arena, as planning concepts were developed and then debated and modified. Most striking, to modern eyes, is the degree to which citizen participation was actively solicited, through public meetings, circular letters to prominent organizations, and the distribution of printed copies of the plan. The main open debate, though, occurred in Step 2—Contention. Further participation was invited in Step 3, but almost none was forthcoming. The debate, by then, was confined to the council chamber.

(ii) The key figure, particularly in the first two steps, was Edinburgh's Lord Provost, without whom Littlejohn's initiative would have lost momentum. William Chambers, a man who had never held political office, was invited to become Lord Provost in 1865 because of his reputation as a reformer; he accepted because of the opportunities which Littlejohn's report appeared to offer[31]. For the next two years he devoted himself to the task of building a base of popular and political support for the scheme, but

MODEL OF THE PLANNING PROCESS, EDINBURGH IMPROVEMENT SCHEME 1867

	TIME	PRINCIPAL ACTORS	PURPOSE	OUTCOME
STEP 1 - IMPULSION				
(a) Technical phase	December 1864 August 1865	Medical Officer of Health	Sanitary survey of city	Redevelopment concept described
(b) Political phase	October 1865 December 1865	Lord Provost	To win Council's support	Plans "to be matured"
STEP 2 - CONTENTION				
(a) Technical phase	January 1866	Lord Provost Burgh Architect	To develop a physical planning concept	Preliminary plan
(b) Political phase	January 1866 April 1866	Lord Provost Town Council committees Public organisations Citizens' groups	To win political and popular support	Acceptance of preliminary plan with some modifications — parliamentary plans to be prepared
STEP 3 - AUTHORISATION				
(a) Technical phase	May 1866 July 1866	Planning consultants	To refine the plan for final debate	Refined plan — printed version widely distributed
(b) Political phase	July 1866 May 1867	Lord Provost Town Council and its committees Parliament	To win definite commitment	Modifications to refined plan — Edinburgh Improvement Act, 1867
STEP 4 - IMPLEMENTATION				
(a) Technical phase	September 1867 1887	Improvement Trust Planning consultants	(a) To acquire and clear sites (b) To prepare detailed layout plans and building specifications	Disposal of building sites for redevelopment

FIGURE 6.1.

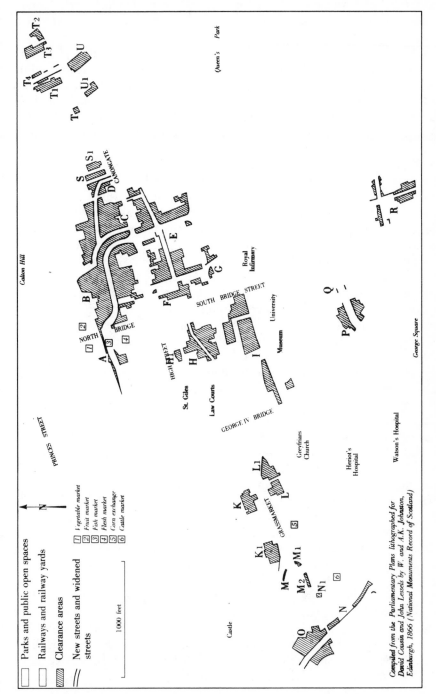

FIGURE 6.2. Areas designated for acquisition and clearance under the Edinburgh Improvement Act, 1867.

his identification was even closer than that suggests. The physical planning concept which was developed in Step 2, and which was largely followed in the final plan, was essentially his[32].

(iii) The plan authorized by Parliament in 1867 was a clearance plan, not a redevelopment plan, which meant that the detailed planning was left until the implementation stage (figure 6.2). As each project area was cleared, the Improvement Trust had to decide how the land was to be used, and the planning consultants had to prepare detailed layout plans and building specifications. Inevitably, in a process that spanned more than twenty years, decisions were made in an *ad hoc* fashion, reflecting the exigencies of current conditions rather than some preconceived blueprint.

To a surprising degree, the same conclusions can be drawn from the Leith improvement scheme of 1880—surprising because this scheme was conducted under the first Cross Act and new constraints on local action might therefore have been expected. In fact, the planning process took on essentially the same form as in Edinburgh (figure 6.3), even to the emergence of a key figure, Provost John Henderson, who not only salvaged the scheme after its popular rejection but designed the compromise plan which was eventually implemented[33]. This parallel between the Edinburgh and Leith experiences leads to an obvious conclusion: not only was political leadership necessary, even under the Cross Acts, but political effectiveness was greatly enhanced by the leader's close personal identification with the scheme, and the strength of his commitment to it. At the technical level, too, the parallels were strong. Once again, the plan which was actually approved by Parliament was a clearance and street improvement plan. It specified that new sanitary housing had to be built, somewhere, to accommodate the displaced population, but did not actually order the cleared area to be redeveloped for housing[34]. In fact, it was taken for granted that the site would be used for working-class tenements of some kind, but the form of the redevelopment and all related technical decisions were entirely at the Town Council's discretion. An overall layout plan was decided upon through an architectural competition in 1881[35], but even this left a great deal undetermined. The final decisions were made, in an *ad hoc* manner, as development applications were received over the next thirty years.

It appears then, that despite the special statutory framework of the Cross Act, the planning systems which evolved in Edinburgh and Leith were essentially an adaptation of customary procedures to a new practical problem. And inevitably, in long-drawn-out processes, the adaptations themselves came to acquire the force of established institutions in the hands of an effective and experienced bureaucracy. The significance of this point is revealed in the three renewal schemes for which the Edinburgh Corporation was responsible under the Housing Act of 1890. Beginning with the 1893 scheme, a much simpler routine was followed, and it was largely in the hands of technical officials. These were the medical officer of

MODEL OF THE PLANNING PROCESS, LEITH IMPROVEMENT SCHEME, 1880

	TIME	PRINCIPAL ACTORS	PURPOSE	OUTCOME
STEP 1 - IMPULSION				
(a) Technical phase	January 1876	Medical Officer of Health	To determine whether some areas were legally unhealthy	Official representation under 1875 Act
(b) Political phase	February 1876 July 1877	Public Health Committee	To evaluate the official representation	Representation accepted — improvement scheme to be prepared
STEP 2 - CONTENTION				
(a) Technical phase	August 1877 October 1877	Burgh Surveyor Architectural Consultant	To develop a physical planning concept	Preliminary plan
(b) Political phase	October 1877 November 1877	Town Council Ratepayers	To win political and popular support	Rejected by plebiscite — to prepare plan for smaller area
(c) Technical phase	December 1877 January 1878	Burgh Surveyor	To develop a modified planning concept	Revised plan
(d) Political phase	February 1878 May 1878	Town Council Ratepayers	To win political and popular support	Plan abandoned — petition
(e) Technical phase	May 1878	Medical Officer of Health	To prove that some areas were legally unhealthy	Official representation under 1875 Act
(f) Political phase	June 1878 November 1878	Public Health Committee Home Secretary's Office	To win political and popular support	Wait for new Council to be elected
STEP 3 - AUTHORISATION				
(a) Technical phase	December 1878	Provost	To develop a modified planning concept	Revised plan
(b) Political phase	January 1879 August 1880	Provost Town Council Home Secretary's Office Parliament	To win definite commitment	Revised plan accepted — Leith Improvement Scheme Confirmation Act, 1880
STEP 4 - IMPLEMENTATION				
Technical phase	September 1880 Circa 1910	Town Council Planning consultants Burgh Surveyor	(a) To acquire and clear sites (b) To prepare detailed layout plans and building specifications	Disposal of building sites for redevelopment

FIGURE 6.3.

health, who decided which areas should be condemned, and when; the burgh engineer, who drafted the physical plans and supervised their implementation; and the central government's inspector (a retired army engineer) who conducted the local inquiries and whose reports were always followed exactly in the official authorizations. The schemes had to be sanctioned by the Town Council, and each was administered through a council committee, but the openly political nature of the earlier schemes was a thing of the past. The improvement schemes had ceased to be controversial, either within Council or without; public participation was non-existent and was no longer solicited; and the councillors acted more like technical experts than politicians, particularly in their appearances before the local inquiries. Attitudes had changed substantially, in large part, no doubt, because the benefits of sanitary reform had been proven to everyone's satisfaction. Edinburgh's crude death rate had fallen from a high of 30.4 per 1000 in 1869 to 16.1 in 1894, and the local officials did not hesitate to place much of the credit on the 1867 improvement scheme[36]. Moreover, these officials took care not to upset the favourable climate of opinion by embarking on ambitious and expensive schemes on the 1867 and 1880 scale. The public costs of the earlier schemes were at the root of all controversy but, in the 1890s, by proceeding a little at a time, the cost issue was effectively defused[37].

IMAGES OF CITY, SLUM AND IMPROVEMENT

By the 1890s, the institutions of improvement planning were firmly in place in Edinburgh. It might also be expected, as a parallel trend, that the slum problem would have been more clearly understood, and the goals of slum clearance more carefully defined. In part, this appears to be true, but mainly in the sense that the institutional purpose of the improvement schemes had been narrowed appreciably. The fundamental questions of need, and the relevance of the improvement-scheme approach, were simply assumed away. Only in the 1860s, before there was national legislation to provide a *raison d'être* for municipal action, was there much attempt to justify the need for renewal.

A number of simple questions will serve to set this issue in context. What were the improvement schemes meant to improve? Who was meant to benefit? What attitudes were held towards the slums and their inhabitants, and how did these motivate and shape the actions that were taken? To what extent, if at all, was there a genuine desire to help the slum residents, as a moral or compassionate end?

These questions can be answered only by inference but, as a first step, it must be realized that the slum residents themselves were never heard from in the planning exercises, nor were they expected to be heard from. When participation was solicited, it was participation by the elite, particularly those members of prominent organizations who could be expected to influence the only population that mattered, the enfranchized householders who would have to bear the public costs. Even at the statutory inquiries of the 1890s, the residents of the clearance areas were never represented; the hearings were solely for the benefit of the absentee landlords.

To the powerholders, the slums were known only by evil reputation. The Leith slums, wrote one local historian in the 1890s, were a *terra incognita,* a backwater of 'squalid lanes and closes' which few people had cause to penetrate[38]. William Chambers's first action as Lord Provost of Edinburgh was a close personal inspection of some of the city's worst quarters, a horrifying revelation which he forced his officials to share and which reinforced the deterministic beliefs of the time[39]. 'To the unclean and miserable homes of too many of the poor', wrote Provost Lindsay in 1865, 'may be traced much of the moral degradation into which they fall'[40]. Another Edinburgh sanitarian, Dr. Alexander Wood, expressed it more passionately and more personally: 'If you treat human beings worse than beasts, what can you expect them to become? . . . Would I be myself better in similar circumstances?'[41] There were others, though, who argued that poverty was the root cause of the slum problem, and that disease and bad housing, filth and depravity, were merely its symptoms[42]. Even Chambers seems to have had some glimpse of this. The slum residents, he remarked in one speech, were 'vagrants and semi-pauperized orders from all parts of the country'[43], a mixture of rural Scots and Irish migrants who were befouling Edinburgh's proud face by their dissolute behaviour. But while Chambers saw this as a reason for cleaning out the slums, it could also be used to argue that the improvement scheme approach was the wrong one for the time. The Parochial Board of St. Cuthberts, out of years of experience with poor law administration, seized on the fact that the 1867 scheme would destroy much of the city's cheapest housing, and so worsen rather than improve the lot of the poor[44]. Another practical reformer, the Reverend James Begg, carried the argument a step further[45]. Although the slums must eventually be cleared, he said, the immediate need was for *more* cheap houses, not fewer. Public funds should be spent on construction rather than demolition, so that population could be siphoned away from the slums and congestion ended.

Implicit in these views, of course, was the expectation that the slum residents were the intended beneficiaries of the 1867 scheme, an expectation that was not warranted by events. Although, in deterministic vein, sanitary improvement was described as a step towards 'moral amelioration'[46], there was little overt concern for the people whose homes were destroyed. Only Littlejohn took it for granted that clearance areas would be redeveloped with cheap houses for the displaced population[47]. Generally, it was assumed that the local authorities had no obligation, legal or moral, towards the residents of their clearance areas, as long as they did not evict too many of them at the same time. The point was demonstrated most convincingly in 1885, before the Royal Commission on the Housing of the Working Classes, where the Town Clerk of Leith had to endure particularly tough questioning, based on the assumption that the Town Council was required to rehouse all the original population of the improvement scheme area on the actual clearance site[48]. The Town Clerk not only denied this but asserted that the Council had no intention of trying to meet such a condition. Quite apart from the undesirability of rebuilding to the original density, the 1875 Act could not be used in the way that Cross and the Commission apparently thought it should[49]. In Leith, as in Edinburgh under the 1867 scheme, the substitute accommodation was provided by vacancies in the standing housing stock, and the evidence that this was effective was simply that people were absorbed by the open market with no known fuss or stress[50]. From the outset, it was taken as self-evident that the displaced population could not be rehoused through redevelopment. It was quite impossible for private enterprise to satisfy all the sanitary requirements in new buildings, and to secure a reasonable return, by charging rents that the poorest slum dwellers could afford. When housing was built, it was intended for the superior working classes, the artisans and tradesmen, not for casual labourers or rag-pickers, and certainly not for the drunkards, prostitutes and criminals of all descriptions which the slum population was so widely believed to comprise.

Thus, although the reform leaders might be stirred by humanitarian and moral considerations, there was little place for such sentiments in the world of practical decisions. In that world, public money was to be spent with due care and economy; redevelopment had to march to the dictates of the market place; public authorities were obliged to secure the best possible return on their investments in cleared land, no matter how long they had to wait; and success was measured by the disappearance of known centres of pestilence. In practice, attention was focused on insanitary *areas* rather than their inhabitants, a point which became explicit in 1890. In the Cross Act of 1875, renewal was to be motivated by considerations of 'moral and physical welfare'. In the 1890 Act, the reference to moral welfare was dropped, and the rehousing requirement could be satisfied by declaring that a sufficient number of existing low-rent houses was known to be vacant. In short, the improvement scheme was accepted as a public health measure rather than a device for providing the poor with better houses, which is another reason why it became so non-controversial and routine. The legislation provided a pat formula for declaring areas to be unhealthy, a formula that was no longer cluttered by vague considerations about the morality of the poor or the social desirability of raising their housing standards.

For all its apparent clarity, though, the 1890 Act still begged a long unanswered question: who was to benefit from the clearance of unhealthy areas? The intent of all the legislation appears to be directed at the resident population, but the practice, once again, was otherwise. Since there was no control over the relocation process, at least until late in the 1890s in Edinburgh's case, there could be no guarantee that the displaced families would find new homes that were any better than the old[51]. Some other interest had to be served, then, to impel the Corporations of Edinburgh and Leith to act as they did. Two possibilities stand out from the contemporary documents and, intuitively, each looks more persuasive than any concern for the slum dwellers. The first was described by the Leith Inspector of Nuisances, in a report to Provost Lindsay. Put crudely, it was fear. The slums were a breeding ground for disease, but could not contain it: 'overleaping all barriers, it carries death into the most favoured districts beyond', setting the whole city at risk[52]. The slum problem, in this view, was reduced to a problem of epidemic contagion, and Littlejohn demonstrated how much there was to lose in his evidence that death rates ranged from a low 14 per thousand in one of the affluent suburbs to between 30 and 38 in the worst quarters of the old town[53]. A similar contrast was reported by Lindsay in Leith.

And yet, on its own, fear seems not to have been a particularly effective spur to government action. Rather, it served to reinforce other interests, the chief of which was civic pride. Even Leith was not immune[54], but the clearest illustration is afforded by Lord Provost Chambers of Edinburgh. Indeed, for all the sincerity of his humanitarian impulse, Chambers's own writings leave no doubt that his pride in Edinburgh was his strongest practical inspiration[55], and his most effective line of argument with his supporters. The slums had to be redeveloped because they were a disgrace to a city of Edinburgh's stature, at once undermining its contemporary reputation and its symbolic value as the repository of 800 years of Scottish history. The theme had powerful emotional appeal, and typically took the form that the old town of Edinburgh could not be restored to its proper place in the community until it was once again lived in by 'a superior class of people'[56].

There is no cause to be surprised by this interpretation. The persistence of the word 'improvement' is revealing of the continuing force of the progressive spirit. Under the 1862 Act, for instance, local authorities were empowered to impose a general improvement tax on their ratepayers, and Lindsay's own recital of the things that the Leith levy paid for in its first year is remarkable for its diversity[57]. It must therefore be realized that improvement, itself, sweepingly conceived, was the key notion which engaged practical reformers like Chambers and Lindsay. An improvement scheme could serve many ends, and no real attempt was made to think them through and separate them. Simple order was not imposed on the improvement idea until the 1890s when, by reducing the improvement scheme to a sanitary device, it was also reduced to a technical duty of the sanitary officials, serving only one interest, the *public* health. And progress in the public health could be charted directly in the falling track of the crude death rate, which, in its time, became as great a source of pride as any of the better-known symbols of Edinburgh's status.

RENEWAL CONCEPTS IN THE IMPROVEMENT SCHEMES

Just as the slum problem was conceived largely in physical terms, so too was slum renewal. The emphasis in the renewal plans was on the layout of streets and building plots, the style and quality of new construction, and, always, public costs and returns. Above all, in the two large schemes of 1867 and 1880, where civic pride was the dominant motif, the opportunity to 'regularize' the street network stands out as the central planning conception. Initially, though, as envisaged by Littlejohn, new streets were no more than a neat tactic for making the disease-ridden quarters of the city healthier. In the planning catch-phrase of the day, the slums would be 'opened out'. As local illustrations he cited the 1827 improvement scheme, which provided several major roads into and through the old town, and a private project of the 1850s, in which Edinburgh's ancient High Street was linked to a new railway station[58]. As a by-product, in both cases, foul and congested quarters, which normally lay behind the main street frontages, were thrown wide open to 'improving influences'. In the 1867 scheme, the procedure and the results were the same, but the rationale was reversed; sanitary improvement was the stated purpose and street improvement the by-product. In the long-term, though, the new and widened streets are the best-remembered benefit, and the individual clearance areas seem to have been selected as much for their value to the inner-city road network as for any sanitary reason. Were they necessarily the worst slum areas? The documentary records are silent on this question. All that can be said for sure is that neither Chambers nor the Trust's architects attempted to disguise the importance which they attached to the street plan[59]. Progress and civic pride demanded that the street network should be modernized; the sanitary reform movement provided the opportunity.

The same spirit is evident in the Leith scheme. From the outset, the chief planning emphasis was on the need to secure a cross-town link through an otherwise impassable quarter[60], and the boundary of the clearance area (figure 6.6) was obviously drawn to fit the route of the new street.

Does this, then, mean that the corporations of Edinburgh and Leith were being devious when they framed their clearance schemes of 1867 and 1880, because street improvement was their goal all along? That would be an unduly cynical interpretation. In accordance with the broadly-based conception of improvement, new streets were regarded as a legitimate benefit of slum clearance for sanitary purposes. Even the general

FIGURE 6.4. Chambers Street was the major architectural creation of the 1867 improvement scheme. The street is eighty feet wide and is lined on the north side with public buildings in the style of the Renaissance revival.

FIGURE 6.5. Henderson Street, the main through-street in the Leith improvement scheme. Like Chambers Street in Edinburgh, it was named after the Provost whose leadership was essential to the scheme's success.

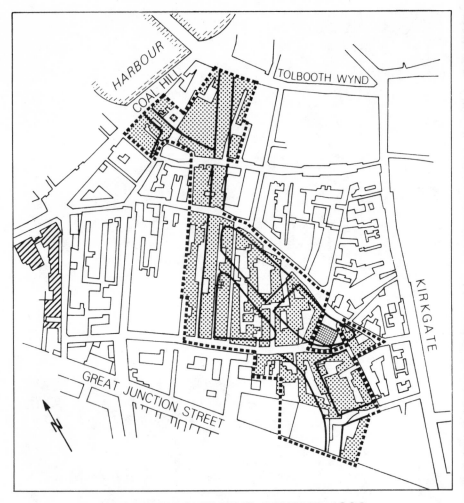

LEITH IMPROVEMENT SCHEME, 1880

•••••• Boundary of improvement scheme area

Condemned buildings

Street layout after redevelopment

Hospital

School

FIGURE 6.6. Areas affected by the Leith improvement scheme, 1880.

FIGURE 6.7. St. Marys Street was the first achievement of the 1867 scheme. A narrow and irregular wynd was opened into a fifty-foot-wide street, with new shops and artisans' tenements along one frontage. The 'picturesque' roofline was one of the architects' most distinctive contributions.

FIGURE 6.8. A plainer version of the stone-built tenements of the 1867 improvement scheme, and truer to the Scottish urban vernacular then St. Marys Street.

legislation accepted this principle. In the 1875 Act, and in all succeeding acts, local authorities were given the right to demolish healthy properties to obtain access into and through an improvement-scheme area, as long as compensation was awarded at full market value. At the same time, as improvement scheme planning became more routine and technical, and more sharply focused on the public health, so it narrowed as a planning concept. 'Improvement scheme' ceased to be a metaphor for a wide-ranging vision of municipal progress, and became, instead, a legal title for a specialized function of local government, by which the pockets of bad housing were cleaned out, one by one. Simultaneously, the welfare of the poorer elements of the population was thrown into sharper focus, as the later renewal plans demonstrated in three ways.

(i) Under part 3 of the 1890 Act, which gave local authorities the right to own 'lodging houses'[61], the Corporation of Edinburgh began to experiment with cheaper forms of construction. In the previous schemes, one of the major design considerations had been that new housing should be built in the Scottish vernacular style. The authorities therefore insisted upon the construction of traditional tenements in good quality stone, often handsomely faced and with much attention to ornamental detailing. Particularly in the 1867 scheme, the Trust's architects deliberately tried to recreate the historic atmosphere of old Edinburgh, with due deference to the Gothic taste for the picturesque. Builders might complain about the extra costs which were being forced on them, as they did also in Leith in the 1880s, but standards were lowered reluctantly[62]. In the 1890s, by contrast, the Corporation of Edinburgh deliberately cut every corner that it could. Brick and stucco replaced the traditional stone; flatted cottages replaced the traditional tenement; external iron galleries replaced interior stairs and corridors; and frills and ornaments of all kinds were eliminated. Cost became the first design criterion, within the bounds of the sanitary regulations[63].

(ii) For the first time, rehabilitation was used as a serious alternative to redevelopment. Sometimes it was the response of the owners, under the threat of condemnation and expropriation[64]. In other cases, the Corporation itself restored an expropriated building, perhaps to save on time as much as on cost. The earlier schemes, which were completely captive to the building industry's willingness to take over the cleared sites, had demonstrated that redevelopment could be an exceedingly drawn-out process, as well as a costly one. It is also worth noting, as an aside, that part of the rehabilitation initiative came from Patrick Geddes, who persuaded the Corporation to let him take over a tenement which was scheduled for demolition under the 1893 scheme[65].

(iii) On some sites under the last schemes, the renewal plans included amenities which demonstrate an emerging sensitivity for the needs of the slum population. In the 1867 scheme, there was nothing comparable.

FIGURE 6.9. One of Edinburgh's earliest examples of public housing, built on a site cleared under the 1893 improvement scheme.

Where amenities, like churches, were provided, it was entirely on the initiative of their sponsors who had to pay the full market price for their sites. In the Leith scheme, a further step was taken, albeit a misguided one. A large ornamental park was created, as a poor man's version of the residential squares and 'places' of the New Town of Edinburgh; civic pride was expressing itself again, when the real need was for somewhere for children to play. Only in the 1890s did playgrounds become an integral part of renewal plans. Public wash houses were also introduced, in long overdue recognition of the difficulty of improving personal hygiene in dwellings that had neither bathrooms nor laundries (figure 6.12).

This last point highlights another one: even in the improvement schemes, the acceptable standards of housing in the 1890s were very low. The units might be structurally sound, damp-proof and reasonably well lighted, but they were still small and deficient in the most basic hygienic amenities. The chief debate during these late schemes addressed just these issues, in hard practical terms: How many families could be permitted to share a water closet? Should one-roomed houses be tolerated, or should two rooms be the minimum size?[66]. In their own way, the Edinburgh politicians were confronting the classic planning paradox, that improvements in quality standards impose additional costs which put the improvements beyond the reach of those they are intended to benefit.

In the 1867 scheme, in keeping with the progressive spirit of the time,

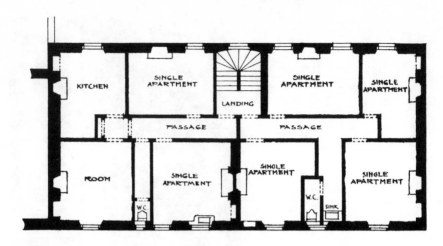

PLAN before RECONSTRUCTION

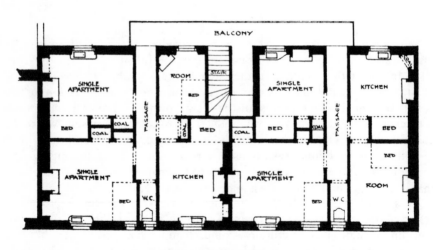

PLAN as RECONSTRUCTED

FIGURE 6.10. Tenement rehabilitation by Edinburgh Corporation in the 1890s: plans.

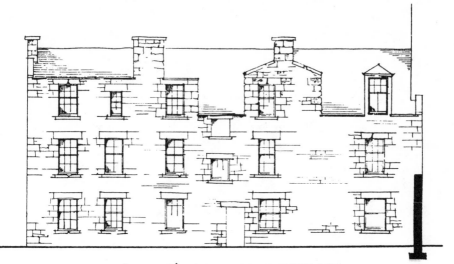

BACK ELEVATION before RECONSTRUCTION

BACK ELEVATION as RECONSTRUCTED

FIGURE 6.11. Tenement rehabilitation by Edinburgh Corporation in the 1890s: elevations.

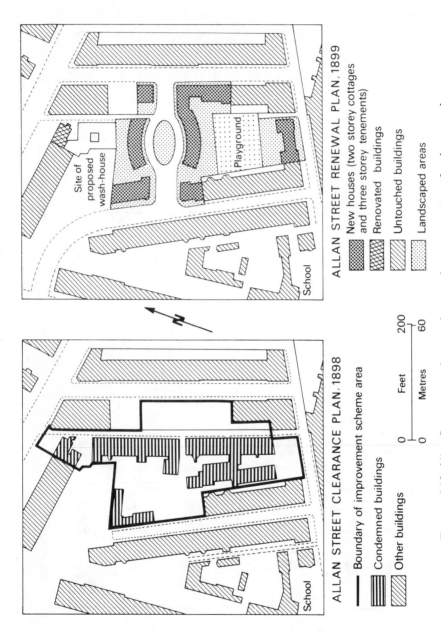

ALLAN STREET RENEWAL PLAN, 1899

Site of proposed wash-house

Playground

School

▓ New houses (two storey cottages and three storey tenements)

▨ Renovated buildings

⬚ Untouched buildings

⋮ Landscaped areas

ALLAN STREET CLEARANCE PLAN, 1898

School

━ Boundary of improvement scheme area

▥ Condemned buildings

▨ Other buildings

0   Feet   200

0   Metres   60

N

FIGURE 6.12. Allan Street renewal areas, showing the incorporation of a playground.

aesthetic images of the reconstructed city dominated over social conscience. The quality standards which were derived from those images were not easily relaxed, regardless of their impact on redevelopment costs and no matter how large a section of the working-class population was excluded. In fact, only once did the Improvement Trustees allow social needs to intrude at all upon their redevelopment planning. In response to considerable external pressure, they used some of their own funds to build four mean tenements of one-roomed houses on an out-of-the-way street[67], but even these were too expensive for the displaced population. When they were sold, at cost, it was to 'artisans of a superior class'[68].

The attitudes of the Improvement Trustees during the twenty-five year implementation phase of the 1867 scheme stand clearly revealed by their redevelopment achievements. Four points deserve particular emphasis.

(i) Housing had a low priority in the redevelopment plans. In 1866, the Trust's architects forecast that redevelopment would produce almost as many houses as were condemned[69], but only in the first project, under-taken when the reform interest was still at its peak, was housing the dominant concern. Elsewhere, the emphasis was on a wide variety of commercial and institutional buildings, and housing was secondary. By 1885, when the Trust was winding down its affairs, 2720 houses had been demolished but only 340 new ones had been built[70].

FIGURE 6.13. The Guthrie Street tenements, the only attempt to build low-cost housing under the 1867 scheme.

(ii) At all times the Trust sought the highest financial return on its land. This is demonstrated in numerous ways, from its standard building conditions to the upset prices that it set at public auctions, and its reluctance to reduce either, even in the face of persistently weak demand. In the day-to-day administration of the Trust, fiscal responsibility was the ruling criterion, not social responsibility.

(iii) In the same vein, to stay within budget, the Trustees quietly failed to proceed with some of the authorized projects. Two were particularly striking. Although their congestion was as bad as any of the other areas, and they were to be major subjects of the next scheme in 1893, they were unattractive to the Trustees of 1867 because their potential commercial value was limited; they did not offer new street frontages in prime business locations.

(iv) This concern for redevelopment value was not just narrow commercialism. Both of the early schemes were enormously expensive, and required large public subsidies. In the Leith scheme, for example, the gross land costs for acquisition and clearance were £12,500 per acre, which created site values far beyond the reach of the poorer classes[71]. The Edinburgh costs cannot be calculated as nicely but they were of the same general order. In effect, these condemned properties were being treated as though they were still in prime condition, at the peak of their commercial value[72], an attitude which may be interpreted as an unthinking class reaction and an unquestioning use of a customary administrative procedure. At all events, apart from one outburst from Chambers[73], the rightness of the approach was not challenged, even though the financial implications were always obvious to the Trustees. Knowing they could never recoup their costs, they felt obliged to reduce the gap as much as possible by securing the best return that the market would bear. In fact, in the Edinburgh case, the subsidy was roughly 70 per cent, or £400,000 out of gross costs of £550,000[74].

When these financial realities were combined with the desire to recreate 'old' Edinburgh in a more progressive image, the concern for high-quality redevelopment stands fully explained. The ratepayers of Edinburgh had to be given good value for their £400,000, and this was done in three ways: some of the city's unhealthiest and most threatening slum quarters were swept away; the efficiency of the street network was increased; and, in the process, some fine new commercial properties were created and had to be given due architectural expression. The slum warrens gave way to broad streets that were handsome as well as efficient.

By and large, the same attitudes prevailed in the Leith scheme of 1880, although the Leith Town Council was more constrained by the enabling legislation. Again, a disorderly clutter of courts and alleys yielded to a broad through street which demanded an appropriate physical setting, as exemplified in such features as the ornamental park and the well-designed tenements[75]. Nor did the Town Council ever deceive itself into thinking that the clearance area could be restored with the same number of houses, even though this brought it into long dispute with the Home Secretary's office. The paramount physical-planning conception, as in all the Victorian renewal schemes, was one of opening out congested quarters. And 'opening out' was inconsistent with the social end of maintaining the size of the housing stock, just as the site costs under redevelopment were inconsistent with the desire to rehouse the original population, or people like them.

Some Implications for Planning Thought

Of necessity, this review of the Edinburgh experience has been highly generalized, but it nonetheless casts some light on the paradoxical evolution of planning thought in the second half of the Victorian period. As a first point, there is no question that the appeal of the slum-clearance approach was undiluted, for all its political and practical difficulties. Born as it was in a progressive image of the city, the improvement scheme came to be accepted as a progressive institution in its own right, yielding benefits in the public health which were believed to be beyond challenge. And while the initial vision of improvement was to fade, in time, as attention was focused more and more sharply on the goal of sanitary improvement, there was an associated heightening of the inspiration which reform-minded officials continued to draw from William Chambers. To a man, they saw themselves carrying Chambers' 'great work' to its necessary conclusion, sweeping away those slum remnants which it had been politically inexpedient to condemn in 1867[76]. As in Leith in 1880, the original clearance areas were delimited not by need but by the tolerance of the ratepayers, and the planning processes in both communities were dominated by the search for an acceptable compromise between public costs and the desire to restore the slums to 'social and commercial respectability'. Not surprisingly, then, it had been one of Chambers' fondest hopes that private enterprise would follow where he had led[77], a failed dream which was to give a later generation of officials their most obvious line of argument. A simple scenario was composed: slum clearance had made Edinburgh a healthier city; the removal of the remaining slums would make it healthier still; from which emerged the practical target of reducing the crude death rate of the old town to the level of the rest of the city.

Despite the practical effectiveness of this model, however, contradictory insights were beginning to emerge, even as early as the 1880s. The first was the realization that Edinburgh's slums were dynamic, and that the improvement scheme system might actually be perpetuating them. Initially, in Leith as well as Edinburgh, all faith was placed in the filtering mechanism; it was believed that the construction of new houses with higher sanitary standards would result in an upward shift in housing quality, from which even the poor would eventually benefit. To an extent, as revealed by census housing statistics, this upgrading did occur, but the public health officials also accumulated a great deal of first-hand evidence about the deterioration of filtered-down houses in the 1880s and 1890s[78]. They therefore developed a new mental model in which the slums were relocated with the slum population.

An obvious question then arises: how did Edinburgh's officials rationalize the contradiction which they had now posed? The answer seems to lie in the 'habits of the people' hypothesis, or the belief that it was the poor themselves—shiftless, dirty and drunken as they were considered to be —who were largely to blame for the persistence of the slums. 'The habits of the people and the conditions of their dwellings have ... kept pace with each other in their downward course', wrote Thomas Cooper, the burgh engineer[79], loading the poor with guilt for failing to take advantage of the opportunities for environmental betterment which had been extended to them. The judgment was a moral one, a latter-day demonstration of the unforgiving side of Scottish puritanism, and it had the paradoxical effect of reinforcing the single-mindedness with which the goal of the *public* health was pursued. The creators of slums deserved no consideration; 'society must do something to protect itself against disease and vice'[80]. William Chambers had said that in 1866, and it was held to be no less true at century's end.

The larger implication of these developments, with respect to the progressive interpretation of planning thought, is that the improvement ethic in Victorian Edinburgh was marked by an intense conservatism. Not only did it become narrower in purpose but it continued to be permeated by the moral prescriptions of the evangelical revival. If anything, in fact, the moral perspective also narrowed, in a regressive fashion. During the 1867 scheme, the Corporation's actions could always be justified under the criterion of responsibility to the ratepayers, which was obviously perceived to be a greater good than the welfare of the slum population. In the later schemes, however, this moral weighting was by no means so clear, and slum clearance began to look uncomfortably like a punishment for unrespectable behaviour.

At the same time, at the risk of piling contradiction upon contradiction, there is evidence from the last years of the nineteenth century that the special needs of the slum population were being seen in a more humane light. The Housing Commission of 1885 was probably the critical catalyst, because of its forceful attention to the issue of rehousing displaced families, but the new social concern was manifest in all the physical achievements of the schemes under the 1890 Act. The legislation itself played some part, of course, but there were also changes in local attitudes which went far beyond the new legal prescriptions. There was nothing in the Act, for example, which required the City of Edinburgh to build houses more cheaply than had previously been thought possible, or to provide drying greens, wash-houses and playgrounds as part of its redevelopment programme. Local planning practice was evolving in a progressive direction, in response to the first effective stirrings of corporate social conscience.

And how is that practical evidence to be reconciled with the regressive interpretation which has already been advanced? The most obvious point is that it fitted the concern for public health, since the amenities at the redevelopment sites could all be justified as aids to cleanliness and fitness. Social justice was being served, but in a cautious and circumscribed fashion. The poor did have some rights, but only if they could demonstrate their willingness to live by the canons of respectability. Only 'good' tenants were welcome in the Corporation's houses, and even they had to submit to a management policy which came direct from Octavia Hill's brand of benevolent despotism[81]. Deterministic beliefs continued to be strong, as well. 'It is not to be expected that human nature can be "dragooned" into reformation', said Cooper[82], but environmental improvement was nonetheless held to be a mediator in moral reform, as an essential first step. Littlejohn had argued in exactly the same vein thirty years earlier[83].

The force of the *laisser-faire* ethic must also be allowed for. Repeatedly, over the years, the public officials of Edinburgh reiterated their horror at any thought of enlarging the scope of public responsibility. Two points, in particular, emerge. The first, which was deeply embedded in Scottish evangelicalism, was the belief that the highest form of benevolence was that of helping the poor to help themselves. Charity was both a moral duty and a moral test for the affluent, but it was by no means a right of the poor; that raised the spectre of a population lost in abject dependency. The second point concerns the division of responsibility between public and private enterprise, in the conventional commercial sense. Public enterprise should do nothing that private enterprise was willing and able to do, which meant, in particular, that it should not build houses. The role of local government, was to destroy bad property, not to reconstruct it, the Housing Commission was told[84], and only with great reluctance was this opinion moderated over the next fifteen years. The barriers to private action were apparent from the beginning of the 1867 scheme, but it took a long time for public authorities to admit that they could do something to reduce the gap between financial realities and housing need, without undermining the moral fibre of the nation.

Concomitant with that breakthrough there came another which was to bear even more directly on the development of the planning idea. During the 1890s in Edinburgh, it began to be argued that the improvement of the slum environment could not be confined to the slums themselves. If, indeed, private enterprise was unable to build cheap houses on cleared sites, and if the improvement-scheme approach was merely perpetuating the slums, some different technique was required. Again, it was found in the past, in the notion of cheap suburban land which James Begg had advocated in the 1850s and 1860s. By 1894, even Thomas Cooper could use one of his official reports to charge Edinburgh's suburban land owners with the responsibility for maintaining the city's slums, because of the binding cordon of high-cost land which they refused to break[85]. Social idealism also began to show itself, in at least one official mind. Municipal ownership of land was inevitable, said Cooper, if slums were to be ended and the poor housed decently. The practical realization of these dreams was still decades into the future, waiting on such national legislation as the Housing and Town Planning Act of 1919 and the Housing Act of 1930, but some radical seeds were germinating for all that—seeds which owed their conception to the Victorian experience with environmental improvement.

NOTES

1. For an exception see Tarn, J. N. (1969) Housing in Liverpool and Glasgow: the growth of civic responsibility. *Town Planning Review*, **39** (4), pp. 317–34.
2. See, for example, the debate on the second reading of the Artizans and Labourers Dwellings Improvement Bill (1875) *Hansard's Parliamentary Debates*, Third Series, **244**, pp. 449–62.
3. Ashworth, W. (1951) *The Genesis of Modern British Town Planning*. London: Routledge and Kegan Paul.
4. Benevolo, L. (1967) *The Origins of Modern Town Planning*. London: Routledge and Kegan Paul.
5. Choay, F. (undated) *The Modern City: Planning in the 19th Century*. London: Studio Vista, p. 15.
6. Dyos, H. J. (1957) Urban transformation: a note on the objects of street improvement in Regency and early Victorian London. *International Review of Social History*, **2**, pp. 259–65; Dyos, H. J. and Reeder, D. A. (1973) Slums and suburbs, in Dyos, H. J. and Wolff, M. (eds.), *The Victorian City*. London: Routledge and Kegan Paul, pp. 359–86.
7. Giedion, S. (1959) *Space, Time and Architecture*. Cambridge, Mass.: Harvard University Press, p. 648.
8. To cite just one example, the Edinburgh Improvement Act of 1876 was concerned with the enlargement of Princes Street Gardens.
9. Lindsay, J. (ed.) (1914) *Municipal Glasgow: Its Evolution and Enterprises*. Glasgow: The City Corporation, p. 48.
10. Cherry, G. E. (1972) *Urban Change and Planning: A History of Urban Development in Britain since 1750*. Henley-on-Thames: G. T. Foulis, pp. 69–70; Wohl, A. S. (1977) *The Eternal Slum: Housing and Social Policy in Victorian London*. London: Edward Arnold, pp. 26–7.
11. Ashworth, W. (1951) *The Genesis of Modern British Town Planning*. London: Routledge and Kegan Paul, pp. 96–110.

12. Tarn, J. N. (1969) Housing in Liverpool and Glasgow: the growth of civic responsibility. *Town Planning Review*, **39** (4), pp. 317–34; Lindsay, J. (ed.) (1914) *Municipal Glasgow: Its Evolution and Enterprises*. Glasgow: The City Corporation, pp. 50–7; Allan, C. M. (1965) The genesis of British urban redevelopment with special reference to Glasgow. *Economic History Review*, **18** (3), pp. 598–613.
13. Briggs, A. (1963) *Victorian Cities*. London: Odhams Books, pp. 228–33.
14. (1877) *The Builder*, **35** (1802), p. 842. This is merely the first of many references to the problem.
15. See, for example, (1879) *The Builder*, **37** (1904), pp. 845–6.
16. Bell, J. and Paton, J. (1898) *Glasgow: Its Municipal Organization and Progress*. Glasgow: James MacLehose and Sons, pp. 218–20.
17. Tyrwhitt, J. (ed.) (1947) *Patrick Geddes in India*. London: Lund Humphries, p. 45.
18. *Ibid.*, pp. 40–1.
19. Tarn, J. N. (1969) Housing in Liverpool and Glasgow: the growth of civic responsibility. *Town Planning Review*, **39** (4), p. 331; Allan, C. M. (1965) The genesis of British urban redevelopment with special reference to Glasgow. *Economic History Review*, **18** (3), p. 609. It is also evident, from the large number of reports in *The Builder* in the late 1870s and early 1880s, that the hardship of displaced families was exciting a great deal of contemporary concern.
20. Kitchen, P. (1975) *A Most Unsettling Person: An Introduction to the Life and Ideas of Patrick Geddes*. London: Victor Gollancz. See also Edinburgh City Corporation, *Miscellaneous papers relating to transactions under the Improvement Scheme 1892; also correspondence with Professor Geddes anent various subjects 1892–1895*, City Archives, Bundle 34.
21. Report of an address by Professor W. T. Gairdner, (1883) *The Builder*, **45** (2122), pp. 446–7. For a contrary view see Muir, G. W. (1884) *The Sanitary Condition of Glasgow and the Failure of the Improvement Act in Improving the Health of the Community*. Glasgow: W. Porteous & Co.
22. Leith Town Council (1860) *Council Record*, 4 (July 3).
23. Section 161, *The Police and Improvement (Scotland) Act*, 25–26 Victoria, c. 101, 1862.
24. Lindsay, W. (1865) *Address by Provost Lindsay to the Town Council of Leith*. Printed privately, pp. 20–1.
25. *The Edinburgh Improvement Act*, 30–31 Victoria, Cap. 44, 1867.
26. Best, G. (1968) The Scottish Victorian City. *Victorian Studies*, **11** (3), p. 335.
27. Edinburgh Town Council (1862) *Report by the Lord Provost's Committee as to the General Police and Improvement (Scotland) Act, 1862*. Printed privately, September 30.
28. *Edinburgh Provisional Order Confirmation Act*, 30–31 Victoria, 1867.
29. Edinburgh Town Council (1862) *Council Record*, 285 (September 30).
30. Section 5 of 38–39 Victoria, Cap. 49, said, in part, that the local authority 'shall provide for the accommodation of at least as many persons of the working class as may be displaced in the area with respect to which the scheme is proposed, in suitable dwellings, which, unless there are any special reasons to the contrary, shall be situate within the limits of the same area, or in the vicinity thereof, and shall also provide for proper sanitary arrangements'.

31. Marwick, J. D. (c. 1905) *A Retrospect*. Glasgow: printed privately, p. 158. Marwick was Town Clerk of Edinburgh during Chambers' tenure. Chambers, himself, said that Littlejohn's report had convinced him 'that the time had come when the whole subject of sanitary improvement ought to be grappled with, no matter at what cost, or at what amount of trouble'; Chambers, W. (1866) *Adress to the Architectural Institute of Scotland*. Printed privately, December 12.

32. Edinburgh Town Council (1866) *Minutes of the Lord Provost's Committee . . . with Explanatory Statement by the Lord Provost*. Printed privately, February 13; Cousin, D. and Lessels, J. (1866) *Plan of Sanitary Improvements of the City of Edinburgh*. Printed for the Town Council, p. 4.

33. Leith Town Council (1879) *Council Record United Series*, 2 (February 4).

34. *Leith Improvement Scheme Confirmation Act*, 43–44 Victoria, Ch. 175, 1880. The provisional order which was confirmed by this Act was signed by Home Secretary Cross on March 24, 1880, and included the following provision: 'The buildings on the lands constituting the improvement areas . . . shall be taken down and removed gradually, new houses for the accommodation of the population of the working class now occupying these areas being built simultaneously with the taking down and removing of the existing buildings'.

35. Leith Town Council (1881) *Leith Improvement Scheme: Letter Book* 3 (September 19), pp. 121ff.

36. These statistics are quoted in the first annual report of the Public Health Committee of the Edinburgh Town Council, in May 1896. The report also notes that there were fewer deaths in Edinburgh in 1895 than there were in 1865, although the population had increased by more than fifty per cent. Many possible reasons are noted but 'chief, of course, among the causes of our improved sanitary condition have been the improvement schemes under the Provostships of Dr. William Chambers and Sir James A. Russell [the 1893 Scheme]'.

37. Pollard, J. (1895) *Thirty Years' Sanitary Progress in Edinburgh*. Edinburgh: printed privately, pp. 8–9.

38. Irons, J. C. (1897) *Leith and its Antiquities from the Earliest Times to the Close of the Nineteenth Century*, vol. 2. Edinburgh: printed for the subscribers, p. 336.

39. Chambers, W. (1865) *The Lord Provost's Statement to the Town Council Respecting Sanitary Improvement*. Printed for the Town Council, December 5.

40. Lindsay, W. (1865) *Address by Provost Lindsay to the Town Council of Leith*. Printed privately, p. 28.

41. Wood, A. (1868) The condition of the dwellings of the operative classes in Edinburgh, in *Report on the Condition of the Poorer Classes in Edinburgh, and of their Dwellings, Neighbourhoods and Families*. Edinburgh: Edmonston and Douglas, p. 110.

42. Edinburgh Association for Improving the Condition of the Poor (1867) *How to Relieve the Poor of Edinburgh and Other Great Cities without Increasing Pauperism*. Edinburgh: Edmonston and Douglas.

43. Chambers, W. (1866) *Address to the Architectural Institute of Scotland*. Printed privately, December 12.

44. Parochial Board of St. Cuthbert's (1866) *Report of the Chairman's Committee*. Printed privately, March 19.

45. Begg, J. (1870) *The Causes and Probable Remedies of Pauperism in Scotland*.

Edinburgh: Chalmers Association for Diffusing Information on Important Social Questions, p. 21.

46. Edinburgh Town Council (1866) *Report by the Subcommittee of the Lord Provost's Committee as to the Sanitary Improvements of the City.* Printed for the Town Council, March 29 to April 9.
47. Littlejohn, H. D. (1865) *Report on the Sanitary Condition of the City of Edinburgh.* Edinburgh: printed by Colston and Son, p. 113.
48. The Royal Commission on the Housing of the Working Classes (1885) *Minutes of Evidence, Appendix, and Index as to Scotland,* Cmnd 4409-1. London: HMSO, questions 20,272–587.
49. The explicit rehousing requirement in the Leith Provisional Order (footnote 34) went beyond the vague wording of the 1875 Act and the Town Council, in effect, was arguing that this was unfair. It was enough to live up to the less confining spirit of the enabling legislation.
50. For the Edinburgh response see The Royal Commission on the Housing of the Working Classes (1885) *Minutes of Evidence, Appendix, and Index as to Scotland,* Cmnd 4409–1. London: HMSO, questions 18,709–12.
51. Only in the schemes of 1898 and 1900 could construction and renovation be phased so that there was the option of offering definite accommodation to evicted families. And even then it was emphasized that the Corporation was under no legal obligation, since there were sufficient vacant houses in the city. See, for example, precognition of Bailie Brown before the local inquiry into the 1900 improvement scheme; Edinburgh Town Council (1900) *Documents on the 1900 Improvement Scheme Inquiry,* City Archives, miscellaneous bundle D5/2.
52. Lindsay, W. (1865) *Address by Provost Lindsay to the Town Council of Leith.* Printed privately, p. 10.
53. Littlejohn, H. D. (1865) *Report on the Sanitary Condition of the City of Edinburgh.* Edinburgh: Printed by Colston and Son.
54. Lindsay, W. (1865) *Address by Provost Lindsay to the Town Council of Leith.* Printed privately.
55. See, particularly, his address to the Architectural Institute. In the words of a later admirer, Chambers was 'proud of [Edinburgh's] history and traditions, devoted to her welfare, grateful to her as the home of Scottish literature, and sure in the belief that it was possible to make her as healthy as she was famous': Pollard, J. (1898) *The Care of Public Health and the New Fever Hospital in Edinburgh.* Edinburgh: University Press, p. 15.
56. Miller, P. (1866) *Suggestions for the Sanitary Improvement of the Old Town of Edinburgh.* Edinburgh: Andrew Elliot, p. 17.
57. Lindsay, W. (1865) *Address by Provost Lindsay to the Town Council of Leith.* Privately printed, pp. 16–20. He also described numerous other 'improvements' being carried forward under other legal powers.
58. Littlejohn, H. D. (1865) *Report on the Sanitary Condition of the City of Edinburgh.* Edinburgh: printed by Colston and Son, p. 112.
59. Cousin, D. and Lessels, J. (1866) *Plan of Sanitary Improvements of the City of Edinburgh.* Printed for the Town Council.
60. Leith Burgh Surveyor's Office (1878) *Plan Showing Proposed Improvements,* January 22.
61. In Edinburgh and Leith, the term 'lodging house' had previously been restricted

to overnight hostel accommodation, but in section 53 of the 1890 Act it was defined to include 'separate houses or cottages for the working classes'. This much broader definition was taken to mean that municipal corporations had the right to own and manage any form of rental housing for the working classes.

62. Edinburgh Improvement Trust (1870) *Minute Book,* 2 (April 1 and April 13); Leith Town Council (1884)*Council Record,* September 2.
63. Edinburgh Town Council (1901) *Report by the Improvement Scheme Committee: Erection of New Houses for the Working Class at Portobello,* April 3. See also precognition of Bailie Brown: Edinburgh Town Council (1900) *Documents on the 1900 Improvement Scheme Inquiry.* City Archives, miscellaneous bundle D5/2.
64. Baily, F. (1898) *Report as to Edinburgh Improvement Scheme,* printed privately.
65. Edinburgh Town Council (1900) *Council Record,* May 8.
66. See, for example, Edinburgh Town Council (1898) *Council Record,* October 11.
67. Edinburgh Improvement Trust (1871) *Minute Book,* 2 (November 2) and (1872) *Works Committee Minute Book,* 1 (November 21).
68. The Royal Commission on the Housing of the Working Classes (1885) *Minutes of Evidence, Appendix, and Index as to Scotland,* Cmnd 4409–1. London: HMSO, question 18,738.
69. Cousin, D. and Lessels, J. (1866) *Additional Statement Relative to Proposed City Improvements,* printed for the Town Council.
70. The Royal Commission on the Housing of the Working Classes (1885) *Minutes of Evidence, Appendix, and Index as to Scotland,* Cmnd 4409–1. London: HMSO, question 18,706.
71. The actual expenditures by 1883 were in excess of £110,000 for an area of about 9 acres: Leith Town Council (1883) *Leith Improvement Scheme: Letter Book,* 3, pp. 856ff.
72. Edinburgh Improvement Trust (1869) *Minute Book,* 1 (April 7).
73. Edinburgh Town Council (1866) *Minutes of the Lord Provost's Committee . . .* with Explanatory Statement by the Lord Provost. Printed privately, February 13.
74. The Royal Commission on the Housing of the Working Classes (1885) *Minutes of Evidence, Appendix, and Index as to Scotland,* Cmnd 4409-1. London: HMSO, question 18,732.
75. One tenement block was approved by the Town Council with the following commendation: 'The elevations . . . are ornate and imposing in character, and . . . will present a pleasing effect'. Like other buildings in the scheme, it consisted of shops on the ground floor and three-roomed artisans' dwellings above. Leith Town Council (1890) *Council Record,* May 6.
76. Littlejohn's testimony (1893) *Inquiry with Reference to the Edinburgh (Housing of the Working Classes Act) Improvement Scheme,* City Archives, miscellaneous bundle D3/1.
77. Chambers, W. (1865) *The Lord Provost's Statement to the Town Council Respecting Sanitary Improvement.* Printed for the Town Council, December 5, p. 10.
78. See, for example, Bailie Dunlop's testimony at the public inquiry in 1893 (footnote 76).
79. Edinburgh Town Council (1885) *Council Record,* October 6.
80. Edinburgh Town Council (1866) *Report by the Subcommittee of the Lord Provost's Committee as to the Sanitary Improvements of the City.* Printed for the Town Council, March 29 to April 9, p. 9.

81. See, for example, Cooper, T. (1894) *Report on the Work of the Burgh Engineer's Department for the Year 1893–94.* Printed for the Town Council.
82. *Ibid.*
83. Littlejohn, H. D. (1865) *Report on the Sanitary Condition of the City of Edinburgh.* Edinburgh: printed by Colston and Son, p. 120.
84. The Royal Commission on the Housing of the Working Classes (1885) *Minutes of Evidence, Appendix, and Index as to Scotland,* Cmnd 4409–1. London: HMSO, questions 19,727-32. This explicit comment was made by a Glasgow witness, but it conformed closely to the tenor of the remarks of many Edinburgh witnesses.
85. Cooper, T. (1894) *Report on the Work of the Burgh Engineer's Department for the Year 1893–94.* Printed for the Town Council.

7

A patriarchal utopia: the garden city and housing reform in Germany at the turn of the century

FRANZISKA BOLLEREY
and
KRISTIANA HARTMANN

The history of German housing and town planning during the nineteenth century, like that of developments in England, France, Belgium and other modernizing countries, is tightly bound up with the progress of industrialization. In consequence a number of parallels can be detected between the various national movements of housing reform in Europe. These numerous overlaps and common strands by no means blot out, however, the distinctive national characteristics of the history of public housing in each country. In the family of European movements, English 'housing reform' played the role of a generous mother and father. The French and Belgian version, which we can call *'habitations à bon marché'* or (in the term originally coined at Mulhouse, in Alsace) *'cité ouvrière'*, assumed the function of a distant relative. The German housing-reform movement adopted the role of an ambitious son and long suffered from an oedipal syndrome in relation to its English parent which outshone it and, in consequence, had to be overcome.

Throughout the whole history of housing-reform efforts in Germany we encounter a compulsive desire to make comparisons with England. Always present, this desire could on occasion burst forth with great intensity. At

135

the height of the German housing debate, shortly before the turn of the century, a German architect was attached to the German embassy in London. His instructions were to appraise, on behalf of the German emperor and nation, the example of English housing. This architect, Hermann Muthesius, delivered his report in a three-volume work, *Das englische Haus,* published in 1904[1]. He thus established himself, at a stroke, as both an outstanding expert on English practice and a much-respected and oft-quoted mentor of reform in housing, art, and town planning in Germany.

EARLY DEVELOPMENTS IN GERMAN HOUSING REFORM

Half a century earlier, with German industry still at a very early stage of its development, the first stirrings of unrest among an infant working class had begun to make themselves felt with the Silesian weavers' rebellion of 1844 and other disturbances. The conservative professor of philology, Victor Aimé Huber, responded to this disconcerting climate with a series of reformist writings and appeals. In 1845, on his return from a journey to England, he launched a journal, *Janus: Jahrbücher deutscher Gesinnung, Bildung und Tat,* with the intention of steering German counter-revolutionary forces in the direction of spiritual, moral and economic education[2]. He sharply disputed Friedrich Engels's portrayal, *The Condition of the Working Class in England,* which appeared for the first time in 1845[3]. His chief work on the housing question was *Die Selbsthülfe der arbeitenden Klassen durch Wirtschaftsvereine und innere Ansiedlung* (Working-class self-help through trade associations and domestic settlements), published in 1848. Huber wanted to see a self-help organization set up distributive societies which would not only organize consumption on a socially-oriented basis, but would lay the foundation for cooperative production. Rigorous selection ('only members of moral integrity and responsiveness') and strong, autocratic leadership were regarded by Huber as important preconditions for the success of his plan. He wanted the Prussian State to take up the direction of his associations and he would have nothing to do with the 'daydreams of the Fouriers, the Owens and the Cabets'[4] who did not regard the family, as he did, as something sacred.

   Huber envisaged a basic block of two, or at the most four, single-storey 'hut dwellings' (*Hüttenwohnungen*) arranged on a cruciform plan. A number of these blocks would be grouped around a central building in which all communal services would be concentrated. From it '... hot and cold water, gaslight, and possibly warm air or steam flow to the individual huts. The single furnace will also serve a communal bakehouse and will heat the water for a bath-house and perhaps a wash-house as well. This building should also serve as the centre of the life of the community'[5].

The idea of a four-dwelling unit was realized in 1851 by the architect, Henry Roberts, when he designed a model workers' housing block for the Great Exhibition in Hyde Park, London, under the patronage of Prince Albert. The dwellings were not, however, grouped on one level as Huber had proposed. Instead, they were in a two-storey building of two flats on each floor. A few years later, however, an arrangement similar to Huber's was adopted for the workers' housing built in the *Cité ouvrière* at Mulhouse; Huber himself reported on it in 1861 in an essay entitled *Die Wohnungsnot* (The housing shortage)[6].

In the meantime, Huber's ideas produced the *Berliner gemeinnützige Bau-Gesellschaft* (Berlin Cooperative Building Association), which he founded in 1847 with the Prussian government architect, C. W. Hoffmann[7]. As the first cooperative housing-reform association in Germany, it was graced by the honorary membership of the English Prince Consort, Albert von Sachsen Coburg-Gotha. The authoritarian art lover, King Friedrich Wilhelm IV of Prussia, donated 2000 talers[8]. From Czar Nicholas and Czarina Alexandra, the former Prussian princess, it received not only 1000 ducats but the name 'Alexandra Foundation'[9]. Yet this promising start had come to nought almost before the London exhibition of 1851 had closed its doors. The time was not yet ripe for reform in Germany. First the conditions had to be such as to make corrective measures a necessity. As the London exhibition had demonstrated, industrialization had to be allowed to proceed if any kind of control were to be exercised over the future. Putting little people into little houses was irrelevant to this kind of progress, which depended on the creation of a system of large-scale industry in a united Germany. The strenuous efforts of Huber and Hoffmann failed because of the incomprehension of their contemporaries. Disappointed, both of them left Berlin in 1852. Huber tried, with little success, to found a model economic community in Wernigerode. Hoffmann was transferred to the provinces. Paternalism had nevertheless taken root in housing reform; in 1878 the Hamburg author, Julius Schultz, published a book on the *Cité ouvrière* which he entitled *The Mulhouse System of Workers' Housing: A Call for the Emulation of This Humane Means of Combating Socialism.*

THE IMPACT OF INDUSTRIALIZATION

In the middle of the nineteenth century German human and capital resources began to concentrate on the creation of manufacturing industry. In fact, the initial rise of the West-Prussian economy in the 1850s was largely the product of the efforts of foreign companies. Belgian, Irish and English concerns were prominent among the creators of the legendary industrial explosion in the coal and iron-ore fields of the Rhineland and

Westphalia[10]. Through exploratory visits to England like those of Krupp, and cooperation with Belgian firms, German industrialists acquired the know-how which after 1871 allowed them to take over the direction of industrial development. From the 1860s there was an increasing shift of emphasis from agriculture to industry, and from the manufacture of consumer goods to that of capital goods. There was a corresponding shift from small and medium-sized to large enterprises. By 1900 the large-scale enterprise was a characteristic feature of the Germany economy, with the 500 largest firms employing a total of one million workers. 'The concentration of capital began to exercise a decisive influence on the shaping of the economy'[11]. In the years between the turn of the century and the First World War, free competition was substantially eroded by the growth of monopoly, with production and prices fixed by mutual agreement between firms. The involvement of industry with the big banks further sustained this national-imperialistic process of concentration[12].

Industrial development produced an alarming rate of population growth in the towns. The population of Germany more than quadrupled between 1816 and 1914, rising from fifteen to sixty-four millions. As a result of industrial development this increase was mainly concentrated in established and newly-created urban agglomerations. In 1871 36.1 per cent of a total of forty-one million inhabitants of the newly-created German Empire lived in urban areas; by 1914 60.1 per cent was urbanized. In a society dominated by *laisser-faire* ideas, nothing was done to regulate the internal migration which lay behind these figures, and which increasingly took the form of a movement from east to west. In 1851 there were only five cities of more than 100,000 inhabitants in the territory which later became the German Empire; in 1910 there were forty-eight such cities. More than a quarter of the population of the Empire lived, in 1910, in cities of more than 100,000 people. Population growth between 1867 and 1900 took the following form[13]:

Rural districts (<2000 inhabitants)	1 per cent
Small and medium-sized towns (2000–100,000 inhabitants)	163 per cent
Large cities (>100,000 inhabitants)	234 per cent

The increase in population was at its fastest and most overwhelming between 1895 and 1900. In the Prussian provinces of Rhineland and Westphalia the population grew by 395,000, while East Prussia lost 500,000 inhabitants in the same period. Berlin, the capital of the Empire, grew by 127,000 in this five-year period thanks partly to the efforts of industrialists such as Borsig, Siemens and Halske[14].

Economic and demographic growth, acting as two opposing but interdependent poles, created problems which the imperial government, founded on liberal principles imported from England, could not master. Social policy, as Huber understood it, was not pursued. The constitutional monarchy established by Bismarck made it difficult for the imperial

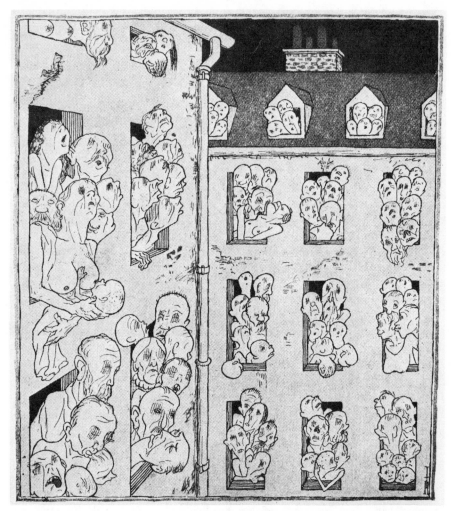

FIGURE 7.1. In Berlin intensive site usage was accompanied by serious overcrowding of the buildings, with numerous single-room and cellar dwellings.

parliament to exercise an effective influence over the arbitrary and undemocratic actions of the executive[15]. Effective parliamentary participation was further hindered by restrictions on the franchise. Consciousness of the discrepancy between booming industry on the one hand and inequalities in social and housing policy on the other was further aroused by the ban on the organization of the Social Democrats (*Sozialistengesetz*) between 1878 and 1890[16]. Poor housing conditions, revealed as early as the 1861 census, were countered by building codes, regulations and town-extension plans which, far from imposing order on the dynamics of urban growth, merely added to the confusion[17]. The alarming numbers of inhabited cellars and of

FIGURE 7.2. This view of a Berlin one-room dwelling was taken on the eve of the First World War.

unheated and unhealthy dwellings were a matter of common knowledge. Doctors, economists and educationalists drew attention to the undesirable consequences of the sharing of family accommodation by lodgers and the over-intensive use of urban building sites[18]. But very little was actually done to prevent the direct exploitation of the working classes and the intensification of the work process in the factories. As a result, the harmful physical and psychological effects of these processes in the sphere of human reproduction were neither eradicated nor reduced. For the time being, action did not extend beyond the expression of regrets and the making of exhortations in which even the sovereign, Kaiser Wilhelm II, joined towards the end of the century[19].

Owing to the decentralized system of administration there were no standardized building regulations in the German Empire. The most heavily industrialized areas, and above all the Ruhr, suffer even today from historic deficiencies in planning and administration which produced a visually and physically disturbing intermixture of working, living and recreational space. Berlin, on the other hand, capital of the German Empire and seat of the Kaiser, was to be designed on a more costly and monumental scale to provide a backdrop for the display of imperial might. Berlin's planned extensions and monumental building ordinances dated back to the

FIGURE 7.3. This aerial view of typical Berlin *Mietskasernen* of the later nineteenth century clearly reveals the extent of the interior courtyards which the great distances between the streets of the Hobrecht plan tended to generate. Note that the maximum building height, fixed in relation to the width of the street, applied also to buildings sited within the block.

seventeenth and eighteenth centuries, and the new districts such as Dorotheenstadt, Friedrichstadt, and Friedrichswerder were respected throughout Germany and well-known abroad. This Prussian, Hohenzollern tradition was to be maintained despite the restructuring of the urban organism brought about by developments in industry, population, and communications. The building regulations of 1853, 1887, 1892, 1903 etc.[20] and the extension plan of 1862, which has gone down in history as the 'Hobrecht Plan', partly reinforced and partly created the Berlin pattern of high-density housing which made it 'the biggest tenement city in the world' (*die grösste Mietskasernenstadt der Welt*)[21]. 'It is disgraceful', wrote the historian of Berlin, Werner Hegemann, 'that the valuable experience accumulated through largely successful town-planning efforts abroad [he had mainly France and England in mind here] should have failed to stop the same serious defects being repeated in Berlin after 1840, when industrializ-ation set in with unprecedented force . . .'[22]. Another town-planning critic, Rudolf Eberstadt, provided a sharper analysis: 'This general introduction of the tenement block (*Mietskaserne*) was quite intentional; it was seen as . . . the appropriate housing form for the working classes . . .'[23].

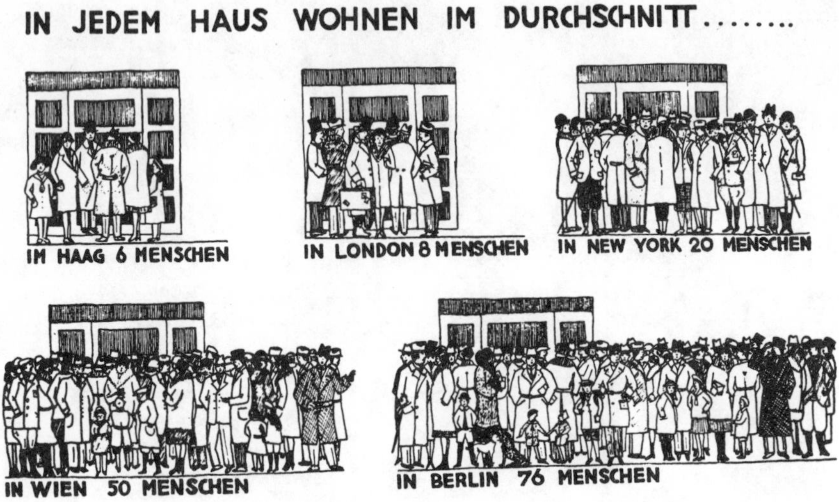

FIGURE 7.4. 'The average house accommodates . . .'. Graphic portrayal of variations in residential densities between major cities. The cartoon dates from after the First World War, but the figures were much the same before 1914.

With the *Reichstag* indifferent to reform on an imperial scale, German urban conditions came to be discussed in a multitude of small societies, associations and organizations[24]. The socio-political objectives of these reformers, influenced by Huber's ideas, lay in the direction of self-help organizations, and they strongly advocated working-class home ownership[25]. The first German law on cooperative societies, based on the principle of unlimited liability advocated by Schultze-Delitzsch and Faucher, produced little effect; between 1879 and 1888 the number of cooperative building societies *fell* from forty-six to twenty-eight. In 1889, however, the second law on cooperatives was passed, this time on the basis of limited liability. The number of building societies now increased more than ten times between 1890 and 1905, rising from fifty to 588. Further legislation, including the disablement insurance law and old-age pension scheme of 1889, the income tax law of 1891, the stamp duty laws of 1895 and 1899, and their subsequent amendments gave extra encouragement to the building societies[26]. However, these statutes did virtually nothing to relieve what had become a massive housing shortage. The same was true of the self-help organizations proposed by Ernst Sax in *Wohnungszustände der arbeitenden Klassen und ihre Reform* (Housing conditions of the working classes and their reform)[27], and the analysis put forward under the pseudonym 'Arminius' by Countess Adelheid Dohna Ponisky in *Die Großstädte in ihrer Wohnungsnot und die Grundlagen einer durchgreifenden Abhilfe* (Big cities, their housing problems, and the basis of a radical remedy)[28]. These studies only described the problem; they did not solve it. They were based on the conviction that the housing shortage was the principal cause of distress among the working classes. Solve the housing problem, they thought, and proletarianization would be halted. The representatives of scientific socialism dismissed such proposals as mere philanthropy, intended to disguise reality. Bourgeois reformers, they maintained, sought to abolish all evil from society but their proposals would in fact root it even more strongly. Friedrich Engels emphasized

> In such a society the housing shortage is no coincidence; it is a necessary institution. The housing shortage and all its associated implications for health etc. can be abolished only if the whole social order from which it originates is fundamentally changed.[29]

EMPLOYERS' HOUSING IN THE RUHR

The controversy over the implications of housing reform and its relationship to evolutionary and revolutionary change had least scope for development in the Ruhr, where nineteenth-century industry had transformed the environment more brutally than anywhere else in Germany. There, purely paternalistic methods were used to produce a pragmatic, utilitarian solution to the housing problem. Over 2000 industrial settlements were built in the Ruhr between the 1850s and the Second World War, with an increase in the scale of development in the 1880s and 1890s. Planned from scratch by the coal and iron companies, they were built hurriedly. The settlements of the early Ruhr mining period were distinguished by very dour, aesthetically unpretentious rows of virtually identical, unrendered four-family houses of the well-known Mulhouse four-in-a-block type. They always reflected the economic objective of the industrial concerns, which was to provide new labour and to reproduce spent labour for production units which were often located not only outside the towns, but also away from existing rural settlements.

Industrial development generated an explosive increase in the size of the workforce and the total population. About 1500 miners had been working in the Ruhr in 1800; by 1900 this figure had risen to 226,000 and, by 1913, to 424,000. The number of inhabitants increased correspondingly. The population of a Ruhr region of 4582 square kilometres, defined in 1920 when a regional planning organization, the *Siedlungsverband Ruhrkohlenbezirk* (SVR), was set up, rose as follows:

1871	912,000
1885	1,334,100
1895	1,848,600
1905	2,929,800
1925	2,202,100

FIGURE 7.5. The *Cité ouvrière* at Moulhouse, built from 1853, became an important example for employers' housing efforts in Germany. The communal facilities pictured here were not, however, widely reproduced.

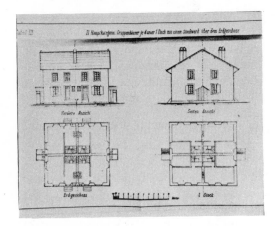

FIGURE 7.6. The four-in-a-block arrangement typical of much of the housing provided by employers in the Ruhr and other German industrial areas in the mid-nineteenth century.

This increase could not be recruited from the immediate vicinity, and much of the 'labour factor' was imported from East Prussia, Masuria, Lithuania, Poland, Czechoslovakia and other areas. The mixture of peoples, languages and religions reached an almost unimaginable complexity in the Ruhr around the turn of the century. In Gelsenkirchen, for instance, a town which had sprung up from nothing as a result of industrial development, nearly sixty per cent of the population were of East European origin in 1900.

As far as planning was concerned, nothing happened in the Ruhr area apart from an uncoordinated accumulation of industrial buildings and housing. However, the pragmatic multiplication of rows of houses gave way to more sophisticated designs after 1890. The architects and mining engineers of the Ruhr region took note of the debate on the 'artistic principles of town planning' launched by Sitte in 1889. They stopped designing settlements as mere accretions of houses which could be extended at will, and

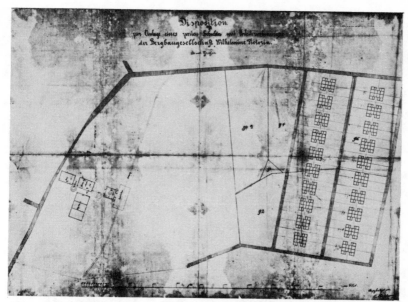

FIGURE 7.7. Plan of the Klapheckenhof mining colony, Gelsenkirchen, built from 1885 close to a new shaft of Wilhelmine-Viktoria colliery company, visible to the left of the houses.

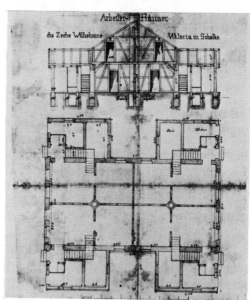

FIGURE 7.8. Plan and elevation of a variance of the four-in-a-block housing favoured by the Wilhelmine-Viktoria colliery company. The inclusion of a lean-to stable (*Stall*) was quite normal, for many families kept one or more animals on their allotments.

began to create planned urban units with squares, various aesthetic elements, and other complementary features. The quality of planning and design in the settlements of the Ruhr was then decisively improved by the serious discussion of town planning, promoted by the Garden City movement after

FIGURE 7.9. Four-in-a-block houses at Klapheckenhof. Rents in such employer-built accommodation were often half those charged for similar homes on the open market. The tree-trunk hides the allotment gardens which were usually included in such colonies as an additional attraction to workers, many of whom welcomed the chance to maintain a link with cultivation after migrating to the Ruhr directly from East Prussia or other backward areas.

1900. The overall planning of urban areas was, however, still neglected.

The older settlements of serial houses were now rejected as monotonous and barrack-like, and the new debate generated a new settlement type. The dominant modes of design were now the creation of multiple and individual spaces, adaptation of the road layout to the site and the enhancement thereof, and the introduction of pre-industrial and of arcadian architectural details. As elsewhere in Germany, these formal and aesthetic innovations in planning and design were introduced in the belief that the social values of the 'New Homeland' could be sensorily induced in the residents by qualitative and quantitative improvements in the design. However, the socio-political objectives of the Garden City movement, which sought to stimulate participatory democracy, were not incorporated in the new industrial settlements. Their creators had different structural objectives which continued to revolve around the creation of proprietary settlements dependent upon the works, in conditions of strict paternalism.

In contrast to the development of Berlin and other big industrial cities, where corridor streets of four- and five-storey blocks were the unvarying product of the economic and administrative conjuncture, the Ruhr produced, much as did the industrial districts of Upper Silesia and Saxony, an extensive and often generously planned form of building. The predominant house-type was of two storeys, or one storey plus an attic floor, occupied by one family, and sometimes arranged in rows. This type of housing, which many housing reformers wanted to see adopted throughout Germany, was not primarily the product of humanitarian considerations. Mining subsidence, or the risk of it, ruled out high building in the Ruhr and the single-family house was the only solution. Allotment gardens were provided as a concession to the agrarian inclinations of the immigrant labour force from the eastern provinces. Land was readily available because the mine-owners, in particular, were accustomed to acquiring extensive estates to protect themselves against third-party claims for structural damage. Progressive reformers criticized the practice of works housing, because the linking of employment and tenancy was thought to restrict the worker's ability to form independent political opinions and to lay him open to deliberate efforts of regimentation. The reformers wanted to see housing provided independently of the employers, or by public authority as it was, for instance, at Ulm.

A number of settlements in the Ruhr have a spacious quality that can be experienced and appreciated even today. Many firms, affected by structural decline and the energy crisis, are now trying to dispose of their housing. Area clearance and a more intensive use of building land are now the order of the day. Resistance takes the form of numerous citizen protest initiatives against the demolition plans, which form one element of the extra-parliamentary participatory democracy which flourishes in the Federal Republic.

THE GARDEN CITY MOVEMENT

The rise of German industrial capitalism on the one hand, and the proletarianization of the urban agglomerations on the other, determined the antagonistic character of the German Empire. The open-minded, professional middle class (*Bildungsbürgertum*) stood between the two opposing sides. Though divided between various allegiances, it formed as a whole an anti-capitalist phalanx. From the mid-1880s onwards it began to denounce the phenomenon of *Unkultur,* and to campaign against the transgressor, 'Industry', which it held responsible for undermining German national culture by devaluing the individual. The essence of German life, capable of infusing the whole of humanity, had been reduced to a dangerous state of dependence on rationalism, insensibility and mammonism. It put forward, as the alternative to *Unkultur,* an idealized vision of the pre-industrial, Biedermeier period, the good old days when the German peasant tilled his German soil, the age of the 'fully rounded German personality'.

The educated bourgeoisie refused to apply a dialectical analysis to the interpretation of economic events. This barrier to the appropriate theoretical explanation resulted in a mystification of the total social situation. Thus a large part of the German bourgeoisie, even while considering itself opposed to certain dominant tendencies in German society, actually allied itself with its enemy. The closer the country drew to the First World War, the more it provided an intellectual veneer to justify the prevailing ethos of nationalistic capitalism.

> The phenomena of modern mass society were roundly condemned. This unfavourable judgment extended to the 'materialistic' aims of the workers' movement as well as to capitalist 'mammonism' ... To counter this 'dehumanization', which they recognized correctly enough but distorted ideologically, they advocated a radical change of direction towards the irrational, towards innate qualities of moral health and integrity. In doing so, they evoked the romantic concept of 'organism' and sought to base on it their motto of 'Culture, not Civilization'.[30]

Science, enlightenment and socialism were irritants. People looked down on these terms as being of internationalistic, not German, origin. Ever since the radical-conservative Paul de Lagarde[31] had, in his *Deutsche Schriften* of 1878–81, put forward a vision of a Greater German Empire and had pointed to the disastrous political and social effects of industrialization, the feeling had grown that 'only a national religion, a Germanic-Christian faith', could bring about a renaissance of the pre-industrial era. The pervasiveness of these nationalistic tendencies emerges from the writings of the architect, Otto March, who believed that the most important objective of town planning was to care for the hundreds of thousands of workers whose productive and military strength had to be conserved in the national interest[32]. The nation was mobilized to counter the threat of *Unkultur*. Culture was to be saved by a specially-developed culture and art education. Nietzsche's longing for a 'true culture' was widely shared. 'It was not political unity that he desired, but "German unity" in the highest sense, the unity of artistic style'[33]. The art critic, Julius August Langbehn, caused a sensation with his book, *Rembrandt as Educationalist,* which he published under the pseudonym, 'By a German'[34]. He rejected the overrating of the intellect at the expense of the development of the character and the soul. He wanted to see priority given to the encouragement of qualities of loyalty to the homeland, integration into the national community, truthfulness of sentiment, and artistic creativity. Art was popularized, to become the essence of the desired cultural renewal, the great educational innovation of the time. For the art-education movement[35], art was the dominant element in life, and this 'philosophy of life' came to imbue the general reform of school education which was now vigorously pressed forward[36].

For all this, the idea of education through art in the late 1880s and early 1890s was not an original German achievement. It was based on the much-

FIGURE 7.10. 'Grow more potatoes ... the German potato must defeat England!' This German war poster, though aimed at peasants rather than suburban gardeners, manages to combine in tragicomic form two major strands in the German mentality—admiration-cum-envy of England, and belief in the fundamental strength of land and of those who tend it.

quoted model of the English Arts and Crafts movement, the creation of John Ruskin and William Morris. England, in fact, was seen as possessing the culture that Germany lacked. The international exhibitions of the nineteenth century were a particularly persuasive indicator of this apparent superiority, but there were many others. This was why the German educated bourgeoisie, though blinkered by the pomp and circumstance of the early years of the new Empire, and despite the general campaign to develop national consciousness thereafter, paradoxically began from the late 1880s to look to England. England's world hegemony had to be overcome not only on the material but also on the ideological plane.

At the turn of the century reforming circles among the German educated bourgeoisie were alive with nationalist, educationalist, emotionally mystifying and socially committed ideas and programmes. Then, in 1902, the idea of the Garden City was imported into Germany from England[37]. It was taken up with enthusiasm by the Berlin *Neue Gemeinschaft* (New Community) movement, a literary circle led by the brothers Heinrich and Julius Hart, which propagated the culturalist ideal of *'Edel-Sozialismus'* (noble socialism)[38]. At first it was not so much the robust, practical side of Howard's idea that attracted these cranky intellectuals, as its echoes of the nature worship and communal living which they practised in their Schlachtensee community outside Berlin[39]. This first, euphoric phase soon came to an end. The call arose for reforms to meet basic needs. The effete Berlin intellectuals withdrew and the German Garden City movement became infused with the practical reformers' sense of social responsibility. However, it never completely lost its nationalist-educationalist tone.

The promoters of garden cities were convinced that those who lived in them would exercise a positive influence over the whole of society, because they would have come into contact with a democratic atmosphere and an aesthetically stimulating environment. The aim of the Garden City movement was a progressive resettlement of the population and the consequent conversion of an authoritarian, anti-parliamentarian State into a democratic, socially-oriented 'Culture-State'. This social interpretation of town planning was aimed at two targets. On the one hand, the inhabitants of garden cities were supposed to be influenced physically and psychologically by an architecture of scale and space. On the other hand—and this is an important objective—they were to be *actively* involved in the designing of their environment. 'The architectural education of the public'[40] was the educational aim of the international architects' congress which took place in London in 1907.

> The interest of the people is essential to good architecture. Architecture is by no means the exclusive concern of the expert. On the contrary, it is the expression of dominant ideas and needs . . . If the eyes of the public are opened to the glaring defects of today's architecture, then architecture will generally improve . . . A people without needs has no art.[41]

The hope was that these efforts to educate people through art and good housing would 'bring up all sections of the population to form a united whole . . . art is chosen to express the essence of the age, to convey feeling and spiritual content and thus to be educational in the highest sense of the term'[42]. The applied arts and architecture would take up the task on the lines pioneered in England. Hermann Muthesius emphasized:

> One thing is clear; arts-and-crafts is facing an educational task of the highest importance. And in this it already oversteps the boundaries popularly ascribed to it. More than mere applied art, it becomes a cultural means of education. The aim of the arts-and-crafts movement is to re-educate the social classes of today in solidity, truthfulness and simple civic values . . . not only will it change the German apartment and the German house, but it will directly influence the character of the generation, for a process of education which produces proper accommodation for us to live in can basically only be a character education . . . [43]

The Austrian, Joseph August Lux, introduced his book on town planning (1908) with these words:

To build means to educate. A people's potential educational level is revealed in
the way it builds. The purpose of this publication is to promote building as a
means of education.[44]

The German Garden City Association can be regarded as representative of
the outgoing social conscience of the German middle class between the turn
of the century and the First World War. It used its reform programme to
support Adolf Damaschke's movement of general land reform. Its activities
were related on both a personal and an ideological plane to the *Werkbund* and
the *Dürerbund*. They were also influenced by the contemporary revival of
anthroposophic and socialistic philosophies and modes of interpretation. The
Association thus formed an important part of a many-faceted movement
which by introducing the public to a new social aesthetic would, or so it was
hoped, arouse interest in, and awareness of the need for, a planned
townscape. This subtle process of emancipation remained, however, over-
shadowed by more fundamental problems.

HELLERAU

It took six years of untiring and undismayed publicity and propaganda
activity by the German Garden City Association to produce the first German
garden-city company. It was founded in 1908, with capital largely provided
by the state social-insurance organization, to build a garden city at Hellerau,
near Dresden. Hellerau was to become a milestone in the history of German
planning.

In 1898 an ambitious furniture manufacturer, Karl Schmidt, had founded
the *Dresdner Werkstätten für Handwerkskunst* (Dresden Craft Workshops) on
lines suggested by William Morris's arts and crafts movement. At the great
Dresden exhibition of interior decoration in 1906, where not only Schmidt's
Werkstätten but also those of Munich (founded 1902) and Vienna (founded
1903) mounted displays, the German arts and crafts movement revealed both
the form and the ethic of the new German craft production to an interested
public. The foundation of the *Deutscher Werkbund* in the following year was
just the logical consequence of years of intensive, cooperative effort by
practitioners, theoreticians, and industrialists, including Friedrich Naumann,
Theodor Fischer, Richard Riemerschmid, Hermann Muthesius, and Peter
Behrens.

It was in the year of the Dresden exhibition that Karl Schmidt, influenced
by the garden-city movement, decided to move his works and the homes of
his craftsmen to the outlying district of Hellerau, which lay on a beautiful
hillside. One hundred and fifty hectares of land were purchased from a total
of seventy-three owners. From 1911 the settlement and works were linked to
the city centre by a tramway, 6.5 kilometres in length. Admittedly, Hellerau
was established on the initiative of a factory-owner. However, in contrast to
other industrialists who built factory villages, Schmidt handed over full

powers of control and decision-making to an independent, limited-liability Garden City Company. 'The garden-city idea goes a step further than the colonies built on the orders of factory-owners, in that it turns the residents into full participants in the creation of the settlement and virtual owners of it. This is a communal effort independent of the factory, and is something very different ...'[45]. The founders were aware that an enterprise which they described as a social experiment 'should above all else, not make the mistake of confusing the employer-worker and landlord-tenant relationships'.

Hellerau incorporated a number of design-innovations, derived from a set of socially-committed, democratic principles and ideas about popular and art education. The district of terraced houses at the 'Grüner Zipfel', sensitively composed by the architect Richard Riemerschmid in accordance with the theories of Camillo Sitte and Theodor Goecke, was planned on the basis of a prior inquiry into the wishes and ideas of the future inhabitants, and was constructed by the Hellerau Building Cooperative Ltd. A so-called 'Commission of Seven', composed of workers from Schmidt's factory, was entrusted with the preliminary investigations. This idea of a commission of

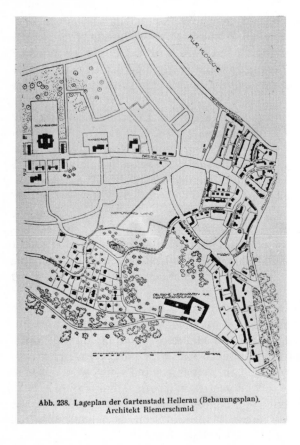

Abb. 238. Lageplan der Gartenstadt Hellerau (Bebauungsplan). Architekt Riemerschmid

FIGURE 7.11. Richard Riemerschmid's development plan for Hellerau garden city.

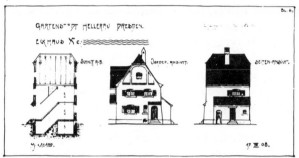

FIGURE 7.12. These house designs for Hellerau garden city, by Richard Riemerschmid, typify the traditional effect sought in this strongly Arts-and-Crafts development. Note the contrast with Bruno Taut's more functional designs for Falkenberg.

inquiry into the living conditions, needs and desires of the workers originally came from Riemerschmid himself[46]. Throughout Hellerau, planning, building and design were controlled by building regulations and ordinances drawn up by a Building and Arts Commission on which sat leading authorities on architecture and town planning. A distinction was made between traffic streets and residential streets in accordance with the latest planning principles. The development plan envisaged four distinct districts: a district of small houses, a villa-district, a central district for communal facilities, including shops and services, and an industrial district. Separate regulations were drawn up for each district.

Hellerau became a much-visited and much-discussed centre of attraction for the whole of the educational reform movement, including its handicraft, gymnastic and musical branches. In 1913 Heinrich Tessenow was commissioned to build the temple-like educational institution of Emil Jacques Dalcroze in Hellerau. Life in Hellerau was ruled by a frenzy of innovation, with inspiration provided by personalities like Paul Claudel and Martin Buber. Hellerau became the shrine of the new spirit[47].

The foundation of Hellerau gave a massive stimulus to the general debate within the German Garden City movement. It strengthened hopes that the spread of the Garden City idea would produce structural changes in the whole of society, and reinforced the view that much-criticized social conditions could be altered, not by political action, but by the gradual introduction of democratic ideas through reforms in town planning, housing and lifestyle[48]. Modes of design were now discussed even more enthusiastically. Comprehensive works of urban art (*Gesamtkunstwerke*) like Venice or Florence received much praise. Inspiration for a comprehensive interior arrangement was sought in Japanese handicrafts[49]. Even the Islamic East was quoted as an example for the separation of residential and traffic streets which Goecke and Eberstadt advocated in Germany[50].

A fundamental disagreement emerged, however. One side idealized the crooked streets, steep gables, half-timbered houses, turrets and walls of the traditional small towns of Germany. Towns like Nuremburg and Rothenburg were mentioned again and again. Pride was taken in the buildings of Hampstead Garden Suburb, in which 'the happy results of study of old German towns' could be detected[51]. The 'Grüner Zipfel' at Hellerau was an expression of this ideal, with its downswept roofs, traditional window and door designs, well-proportioned buildings, and its village–like sense of enclosure. The other side favoured a geometrical mode of planning which drew on established traditions of ideal-town design. They took Karlsruhe as their model[52]. They praised Berlage's extension plans for the Hague[53], and the prize-winning entry which Walter B. Griffin, the Chicago architect and landscape architect, produced for the development plan competition for the federal capital of Australia[54]. Within Germany, they naturally approved the rationalistic layout of the garden city 'am Kugelfang', near Mannheim, the work of Esch and Anke[55].

Muthesius warned the supporters of the *Heimatschutz* (protection of the homeland) movement that for the time being they had been 'misled into thinking that architecture's disease-ridden body could be cured by an injection of "serum" '[56]. Brinckmann, a critic of the romanticizing tendency in town planning, remarked: 'It is absolutely impossible to build a new town on the basis of the reproduction of historic groundplans'[57]. He put forward an alternative, classicist ideal: 'Modern town planning, having plumbed the depths in the nineteenth century, seeks advice from the past. However, a typical German romanticism causes it to disregard the supreme urban art of the eighteenth century'[58]. Karl Ernst Osthaus replied: 'It is by no means an honour for our modern bourgeoisie that almost all the important townscapes of the past go back to princely and, one might almost say, Absolutist origins'[59]. Hans Kampffmeyer justified his interest in historic towns by economic reasoning. For him the argument about an ideal mode of town planning did not merely revolve around architectonics; it was also a question, among other things, of practical organization:

The main feature of the urban phenomenon in the middle ages was cooperative organization, which extended not merely to the political arena but to the whole of economic life. It was a feature of these cooperatively organized towns that they were ruled not by a single individual but by a committee of citizens, or council, which was periodically elected and answerable to the citizenry.[60]

FALKENBERG

The somewhat stuffy Hellerau spirit, the desire to reform everything and everybody, played a smaller part in the foundation of the garden city of Falkenberg-in-Grünau, near Berlin. No paternalistic employer of the Karl Schmidt type was involved here. Instead, the guiding force was the Greater Berlin Cooperative Building Association, founded in 1910 by a small group of middle-class reformers.

Since the 1890s a number of socially-aware groups of people in Berlin had been trying to apply the methods of large-scale planning to come to grips with a phenomenon of building profiteering which legislation alone was no longer capable of controlling. In this they had much in common with Ebenezer Howard's decentralization approach. However, there were no practical results until 1908, when the housing reformer, Karl von Mangoldt, set the ball rolling by founding the *Ansiedlungsverein Gross-Berlin* (Greater Berlin Housing Association). This led to the widely noted Berlin Town Planning Exhibition of 1910, and then to a start on the planning of the Berlin garden city in the same year. After a site and the necessary capital had been obtained in 1912, the young architect, Bruno Taut, produced the master plan[61].

Taut based the main thoroughfares on an earlier plan by Hans Bernoulli,

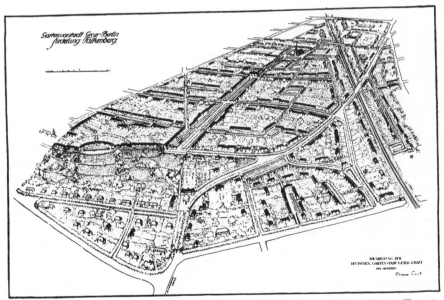

FIGURE 7.13. Bird's eye view of Falkenberg, Berlin, as designed by Bruno Taut in 1913/14. The different housing zones, and notably the villa district in the foreground, emerge very clearly. Much of the layout is strongly reminiscent of Unwin's work but the crescent on the left is pure Taut, and foreshadows his better-known *Hufeisen* at Berlin-Britz.

which in other respects he completely reconstructed. He linked planning elements taken from English garden cities and from traditional German country towns with completely new ones. He incorporated the idea of a semi-circular terrace of houses on the edge of a downward sloping public park. This feature, reminiscent of Bath, was the forerunner of the *'Hufeisen'* (horse-shoe) which Taut designed in 1925 in Berlin-Britz. He said that he borrowed from an old village green in Brandenburg the idea for the street-cum-square, thirty to forty metres wide, which he used at the main street intersection and shopping centre. Lying on a hilltop, and bordered on the east by a public park, it provided distant views. Taut wrote:

> Shops are planned for this street. Local life will concentrate here without being disturbed by traffic, which will be restricted to a narrow strip between four to six rows of trees. At the end of this avenue lies a school with a gymnasium and a house for the teacher, the whole forming a civic complex for which a piece of land will have to be handed over to the local authority. The street then leads on to the church, the tower of which, visible from the village green, will enrich the townscape.[62]

Taut went on to describe the adjoining residential areas:

> The main thoroughfares, twelve to fifteen metres in width, delineate a number of blocks. These are not arranged on garden-city lines. The dominant north-to-south emphasis dictates that interior courts should be created as far as possible. Playgrounds will be laid out here and the official requirement that fifteen per cent of the site should be left free for open space will be observed. Within the blocks there will be paved residential streets, five or six metres wide. As far as possible there will be no sidewalks. An important guideline for the planning of the streets is that they should all interconnect, in order to help people find their way through the area.

As at Hellerau, the content and objectives of the building programme for the first two stages of construction before the war (they were, unfortunately, also the last) were thoroughly discussed with the tenants. Then, in 1913, the building of the 'Akazienhof' (Acacia Court), on the north-east fringe of the area, at last began. The successful Hellerau experience also provided a model for the drawing up of 'principles and regulations' for the 'achievement of architectonic unity' in the Falkenberg estate. In contrast to Hellerau, there was no collective art commission to guide the aesthetic destiny of the estate, but some kind of artistic authority was clearly needed. To avoid possible disagreements, an independent arbitration committee was set up, a 'sort of appeal court' composed of 'town-planning and architectural authorities'. Peter Behrens, Theodor Goecke and Hermann Muthesius took on this task. The planning principles of Falkenberg required the use of 'the simple right-angle' in the layout and a simple outline for the buildings. 'Turrets and the like' were firmly rejected, as were 'all complicated roof-forms', among which the mansard roof was singled out as uneconomic:

We believe that the simplest possible, even a primitive, design is most appropriate to the nature of the task. We can dispense with the monumental-pathetic, the romantic, and even the decorative, arts-and-crafts approaches. This will mean that it will be essential to refrain from purely formal building elements such as classical columns, traditional German half-timbering, and the like.[63]

Taut chose *colour* as the most important artistic element in Falkenberg garden city. His smooth, cubic terraced houses were to be enlivened, not by plastic ornamentation or old-fashioned decoration, but by the red, green, blue, white and brown colours which gave Falkenberg its popular nickname of 'the paint-box estate'.

Riemerschmid's designs for the 'Grüner Zipfel' at Hellerau had shown impressively with what subtle means intimate streets and squares could be created. This endeavour, which drew on the planning tradition of Theodor Fischer, Theodor Goecke, and Hermann Janssen, was renewed at Falkenberg by Taut, who also had been a student of Fischer and Goecke. However, the

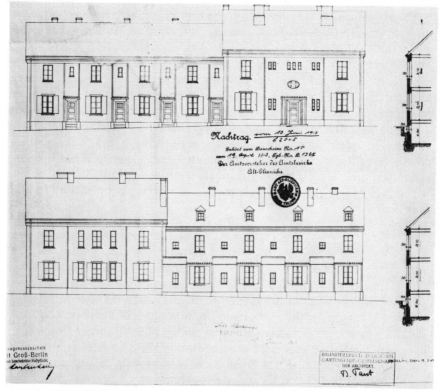

FIGURE 7.14. These stark and slightly neo-classical designs are typical of Taut's work at Falkenberg. The scribbles and stamps indicate that they have received local authority approval, in 1913.

harmonious effect achieved at Hellerau was not the main objective here; instead, all pseudo-harmony of spaces was rejected. The ground floors were emphasized while the upper floors were treated more discreetly, producing a concentrated, close-to-the-earth effect. Symmetry was broken up and thrust aside by varying the shapes of the individual houses and groupings on both sides of the streets or squares, and particularly by the asymmetrical siting of the terminal groups of houses. However, the effect of this disturbance was not chaos but a new quality of image and space, stimulating to sensual perception.

Above all, this pattern for 'a new housing' was not intended to be understood in isolation. 'Formal innovation' was intended principally to express 'social innovation':

> A new idea has been shaped, a really modern idea, an idea which promises to develop into a philosophy of life (*Weltanschauung*), which may even allow us to achieve our greatest and most beautiful ambitions. This idea is a social concept.[64]

The communal spirit burst out in the first Falkenberg festival just before the war, in July 1914—'*uffn Akazienhof*' it was called, in Berlin dialect[65]. Then the field grey of wartime covered up the Falkenberg gaiety, but it revived again in 1919, this time in a republican environment. The tenants' community developed a range of economic and social activities, including the joint purchasing of consumer and household goods in bulk, the establishment of a nursery, a kindergarten and a playground, the foundation of a library and a singing and dancing club, and the organization of 'artistic evenings' for adults. The estate's own sickness-insurance scheme, a health centre and a doctor cared for the residents. The motto was: 'Communal work creates communal life'. The Falkenberg festivals of 1921, 1924, 1926 and 1927 did not attract the tenants alone—thousands of working people came from all over Berlin.

REFORM OR UTOPIA?

The Germany of Wilhelm I and Wilhelm II was obsessed with the town-planning achievements of Britain and France. It lacked the towering vision of a Baron Haussmann, the far-reaching reform plans of a Robert Owen or a Charles Fourier, the integrated planning models of an Ebenezer Howard, and reforming legislation comparable to the British Housing Acts. It also lacked the necessary empirical research; there was, for instance, no German equivalent of Charles Booth's seventeen-volume work, *Life and Labour of the People in London,* published between 1889 and 1897[66]. Germany's uncoordinated and incomplete legislation permitted the planning of Berlin on a scale appropriate to its importance, but it provided no foundation at all for a comprehensively socio-political practice of total town and country planning, a task which in Britain was officially delegated to the local administrations under John Burns's Act of 1909.

Werner Hegemann, in 1910, asked the right question: 'What principles should govern the creation of space?'[67] Rudolf Eberstadt answered him: the city should be planned in the interests of the whole of its population[68]. Thus the problem was grasped theoretically, but as far as practice was concerned—even the practice of the German Garden City movement—Bernhard Kampffmeyer had to admit in 1919 that the pure wine of ideals had to be watered down considerably[69].

Germany, industrializing late in comparison with Britain and France, had to strive hard during the nineteenth century to make up for missed opportunities and to achieve as much as its rivals. The political preconditions were provided by national unification in 1871. Under the rigid and precise organizational control of Prussia, economic and cultural forces would be united and Germany would strive for a position of world leadership. This effort, however, did not involve merely a decision from above to create national wealth and power; it also generated, through the physical and psychological torture of industrialization, a proletariat capable of threatening the State. The division of labour, necessary result of the industrial mode of production, created the phenomenon of alienation. From alienation sprang the short- and long-term objectives of the organized workers' movement, which sought the transformation of the whole system. Those who controlled industrial and state power therefore sought some means of amalgamating the aims of the workers' movement with those of the industrial State.

After the ban on the Social Democratic Party (1878–90) had actually strengthened this alternative force within the State, an attempt was made to absorb the internal enemy by setting up an imaginary external foe. The achievement of late-nineteenth-century and early-twentieth-century nationalism was in fact to divert social frustrations and aggressions onto a foreign enemy before they exploded within the State. The educated bourgeoisie, which was neither involved in the creation of monopoly capitalism nor directly favoured by it, did not analyse this situation. Instead, it supported the chimera of a national threat with all its intellectual and cultural capacity.

The reform movement, sustained by a moral impetus, did not seek a political revolution. It tried by a relay-race through a number of related problem-areas (housing, leisure time, sexuality, education, art) to reach a distant and obscure target. This target was diffusely characterized as 'the new man', 'the new city', or 'the new life'. The way to it was defined somewhat more clearly as a result of the greater public expression, greater participation in decision-making, and more communal life-style that were attempted in the new 'experimental towns'. The paradigmatic character of the new garden cities was to infuse the whole of public life. These objectives were deliberately not connected to an institutionalized opposition within the State, and party allegiance was rejected. Unfortunately, however, the movement linked itself to nationalism.

Hermann Salomon, the medical expert, gave open expression to the nationalist connection when, in a lecture at the Royal Technical High-school in Berlin in 1913, he declared: 'Germany needs garden cities more urgently than England does!' Squeezed between France, Britain and Russia, Salomon went on, Germany had to make sure that the total strength of her people was so conserved and enhanced that, if at all possible, each citizen could achieve more in his work or professional activity than his equivalents in the other leading national states[70]. The first essential was generally to improve Germany's reputation abroad; in the artistic field, for instance, Germany as yet enjoyed little respect. It might seem shocking and un-national to say so, but anyone with a sufficient knowledge of foreign countries knew that Germany counted for little today in painting or sculpture. In architecture Germany was regarded as the most backward of nations, mainly because German taste, in foreign eyes, was considered to be at the lowest imaginable level. The German reputation had sunk so low abroad, that the terms 'German' and 'in bad taste' had become virtually synonymous . . .[71]. Speeches and writings of this type were legion.

Analysis of the reform proposals can be conducted only in the context of a discussion of the intellectual tendencies of the time. It is not, however, the task of research into the history of town planning and related movements to put individual personalities in the dock. Its duty is to analyse general tendencies, to point out trends and dangers. It has to present the historical process in its unvarnished form. The achievement of committed planners, architects, and exponents of arts and crafts must not be obscured by a critical assessment of the conjuncture within which they worked. They materially improved the quality of spatial and architectural creation. Their magnificent effort to build a 'new city' bore some fruit, even if their individual achievement was taken over by a socio-cultural and political tendency the aim of which, in contrast to theirs, was by no means to open society up to an enlightened, liberal democracy. Their political and social miscalculation nevertheless cast a shadow over German housing reform in the early twentieth century.

The German Garden City movement, for all its defects, can be acknowledged as having re-established, albeit briefly, the broken links between urban planning and architecture—links which, incidentally, have again sunk into oblivion in our own day. It showed that the problems of town planning cannot be resolved by individuals, however charismatic, and that this socio-political responsibility can be borne only by an inter-disciplinary, positive and open dialogue between all those involved. It achieved its objectives only in isolated respects. The historical conditions and restrictions of the imperial era strangled its liberating elements. In the

Weimar Republic mainstream town planning came to share the Garden City movement's anti-urban tendency, and the inner city lost its pre-eminence. The Weimar planners progressed beyond the garden city in their resolution of technico-formal questions, thus pressing further ahead with the 'new building' revolution. They did not, however, develop socio-political aspirations comparable to those of the garden-city movement.

Of course, the supporters of the garden city failed to be aware of the dialectical tension between Idea and Execution. They over-estimated their own possibilities. But is it not the prerequisite of all progress, first of all to leap beyond prevailing practical limitations by an effort of the imagination? Any urbanistic movement which is subject to the blessings and curses of a utopian approach deserves our attention.

NOTES

1. Muthesius, Hermann (1904–05) *Das englische Haus*, 3 vols. Berlin.
2. Cf. Huber, V. A. (1894) *Ausgewählte Schriften über Sozialreform und Genossenschaftswesen* (Munding, K. [ed.]). Berlin, p. lxxix.
3. Engels, Friedrich (1845) *Die Lage der arbeitenden Klasse in England*. Leipzig.
4. Huber, V. A. (1894) *Ausgewählte Schriften über Sozialreform und Genossenschaftswesen* (Munding, K. [ed.]). Berlin, p. lxxxvii.
5. Quoted from Herzberg, Ursula (1957) Geschichte der Berliner Wohnungswirtschaft. Unpublished thesis, Berlin, pp. 20–2.
6. Huber, V. A. (1894) *Ausgewählte Schriften über Sozialreform und Genossenschaftswesen* (Munding, K. [ed.]). Berlin, p. 613.
7. 'In fact, it was the proposals contained in a memorial published in February 1847, *The Task of a Berlin Cooperative Building Society, by C. W. Hoffmann*, that earned wide respect.' (Hoffmann, C. W. (1852) *Die Wohnungen der Arbeiter und Armen, 1. Heft: die Berliner Gemeinnützige Bau-Gesellschaft*. Berlin, p. 19); see also Herzberg, Ursula (1957) Geschichte der Berliner Wohnungswirtschaft. Unpublished thesis, Berlin, p. 26: 'The constitution was adopted on 15 November 1847 and officially approved by the royal authority on 28 October 1848'.
8. 'Order of the Royal Cabinet, 26 September 1849. I am actively interested in the efforts of the co-operative building society and to confirm this I have decided to support the enterprise by taking up shares to the value of 2000 talers and making an annual contribution of two hundred talers, payable by my treasurer, Schöning. This order constitutes my response to the representation made to me by the directors of the society whose worthy endeavours will, I hope, achieve every success. Sanssouci, 26th September, 1849. Friedrich Wilhelm.' (Hoffmann, C. W. (1852) *Die Wohnungen der Arbeiter und Armen, 1. Heft: die Berliner Gemeinnützige Bau-Gesellschaft*. Berlin, p. 31.)
9. Herzberg, Ursula (1957) Geschichte der Berliner Wohnungswirtschaft. Unpublished thesis, Berlin, p. 28.
10. See, for example, Wiel, Paul (1970) *Wirtschaftsgeschichte des Ruhrgebiets*. Essen.
11. Kuczynski, Jürgen (1948) *Die Bewegung der deutschen Wirtschaft zwischen 1880–1946*. Maisenheim-am-Glan, p. 93.

12. *Ibid.*, p. 109.
13. For population figures, see Hartmann, Kristiana (1976) *Deutsche Gartenstadt-bewegung: Kulturpolitik und Gesellschaftreform.* Munich, p. 10.
14. See Kampffmeyer, Hans (1913) *Die Gartenstadtbewegung.* Leipzig and Berlin, p. 2.
15. On this point, see Rosenberg, A. (1938) *Die Entstehung der deutschen Republik 1871-1918.* Berlin, p. 15, and Mann, Golo (1966) *Deutsche Geschichte des 19. und 20. Jahrhunderts.* Hamburg, pp. 433ff.
16. See Abendroth, W. (1965) *Sozialgeschichte der deutschen Arbeiterbewegung.* Frankfurt-am-Main, p. 52.
17. Hegemann, Werner (1911) *Der Städtebau nach den Ergebnissen der allgemeinen Städtebau-Ausstellung,* Part 1. Berlin, pp. 19–20.
18. Noack, Victor (1925) *Kulturschande: die Wohnungsnot als Sexualproblem.* Berlin, pp. 15ff.
19. See, for example, Mohler, A. (1950) *Die Konservative Revolution in Deutschland.* Stuttgart, p. 37.
20. See, for example, *Berlin und seine Bauten: Teil 2, Rechtsgrundlagen und Stadtent-wicklung.* Berlin and Munich, 1964.
21. Hegemann, Werner (1930, 1963, 1976) *Das steinerne Berlin: Geschichte der grössten Mietskasernenstadt der Welt.* Berlin.
22. Hegemann, Werner (1911) *Der Städtebau nach den Ergebnissender allgemeinen Städtebau-Ausstellung,* Part 1. Berlin, p. 10.
23. Eberstadt, Rudolf (1920) *Handbuch des Wohnungswesens* (4th ed.). Jena.
24. One such organization was the *Verein Reichswohnungsgesetz,* founded in 1898 by Karl von Mangoldt, and known from 1904 as the *Deutscher Verein für Wohnungsreform.* The aims of the association were: the extension of owner-occupation, the provision of cheap building land, public aid for housing, and socially-oriented rent legislation. They were not incorporated in legislation until the Prussian Housing Law was passed in 1918.
25. On this point, see Vossberg, Walter (1906) *Die deutsche Baugenossenschafts-bewegung.* Berlin.
26. The income tax law exempted from income tax those societies whose commercial activities did not extend beyond the circle of their own members. The stamp tax law exempted from stamp tax and legal fees those societies whose exclusive aim was to provide housing for poor families, whose dividends were limited to four per cent, and whose funds, in the event of the winding-up of the society, were earmarked for co-operative purposes (see Vossberg, Walter (1906) *Die deutsche Baugenossenschaftsbewegung.* Berlin, p. 64.)
27. Sax, Emil (1889) *Die Wohnungszustände der arbeitenden Klassen und ihre Reform.* Vienna.
28. 'Arminius' (1874) *Die Großstädte in ihrer Wohnungsnot und die Grundlagen einer durchgreifenden Abhilfe.* Leipzig.
29. Engels, Friedrich (1970) *Über die Umwelt der arbeitenden Klassen* (edited by Günter Hillman). Gütersloh, p. 180.
30. Hamann, Richard, and Jost, Hermand (1967) *Stilkunst um 1900.* Berlin (East), introduction.
31. On this point see, for example, Stern, Fritz (1963) *Kulturpessimismus als politische Gefahr.* Berne and Stuttgart, pp. 25ff.

32. March, Otto (1913) Stand und Ziel der Städtebaukunst. *Der Städtebau,* 10 (3, 4), p. 31.

33. *Ibid.*

34. The book went through a colossal number of printings. In the first year of publication, 1890, sixty thousand copies were printed in twenty-nine impressions. By 1891 it had gone through a total of thirty-nine printings. Sales fell somewhat from 1893, perhaps because the limits of demand were being approached. By 1909 the cumulative number of impressions had risen to forty-nine. There were further printings between 1925 and 1930, and by 1945 a total of 145,000 copies had been sold (see Stern, Fritz (1963) *Kulturpessimisimus als politische Gefahr.* Berne and Stuttgart, p. 192, and Voss, Liselotte (1926) *Rembrandt als Erzieher* und seine Bedeutung. Unpublished thesis, Göttingen, p. 78).

35. The three well-known art-education conferences, held in 1901, 1903 and 1905, were devoted respectively to graphic art (Dresden), music (Weimar), and sport and physical education (Hamburg).

36. In 1909 Wilhelm II convened a meeting of Germany's leading educationalists to draw up a new teaching programme.

37. See *Gartenstadt,* 1 (9), September 1902, p. 168. It was also in 1902 that Ferdinand Avenarius founded the *Dürerbund,* Theodor Fischer wrote his *Stadterweiterungsfragen,* and Karl Ernst Osthaus founded the *Folkwangmuseum.*

38. See Dietmar N. Schmidt's article on the Hart brothers in *Neue deutsche Biographie,* vol. 7, Berlin, 1966, pp. 706–7.

39. See *Neue Gemeinschaft,* 2 (1–6/7), 1901–2, pp. 158–65.

40. Lux, J. A. (1907) Die baukünstlerische Erziehung des Publikums. *Hohe Warte,* 3, pp. 41ff.

41. *Ibid.,* p. 41.

42. Richter, J. (1909) *Die Entstehung des kunsterzieherischen Gedankens: ein Kulturproblem der Gegenwart.* Leipzig, pp. 73, 85.

43. Muthesius, Hermann (1907) Die Bedeutung des Kunstgewerbes. *Hohe Warte,* 3, pp. 235–6.

44. Lux, J. A. (1909) *Der Städtebau und die Grundpfeiler der heimischen Bauweise.* Dresden, introduction, p. 3.

45. Muthesius, Hermann (1907) *Kunstgewerbe und Architektur.* Jena.

46. Bollerey, Franziska, and Hartmann, Kristiana (1974) Wünsche und Wirklichkeit: Geschichte der Wohnbefragung und eine erste Anwendung. *Bauwelt,* (7), pp. 285ff.

47. For the history of Hellerau garden city, see Hartmann, Kristiana (1976) *Deutsche Gartenstadtbewegung: Kulturpolitik und Gesellschaftsreform.* Munich, pp. 46ff.

48. Osthaus, K. E. (1911) Gartenstadt und Städtebau, in Keller, Karl *et al., Bauordnung und Bebauungsplan, ihre Bedeutung für die Gartenstadtbewegung (Vorträge Jahresversammlung der DGG).* Berling and Leipzig.

49. Lux, J. A. (1907) Nationale Politik. *Hohe Warte,* 3, p. 57.

50. Osthaus, K. E., *ibid.,* p. 39, and March, Otto (1913) Stand und Ziel der Städtebaukunst. *Der Städtebau,* 10 (3, 4), p. 30.

51. Schmidt, Paul Ferdinand (1910) Eine Studienfahrt zu den Gartenstädten Englands. *Kunstchronik,* new series 21, pp. 6ff.

52. See *Der Städtebau,* 8 (12), 1911, pp. 148ff.
53. See *ibid.,* 7, 1910, plates 25, 26.
54. See *ibid.,* 10, 1913, plate 38.
55. See Brinckmann, A. E. (1925) *Stadtbaukunst vom Mittelalter bis zur Neuzeit.* Wildpark-Potsdam, p. 138.
56. Muthesius, Hermann (1912) Wo stehen wir? *Jahrbuch des Deutschen Werkbundes.* p. 21.
57. Brinckmann, A. E. (1908) Moderne Bestrebungen im Städtebau. *Hohe Warte,* 4, p. 338.
58. Brinckmann, A. E. (1910/11) Entwicklung des Städtebau-Ideals seit der Renaissance, in *Transactions of the Town Planning Conference,* vol. 1. London: R.I.B.A.
59. Osthaus, K. E. (1911) Gartenstadt und Städtebau, in Keller, Karl *et al., Bauordnung und Bebauungsplan, ihre Bedeutung für die Gartenstadtbewegung* (Vorträge Jahresversammlungder DGG) Berlin and Leipzig, p. 40.
60. Kampffmeyer, Hans (1913) *Die Gartenstadtbewegung.* Leipzig and Berlin, p. 79.
61. For the planning history of Falkenberg, see Hartmann, Kristiana (1976) *Deutsche Gartenstadtbewegung: Kulturpolitik und Gesellschaftsreform.* Munich, p. 102.
62. Die Gartenstadt Falkenberg bei Berlin. *Gartenstadt,* 7 (5), May 1913, pp. 81ff.
63. *Die architektonische Einheitlichkeit in der Siedlung Falkenberg bei Grünau. Grundsätze und Bestimmungen für ihre Durchführung. Aufgestellt von der Bauabteilung der Deutschen Gartenstadt-Gesellschaft G.m.B.H., gez. Kampffmeyer und Otto* (September 1913).
64. Taut, B. (1913) Kleinhausbau und Landaufschliessung, Vortrag gehalten auf der Generalversammlung der Deutschen Gartenstadt-Gesellschaft, Leipzig, pp. 3ff. (manuscript).
65. On communal life in Falkenberg, see *Der Falkenberg,* 1–8, 1915–24, and *Wohnungswirtschaft,* 1924, 1925.
66. Resumed in Booth, Charles (1902) *Life and Labour of the People in London.* London and New York.
67. Hegemann, Werner (1911) *Der Städtebau nach den Ergebnissen der allgemeinen Städtebau-Ausstellung,* Part 1. Berlin, p. 7.
68. Eberstadt, Rudolf (1909) Die neue Gartenvorstadt in London, Hampstead. *Der Städtebau,* 6 (8), p. 100.
69. Kampffmeyer, Bernhard (1919) *Von der Gartenstadt zur Gartenvorstadt.* Berlin-Grünau, p. 4.
70. Salomon, Hermann (1913) Gartenstädte, in Brix, Joseph and Genzmer, Felix (eds.), *Städtebauliche Vorträge.* Berlin, p. 21.
71. Muthesius, Hermann (1907) Die Bedeutung des Kunstgewerbes: Eröffnungsrede zu den Vorlesungen über modernes Kunstgewerbe an der Handelshochschule in Berlin. *Hohe Warte,* 3, p. 237.

8

The ideology, aesthetics and politics of the City Beautiful movement

WILLIAM H. WILSON

The City Beautiful movement coalesced in the 1890s and waned in the first decade of the twentieth century. Intense city planning activity under the City Beautiful banner flared for little more than a decade, yet the movement was the first self-conscious, nationwide effort to bring order, system, and pattern to the United States' chaotic urban growth. The movement suffered from its limited duration in several ways. Its very brevity is a help, however, in the task of recreating its remarkably insightful and effective ideology, aesthetics and political methods.

Historians of the City Beautiful movement have split into two camps whose cannonades have rattled down the twentieth century. One group locates the origins of the City Beautiful in the neoclassic grandeur of the World's Columbian Exposition, held in Chicago during 1893. It deplores the influence of the Chicago Fair on subsequent city planning. The fair's classicism and axiality were derivative and atavistic, and worse, the translation of the fair's pompous Court of Honor into scores of civic centre and boulevard schemes artfully dodged pressing urban problems in favour of an empty community cosmetic. Some City Beautiful planners contributed to civic melioration, but their achievements were modest at best. The other group does not deny the role of the World's Columbian Exposition in American culture. It does insist that the origins of the City Beautiful movement, while they include the Chicago Fair, are also complex, pervasive, and antecedent. Historians of the second persuasion see positive values in

City Beautiful architecture and planning. They see the movement as an effort to improve the utility as well as the comeliness of cities, to elevate urban citizenship, and to fulfil human needs for transportation, recreation, and residential environment. This study will explicate and extend the position of the second group[1].

The programmatic origins of the City Beautiful movement are to be found in the landscape design, municipal improvement, and civic design movements as they had developed by the late nineteenth century. Most historians have slighted important conceptual and constructivist evolutions in urban landscape design. These largely-ignored developments converted landscape design from concern with large pastoral parks to comprehensive planning for an urban or metropolitan area conceived as an organic, interrelated, interdependent entity. The reasons for this historiographic lacuna may be found, first, in the overconcentration on Frederick Law Olmsted as the representative landscape designer, and second, in the concern for Olmsted's elite reformist writings and what are interpreted to be his increasingly acute adaptations of pastoralism to new sites. Olmsted was really no different from other American landscape architects in his rapid modification of romantic design. Placing Olmsted in the genteel reform tradition through his writings emphasizes his pastoral-romantic prose, merely embellished through time. In contrast to his writings, his landscape design altered significantly. Olmsted's developing designs were more than improved variations on a theme. They were accommodations to the new urban realities of the late nineteenth century, including more active use of parks by the public[2].

Leonard J. Simutis's analysis of Olmsted's designs demonstrates how the pastoral ideal was compromised from the beginning in Olmsted's and Calvert Vaux's first triumph, New York City's Central Park (1858). Malls, promenades, collective recreational grounds, and buildings intruded there, as they did in later parks, although the intrusions were softened by adroit placement and screens of plantings. As Olmsted's insight into the use of his parks grew, he improved his positioning of walks, stairs and other constructions for the purpose of directing and controlling park visitors. His Buffalo park system of 1871, influenced by that supposed *bête noire* of the romanticists, Haussmann, was a quantum leap in city planning. This system and those following from the hands of Olmsted and other designers were far more than traditional landscape parks tied together by boulevards. The boulevards, first linguistically and later often designedly 'parkways', were intended to penetrate the city with a suburban ambience, to spread the rise in desirable homesites and land values through the city, to dampen the jealousies of the urban sectionalism waiting to emerge when one part of the city was improved, and to connect specialized, differentiated parks. At about the same time, the noted landscape designer, H. W. S. Cleveland, offered the boulevard as a device for traffic relief based on his experience in Chicago. Olmsted's parks were deliberately designed for picturesque areas having scenic values but unlikely, because of ravines or hollows, to be developed. Often they were designed for special neighbourhood needs, and occasionally to provide sites for collective recreation safely away from landscape parks[3].

South Park in Buffalo (1888) confirmed Olmsted's shift in emphasis from pastoral-romantic design to naturalistic constructivism. His fundamental reshaping of an unpromising site forecast his landscaper's role at the World's Columbian Exposition. Other landscape architects, including George Kessler in his 1893 park-system plan for Kansas City and Warren H. Manning in his 1901 Harrisburg plan, proposed complex and differentiated constructions. Olmsted and other landscape architects wrapped their naturalistic designs in rhetoric proclaiming pastoral-romantic ideals. As designers, however, they had moved far from the day when they offered the detached landscape park as anodyne for the mental, physical and nervous afflictions of the unnatural city. Park and boulevard systems accepted their urban milieu, offered visual contrasts with scenes of brick and mortar, provided barriers for antagonistic ethnic or racial populations, and restricted, their designers hoped, industrial and commercial uses to 'natural' areas in the organic city. Thus they assisted a logical, functional, urban growth[4].

By the late 1890s landscape architects had widened their concern for urban beauty to include the proper aesthetic development of ordinary residential streets, of home grounds ranging from cottage plots to estates, and of public buildings. The phrase 'outdoor art', describing these concerns, enjoyed a brief vogue. Its proponents stretched 'outdoor art' to include the beautification of school grounds, the school garden movement, the anti-billboard crusade and other efforts to control urban ugliness, and rural scenic preservation, especially in systems of national and state parks. The founding of The American Park and Outdoor Art Association in 1897 by landscape architects, park superintendents, and informed laymen represented a defence of traditional landscape values. But it was more than that. Its founders wished to expand landscape work to most parts of the city. The activities of the APOAA indicated that urban landscape design, settling into the routine of park maintenance and improvement, needed new worlds to conquer. These expanded activities involved more than surface decoration, important as that was. Landscape designers continued to bring hydraulic and sanitary engineers into association with them to solve the drainage and water supply problems of naturalistic construction[5].

Through it all Olmsted and the others clung to older ideals. Olmsted, and landscape designers generally, distrusted the playground movement with its eager grabs for precious park acreage. In his later years Olmsted lashed out at the emerging classicism of the late nineteenth century. The architecture of the World's Columbian Exposition was too starkly white and too busy, he wrote. He sought to keep his precious Wooded Island in the Chicago Fair lagoon free of exhibit buildings but finally capitulated to minor, harmonious construction invading its naturalistic precincts. He denounced the architect Stanford White and his associates, the designers of classicistic entrances to his Prospect Park in Brooklyn. He called them 'cockneys', his expression for ignorant despoilers of natural landscape. But these attacks should not be taken very seriously. In the early 1890s Olmsted, embittered and acerbic, was beginning his sad descent into dotage. His attacks on classicistic architecture promote a false dichotomy between the classicistic and naturalistic modes. His pastoral-romantic writings encourage the mistaken view that landscape architecture embraced dated, unchanging theories and goals, that it was a static profession in the eye of the nineteenth century's social and economic storms. By the 1890s, landscape architects were designing parks and parkways, not as retreats from the cities, but to make cities beautiful. They were helping to fashion the ideological and aesthetic underpinnings of the City Beautiful movement[6].

MUNICIPAL IMPROVEMENT ORIGINS

Municipal improvement formed the second source of the City Beautiful. It began as village improvement with the founding of an improvement society in Stockbridge, Massachusetts, in 1853. By 1870 the old Stockbridge, dreary and dirty, had given way to a well-paved, tree-shaded summer resort town. Its improvement association was a model for the movement, which grew in New England in the 1870s and 1880s, and spanned the continent in the 1890s. Spurred by the village improvement news published in the magazine *Home and Flowers,* improvement proponents gathered at Springfield, Ohio, in 1900 to found the National League of Improvement Associations. In the next two years the organization renamed itself the American League for Civic Improvement and moved its headquarters to Chicago, acts symbolic of its rapid shift away from village improvement. By the early twentieth century municipal improvement was a metropolitan phenomenon, its advocates at all urban size-levels advancing everything from home flower gardening to street cleaning and sanitary engineering. Often women's clubs and their state and national federations organized municipal improvements on the local level. The goals of municipal improvement were practically identical to the functional-aesthetic, small-scale concerns of landscape design: tree planting, residential beautification, anti-billboard crusades, parks and recreation, and various public embellishments[7].

There was some earnestness and a little naïvety in municipal improvement's 'promotion of public beauty'. Yet it made contributions which have been slighted or overlooked. It encouraged women to concentrate on the beautification of the home and its surroundings—house painting, gardening, tree-planting—and to work outward from the home to promote tree-lined, clean streets, public drinking fountains, public baths, billboard control, and improved utilities. It pressed women's organizations to galvanize their communities in the cause of beautification by concentrating upon one practical, carefully-planned, striking improvement. The improvement could be planting home flower gardens with prizes for the best in each of certain categories, keeping a thoroughfare clean, or securing an attractive drinking fountain or watering trough. While advocating realizable goals and one-at-a-time projects, municipal improvement stimulated comprehensive thinking and planning for the community. Its success compelled women not only to think and to plan, but to develop effective propaganda techniques. It joined the landscape design movement in advocating the inseparability of beauty, utility, and municipal financial gain. 'The old saying that beauty is only skin deep is deeply false', wrote Jessie M. Good, an early catalyst of the nationwide movement. 'Beauty is as deep as the bones, the blood, the rosy flesh ... So with the beauty advocated by improvement associations. It is founded on the soundest economic laws. It is the framework on which is founded the science of government ...'. Municipal improvement reflected the nineteenth century's rising living standards. It gave middle- and upper-class women of leisure, refinement, and intelligence an outlet for their energies. It helped to focus community attention on the inutility, ugliness, vulgarity and wretchedness of portions of hundreds of American cities and towns[8].

CIVIC DESIGN ORIGINS

Civic design was the third historic prop of the City Beautiful. Civic design developed from a complex of spatial, visual, economic and social ideas, and resulted in the construction of classicistic public or semi-public buildings singly or in groups. By the end of the nineteenth century it had embraced the civic art movement. Civic art resembled the outdoor art enthusiasms of landscape design and municipal improvement. Professional artists promoted it, however, as a collaborative effort among sculptors, painters, and architects. They argued for the systematic embellishment of utilitarian objects in the city; street lamps and other street furniture, wharves, bridges, and buildings. They urged decorative devices such as park entrances and fountains. The proponents of civic art wished for well-placed sculpture in parks and squares and murals in public and semi-public buildings. They desired permanent artistic achievements outdoors and indoors to enrich the urban landscape, to add dramatic interest to buildings, and to advance the artists' cause with the public[9].

The inspiration for civic art came from Europe, at first funnelled through the Ecole de Beaux-Arts, with its strong collaborative bias. Later it came directly from several European cities. Collaboration advanced under the architect's aegis. H. H. Richardson, a Beaux-Arts student, produced two collaborative structures in Boston, the Brattle Square Church (competition won 1870) and his magnificent Trinity Church (consecrated 1877). Charles F. McKim advanced the ideal of artistic union with his superb classicistic Boston Public Library (1888–95). McKim, a student of the Beaux-Arts and of Richardson, brought into his decorative scheme renowned painters and sculptors. The sculptural and mural elements of the World's Columbian Exposition ratified past collaborative efforts and certified future cooperation. The dean of American architects, Richard M. Hunt, inspired the founding in 1893 of the Municipal Art Society of New York. Though the depression of the 1890s slowed this and other organized efforts to promote civic art, the organizational approach had spread beyond New York by the end of the century[10].

Civic design presumed artistic unity but sought a greater ideal, the subordination of individual genius to a monumental architectonic triumph. McKim's library, Stanford White's Washington Arch (New York City, 1889–95) and other designs from eastern architects heralded the revival of construction in the classicistic mode. Thereafter the classicistic style, decorated by cooperating but subordinate artists, became a common fashion in public and semi-public buildings down to World War II. The individual structure, however well designed, was not the grandest expression of the ideal. Grouped public or semi-public buildings in an axial or symmetrical setting, tied to the city's existing and planned boulevards and parkways, represented its ultimate realization. The World's Columbian Exposition was the immediate visual inspiration. Its major buildings stood shimmering in their white classicistic dress around an axial basin. Transferring the Exposition's temporary plaster vision into permanent 'civic centres' was a significant intellectual leap. Men made the leap. The fact that they did is not entirely due to the Columbian Exposition. Though it is not alone, McKim's Boston Public Library is the best example of a late nineteenth-century building planned in relation to other buildings, and to a court or square. In designing the library to close the west end of Copley Square, McKim treated the space as a developing Renaissance piazza. He adjusted the library's façade elements harmoniously with existing structures, including Trinity Church across the square, the Museum of Fine Arts to the south, and the S. S. Pierce building at the south-west corner. Before the Exposition, then, the conception of grouped buildings was reborn in the nineteenth century mind. The Exposition superimposed on that mind a dazzling vision of freshness and unity. Later expositions sustained it. The plans of Burnham and his associates for Washington, D.C. (1902), Cleveland (1903), San Francisco (1905), and Chicago (1909) were among its most striking renditions[11].

By 1900 the phrase 'City Beautiful' was in widespread use to describe the

congeries of reforms subsumed under landscape design, municipal improvement, and civic design. Then and later its advocates used the phrase retro-
spectively, to include past as well as future planning schemes. The
accelerating velocity and interaction of these reforms was typified by the
Chicago Fair—inspired efforts to improve Chicago and Cleveland in the late
1890s; by the increasing cooperation of the American League for Civic
Improvement and the American Park and Outdoor Art Association, resulting
in their merger in 1904; by a new burst of comprehensive planning after 1900;
and by the appearance, in 1903, of Charles Mulford Robinson's 'bible' of the
movement, *Modern Civic Art, or the City Made Beautiful*[12].

IDEOLOGY OF THE CITY BEAUTIFUL

City Beautiful reformers brought a complex progressive ideology to their
movement. First, they believed in beauty as more than decoration or surface
adornment. They actively sought beautiful buildings and scenes to help
preserve what attractiveness remained in nineteenth-century urban settings.
More, they wished to supplant the pervading ugly, unkempt atmosphere of
the American city. J. Horace McFarland, the leading lay apostle of the City
Beautiful, called it 'the crusade against ugliness'. Turn-of-the-century
American cities were ugly, and dirty too. Retail-commercial downtowns
expressed their vitality by moving as they expanded, leaving backwashes of
ageing buildings given over to second-hand shops, second-rate stores, light
industry, or musty vacancy. Factories and business blocks vomited black,
sooty smoke that loomed over Pittsburg, Chicago, St. Louis. The urban
sections of rivers were treated as sewers, not waterscapes. Junk and rubbish
littered their banks. Many cities had acquired parks but often these were
poorly located, undeveloped, or uncoordinated into park and boulevard
systems. In 1890 Boston and Minneapolis could be proud of their parks but
Chicago displayed just over 2000 acres of parkland, and a pitiful 799
improved acres for its more than one million citizens. Rochester served
133,896 inhabitants with seventy-six improved park acres[13].

Street paving of all types was often conspicuous by its absence. Boston
boasted 100 per cent of its streets paved, though 163 of its 408 street miles
were only gravel covered. Boston was an exception, even for the eastern
seaboard, and in cities farther west paving conditions were much worse. But
fifty of Kansas City's 267 miles were surfaced as were less than five per cent
of those in Dallas. Burgeoning Minneapolis had paved just over three per
cent of its street mileage. In 1903 a resident of Omaha bragged about his
city's advances in street paving. Omaha, he said, embraced 350 miles of
streets and alleys. Eighty-five miles were paved, and ten of those were 'the
remnants of what was once wooden block paving'. The speaker, remember,
was not criticizing. He was boasting of progress. Dirt streets—swirling dust

in summer, gluey, sucking mud in spring, redolent with horse droppings—
were the norm in many American cities[14].

City Beautiful advocates argued for the meliorative power of beauty.
Olmsted's belief in the restorative effects of natural scenery has been demonstrated so often that it needs no repeating. His successors in landscape
design echoed his environmentalism. The municipal improvement wing
applied it to its own concerns. E. L. Shuey of the APOAA contended that
'beauty and healthfulness' were as important as they were inseparable.
McFarland declared that 'beauty came even before food in Eden. And while
we cannot restore man to the garden, we can ... make the city garden-like
...'. Civic design advocate Robinson urged preserving landscape parks,
which 'present the sharpest contrast to the artificiality of the city...'[15].

Beauty was scarcely ever specifically defined, though it was often
illustrated. Well-tended home flower gardens, well-done landscape parks,
street furniture of straightforward but gracious design, monumental public
buildings, all in harmonious relationships, were the basis of civic beauty. City
Beautiful leaders did not wish to go beyond a kind of generalized
Ruskinianism. They knew, by intelligence, breeding and training, what was
beautiful and what was not, be it natural or man-made. What they wanted
was enough influence to exclude 'costly blunders' and 'amateurish
experiment' from the urban landscape. The municipal art commissions
established in many cities after 1900 gave them at least advisory powers over
the design of public structures. While they thus asserted a cultural dominion
over the city, they were hesitant to apply it without regard for neighbourhood
sensibilities or the existing urban environment. Embarrassing contretemps
among arbiters of public beauty, such as the furore over the statue of
Bacchante in the courtyard of the Boston Public Library, occurred rarely[16].

Second, the City Beautiful leadership insisted upon the combination or
blending of beauty and utility. Landscape designers had long argued the role
of beauty in creating a contented urban workforce, attracting a superior
population, and raising property values. That argument continued, best
encapsulated in Burnham's statement that 'beauty has always paid better
than any other commodity and always will'. But by the turn of the century the
assertion that beauty and utility were inseparable meant something more
palpable, direct, and design-related. No structure or scene could be truly
beautiful without being functional as well. Jessie Good's assertion that
beauty was more than skin deep forecast later, almost identical comments
within the municipal improvement camp. McFarland pointed to the clouds of
smoke and soot representing waste in manufacturing, home maintenance,
and cleaning bills. Beauty was simply efficiency, he maintained. McFarland
loved trees, but he believed that the proper tree was also an 'efficient' one.
City Beautiful architects and planners offered designs both attractive and
functional. The city plans of Burnham and his associates concerned traffic
circulation, railroad reorganization, cultural as well as civic centres,

recreational improvements and other functional matters. The Harrisburg plan of 1901 united a report on parks and boulevards with two on mundane but essential street and sewer improvements. A civic centre scheme, the Jarvis Hunt plan for Kansas City (1909), proposed grouping scattered governmental activities into classicistic buildings around a great arc, facing Hunt's spare, monumental, functional Union Station. Arnold Brunner, a sensitive classicistic planner and designer, was so taken with the inextricable natures of beauty and utility that he coined the word 'beautility' to express them. Fortunately, Brunner's coinage never gained much circulation, but he did epitomize City Beautiful functional and aesthetic aspirations[17].

Third, City Beautiful advocates sought expertise in the solution of urban problems. The drive to improve the design and execution of projects by employing experts was characteristic of the era. It advanced in response to growing middle- and upper-class disgust with inept, piecemeal, 'political' patchwork efforts to stay abreast of urban needs. It advanced because experts in the youthful professional fields of architecture, landscape architecture, and engineering were available in sufficient number, training, experience, and eagerness to undertake municipal work[18].

Many desirable aspects of planning clustered around the expert. From the days of Olmsted's work in Central Park, plans from experts had predicted headlong urban expansion, called for the acquisition of public property while land was yet relatively cheap, laid out functional designs of broad scope, subordinated and integrated details, and allowed for gradual, partial improvement within the context of the grand scheme. Without a general plan, Kessler announced in 1893, 'the value of selections for public purposes, their most satisfactory distribution, and the dependence of one improvement upon another, cannot be appreciated ...'. In 1901 the Harrisburg League for Municipal Improvements conceded that 'the financial condition of the city will not at present permit the carrying out of Mr. Manning's system in all its details', but urged a 'substantial beginning'. Two years later the Local Improvement Committee of the APOAA listed 'securing the services of an expert' as of first importance to a successful improvement campaign. An expert 'must be employed if the community hopes to have a beautiful entity'. In *Modern Civic Art*, Robinson called for a commission of experts to plan comprehensively and ensure that each year's construction fitted into the total plan. Burnham's aphorism, 'make no little plans', distilled the experience of City Beautiful experts[19].

Lay devotees of the City Beautiful upheld expertise for two other reasons. They were comfortable with the experts who matured before the second decade of the twentieth century, experts who shared their solid middle- and upper-class backgrounds or achievements. Expert George Kessler could work intimately with layman August Meyer, expert Warren Manning with layman J. Horace McFarland, expert Daniel Burnham with layman Charles D. Norton. This relationship faded as younger experts, more absorbed with professionalism, strove for some distance between themselves and the laity, but it was an important feature of the City Beautiful movement. Further, laymen liked an expert's cachet upon their plans for promotional reasons. City Beautiful bond issue campaigns stressed the practicality of expertly drawn plans. The certitude of expertise could explode like a bomb in the ranks of detractors and doubters. An expert who wrote in sprightly prose provided an excellent prop for bond issue mass meetings and rallies[20].

Fourth, City Beautiful ideologues were class conscious in a non-marxian sense. While insisting, implicitly, on individual mobility and some class fluidity, they accepted the reality of classes in urban America. For practical purposes, they distinguished two classes split along functional lines. The upper group, composed of owners and managers of substantial enterprises, would benefit from public improvements through a general increase in values and ease of living. Through improvements the upper class would recognize class interdependence, and would assume and fulfil the obligations of class leadership. The lower group, composed of manual and non-manual workers and their families, was oppressively city-bound, City Beautiful advocates believed. Unlike the upper group, working-class people could not afford vacations, suburban residences and surcease from the urban environment. These were venerable convictions. Olmsted's creations were partly for the 'tired workers' who lacked alternatives to their hard, harsh surroundings, partly to promote class intermingling on park promenades. Olmsted has been ridiculed for entertaining his vision, but his understanding of dulling toil and his yearning for the re-establishment of human unity were benevolent. Growing awareness of both class and community needs brought a rising emphasis on recreational facilities for the working class. These included playground parks and playgrounds within large landscape parks, public baths, baseball diamonds, picnic areas, tennis courts, and golf courses[21].

In preparing these palliatives City Beautiful ideologues were not impelled by fears of working-class revolt. True, Robinson warned of 'the city slum', where 'smoulders the fire which breaks forth in revolution', but he was practically alone in raising the issue, nor did he pursue it beyond a sentence in *Modern Civic Art*. Governments' ability to contain restiveness during the depression of the nineties, returning prosperity late in the decade, the relatively dispersed character of the country, the reformers' strong sense of community, all quieted the fears of uprising. It does not follow, however, that the City Beautiful movement advanced without a sense of crisis. Its advocates were environmentalists horrified at the lack of urban amenities. Unimproved working-class surroundings, they feared, would eventually demoralize and debase their inhabitants[22].

The movement's fervent optimism, its fifth ideological component, also blanketed fears of class conflict. Its evangelical confidence bubbled up from a compound containing the convictions behind the social, cultural, and ethical outlook of the middle and upper classes. There were yet other elements in the compound, including the grand if partial beautification achievements of pre-Exposition Chicago and a few other American cities, the adaptable grandeur of Paris ascribed to Napoleon III and Haussmann, and the importable architectonic triumphs of Venice and Rome. The urban transformation would depend upon the dynamism of charismatic leaders who were taming scandalous politicians, immigrants, and public service corporations, the dubious moral crustaceans of American cities. Robinson's rhapsodic opening of *Modern Civic Art* was more florid than most City Beautiful declarations but it captured the spirit of them all. 'The darkness rolls away, and the buildings that had been in shadow stand forth distinctly', Robinson exulted. 'The tall façades glow as the sun rises; their windows shine as topaz; ... Whatever was dingy, coarse, and ugly, is either transformed or hidden in shadow... There seems to be a new city for the work of a new day'[23].

Sixth, the City Beautiful shared in what has been called the 'American discovery of Europe'. To thoughtful Americans of the late nineteenth century, Europe was more than a nicely arranged warehouse filled with classicistic models. European cities seemed as dynamic as any in America, yet they were, by American standards, clean, well-administered, attractive, even beautiful entities whose growth and development were well controlled. Political scientist Albert Shaw in 1895 praised the pre-Haussmannic and Haussmannic ruthless destruction of medieval Paris (there were plenty of medieval structures elsewhere in France, he said) but was less enthusiastic about Parisian administrative and sanitary arrangements. German cities, Shaw found, were masterpieces of administration. He praised the Viennese government for forging a beautiful and practical city. Chicago, he noted, muffed a vastly greater opportunity after the devastating 1871 fire. If the municipality had purchased the burned-out district, and planned a civic area with public buildings, parks and boulevards, it could have sold the left-over land for more than enough to pay for the improvements. Since the Columbian Exposition, 'Chicago has had a clear comprehension of the magnificent effects that may be produced as the result of a large initial plan', but, alas, too late. As Shaw dourly concluded, 'it is evident that Chicago would have been the gainer if it could have borrowed some of Vienna's genius for municipal administration'[24].

In the twilight years of the City Beautiful, Frederick C. Howe deplored the rampant individualism in American cities while he praised German municipal ownership, taxes on unearned increment from urban land sales, and zoning. German cities' smooth, powerful administration, he explained, stemmed not from their great age as large cities, for they were in that respect younger than American and British metropolises. German success depended upon home rule and the psychology of responsibility which home rule engendered. Howe's paean to the German expert was an extreme example of American infatuation with European urbanism. Infatuations are impermanent. In 1913 McFarland revolted against an uncritical acceptance of all things German at the expense of a realistic awareness of heavy-handed Teutonic bureaucracy. Just as some municipal reformers stood in awe of European civic administration, so others imbibed European civic design. Both were elements of the awakening to European advances adaptable to American conditions. The parallel is complete even to the later reaction against classicism[25].

The seventh and culminating constituent of the City Beautiful ideology was its acceptance, indeed, its welcome of the American city. The architects, landscape architects, and planners of the era worked in cities and often lived in them or in their suburbs. Some rhetorical attacks on the unnatural city persisted, but these became rarer and more ritualistic as the twentieth century advanced. If American cities could be made beautiful and functional, then they could no longer be thought running sores on the landscape. If the city became the locus of harmony, mutual responsibility and interdependence between classes, mediated by experts, then it would be a peaceful, productive place, no longer a stark contrast to rural scenery. In its comprehensive view of the city and in its non-partisan concern for improvement, the City Beautiful partook of a revived civic spirit. In 1903 McFarland called it 'the great civic awakening'. Three years later he struggled with the problem of 'how civic improvement has become a country-wide movement. Frankly, I cannot answer it, except to voice my own belief, which is that in the fullness of time God has put it into the hands of our American citizens . . . to give us . . . in our urban habitations conditions at least approximating those of the beautiful wild into which our forefathers came a few generations ago'[26].

Imputations of God's design in secular salvation through the recapture of an arcadian past reveal little about the origins of municipal improvement, but they do suggest the similarities between the City Beautiful movement and other progressive developments. City Beautiful planning and progressivism shared a vision of the future based on faith, optimism, and class reconciliation under middle- and upper-class leadership. The City Beautiful movement in its various manifestations was the city planning aspect of early urban progressivism. The later progressive infatuation with professionalism, overarching government, statistics, and immediate melioratives such as improved housing, fragmented the City Beautiful movement, replacing it with the 'city practical'[27].

AESTHETICS OF THE CITY BEAUTIFUL

NATURAL BEAUTY AND NATURALISTIC CONSTRUCTION

The aesthetics of the City Beautiful were as widely ranging as its ideology. Reverence for natural beauty and for naturalistic constructivism, its urban counterpart, stands first in the order of City Beautiful aesthetics. The priority may seem misplaced given the City Beautiful's presumed regard for classicistic forms. When we examine what City Beautiful planners really were thinking and doing, however, we find a reality richer than the classicistic. It was no accident, as Henry Hope Reed, Jr., remarked in 1959, that the scenic preservation and urban beautification movements burst upon the country at the same time. There were precedents. Before the Civil War, Andrew Jackson Downing urged rural or ruralized homes for those urban dwellers who could afford them. The 'rural cemetery' movement, launched in 1831 with the opening of Boston's Mount Auburn, provided stylized romantic landscape retreats for the living who had the leisure and inclination to go to the city's edge. Olmsted personified the juncture of rural preservation and managed conservation with the drive for urban beauty. He offered the suburb to the middle class as the resolution of bleak rural living and the dehumanizing urban environment. Olmsted's work at the Mariposa Estate, his labours to preserve the Yosemite Valley and Niagara Falls, his design for Riverside, Illinois, his achievements at Biltmore, were done in the midst of his civic construction activity. He saw no discontinuity in landscape preservation and conservation, and bringing the 'middle landscape', nature subdued but not civilized, to urban America. Olmsted's environmental-hygienic dicta, the antipollutant role of trees for instance, were creditable if inadequate remedies for urban epidemics[28].

As urbanization, mechanization and commercialization roared into the twentieth century their levy on beauty, wherever located, was too great to ignore. The preservation and accentuation of natural beauty were major motives for the Boston metropolitan park system, Robinson's plan for Raleigh, North Carolina, Kessler's for Dallas, and many others. City Beautiful crusader McFarland was a landscape zealot who fought to save Niagara Falls from continuing commercial threats, and who became one of the country's leading rosarians. The Olmsted brothers, Burnham, and McKim were among those architects and planners who oscillated between intensely urban environments of living or work, and suburban, exurban, or rural retreats. Sculptor Augustus Saint-Gaudens ultimately betook himself to New Hampshire. That appealing mixture of ebullience and exactitude, Stanford White, may once have paid a Long Island farmer $50 per tree to leave standing a grove of potential firewood. Apocryphal or not, the story illustrates White's love of the beautiful. The landscape design and municipal improvement branches of the City Beautiful praised flowers, shrubs, and trees for their enhancing, softening qualities in city settings. Advocates from the landscape design–municipal improvement background espoused corporate beautification, too. They urged grass plots, ground covers, flowers, and naturalistic plant groupings for the grounds of small railroad stations. They praised railroad executives and factory owners who adopted systematic beautification ideas for their properties. Such activities, they noted, often spread beyond the station or the factory gate to home improvement and heightened civic concerns[29].

Civic designers embraced natural beauty and naturalistic constructivism in their urban improvement schemes. Burnham's plans suggested boulevard ties from their civic centres to waterscapes and park landscapes. Each of them proposed new park and parkway schemes unifying and extending the existing landscape-recreational facilities. Robinson's plans for Denver (1906) and Honolulu (1906) offered similar recommendations; so did John Nolen's designs for San Diego (1909) and Reading, Pennsylvania (1910). City Beautiful planners typically treated naturalistic parks and parkways as precious assets, not as relics to be tolerated or disfigured by the imposition of their own designs. The charge that City Beautiful plans scorned natural beauty fits nicely with preconceptions of conflict or dichotomy in city planning, but the charge is simply untrue[30].

CLASSIC BEAUTY

Granting their interest in naturalistic themes, City Beautiful designers believed classicistic architecture to be an important element. Classicistic architecture represented another step in the late nineteenth century's search for an effective, expressive building style. As Carroll L. V. Meeks and others have written, nineteenth-century architects faced a new order of problems represented by the office building, the railroad station, and the need to house expanding, differentiating governments. Architects increasingly concentrated on functional solutions at the expense of bizarre eclecticism. Gothic and gaudy Mediterranean styles gave way to a severe commercial vernacular, and to the Romanesque. Over time, within the Romanesque, turrets softened and shortened, roofs pitched more gently, dormers retreated and lost some excrescences, and ornament flattened into walls. For all its vogue, however, the Romanesque suffered from fatal defects. It was ecclesiastical architecture originally, difficult to adapt to the public and semi-public buildings of a secular culture without severe modifications for which there were no clear guides in proportion and arrangement. The genius of Richardson could impose discipline and order upon the Romanesque, as in the Allegheny County Courthouse and Jail. In weaker hands Romanesque buildings sometimes appeared ill-proportioned and fussily detailed. Their fenestration and the arrangement of horizontal and vertical elements seemed confused and contradictory. Even great Romanesque buildings contain incidents more compelling than their façades: the grace and massing of the rear of Trinity Church; the stylish severity of the Rookery's court; the powerful arch at the servants' entrance of the Glessner House; and the functional arrangement of the backs of Austin Hall and the old Kansas City stock exchange[31].

Classicistic architecture, in contrast, offered basic conceptions of proportion and arrangement. It presented models for adaptation through its range in time and space from classic Greek to the Beaux Arts. 'It was a flexible style', Christopher Tunnard wrote, 'which could make a unity of a building by combining boldness of plan with refinement of detail. It made possible the handling of entirely new building types, frequently of great scale, that a growing democracy required. These were the new state capitals, the railroad stations, and the public libraries, which are part of America's contributions to world architecture'. Classic architecture enjoyed other virtues besides precedent and flexibility. It was ideally suited to any building requiring easy public access on a few floors, controlled vertical movement, and a high degree of functional unity. It was, in other words, a superb envelope for buildings low in proportion to their length and breadth, however much their monumental domes or interior spaces suggested height. Tunnard's list of candidates for classicistic treatment could be extended to courthouses, city halls, museums, art galleries, theatres, banks, post offices, and newspaper offices. Gothic and Romanesque details became distended and trivial on their low, broad surfaces, but classicistic colonnades and arches throve[32].

The classicistic mode encouraged talented architects to pursue their experiments in arrangement and detail within the confines of a discipline. McKim, an architect whom the advocates of picturesque successionism dismiss as a talented copycat, did not 'copy' or 'derive' his buildings in any meaningful sense of the words. The Boston Public Library's multiple origins may be found in Henri Labrouste's Bibliothèque Sainte-Geneviève in Paris, Alberti's San Francisco in Rimini, Richardson's Trinity Church and his Marshall Field wholesale store, and the Roman Coliseum. Charles B. Atwood, answering the charges of plagiarism levelled against his beautiful Art Building at the Chicago Fair, snapped: 'The difference between me and some other architects is that I know what to take and what to leave, and I know how to combine things that come from different sources, while they do not'. Because the designs of these and other classicistic buildings 'come from different sources' we might ask how different such selection is from the obvious borrowings and adaptions among the members of the commercial Chicago and the residential Prairie Schools[33].

The classicistic approach encouraged skilled architects, but as important, its discipline rescued a great many mediocre talents. So long as an architect follows precedent it is reasonably difficult for him to design a bad classicistic building. Weak ones there are, of course: those built without an adequate base above grade on busy city streets, or backed into hillsides, or covered with frivolous detail. Such errors are not typical. Devotees of the classicistic recognized that independent genius in façade design is a scarce commodity among architects. Any large city is infested with hideous buldings, failed efforts at originality, beside which a poised classicistic structure is sweet respite for the eyes. Contemporary failures do not settle the argument against modernism. They do suggest that merely hurling words of dismissal such as 'professional hocus-pocus' at classicistic buildings, does not end the 'battle of styles'[34].

FIGURE 8.1. The City Beautiful movement evokes images of grouped civic centres and decorative effects. For examples see the Burnham and Bennett, Hines, and Reps volumes cited in the notes. City Beautiful programmes in reality, usually included plans for improving the quality of urban life, as the example in these photographs of Harrisburg, Pennsylvania shows.

Lastly, classicistic architecture evoked American history and spoke to the late-nineteenth century urban elite. Classicistic construction was firmly in the architectural tradition from colonial times. It flowered through the late 1840s before giving way to eclecticism. Although the Greek orders were popular, Roman modes also found favour. The differences between the classicism of the early nineteenth century and the classicistic buildings of the American Renaissance are differences of degree, not of kind. Classicistic architecture contained important symbols that the Gothic, Romanesque, or commercial styles never could. As James Early, Neil Harris, and George Heard Hamilton have written, it expressed a romantic attachment to Greece and Rome (and, by extension, the Renaissance city state). This attachment had little to do with governmental forms, more with assumed similarities of political thought and social achievement. At the dawn of the twentieth century it was still possible to believe the United States to be a republic governed in all important respects by European-descended, male-dominated

FIGURE 8.2. Figure 8.1. (left) shows flood-prone, sewage-choked Paxton Creek meandering through an industrial district in about 1900, while in figure 8.2. (above) the same creek in about 1910 flows in a concrete bed, part of a comprehensive beautification, flood control, drainage and recreation scheme approved by voters after a 1901–1902 bond issue campaign.

elites. Despite growing suffragist furore women enjoyed relatively little political participation. Blacks were losing the right to mass involvement in southern politics, and with some exceptions all racial minorities were confined to voting for whites. State houses of representatives as yet elected United States senators. State senators were chosen on a geographic, not a demographic basis. By late-twentieth-century standards the federal government's role was narrow, circumscribed, and remote from the citizen. It was reasonable to emphasize the greatness of the United States by adapting the architecture of past republics[35].

The romantic appeals of classicistic architecture and the romantic yearnings expressed in naturalistic landscape design reconcile those modes of City Beautiful expression. Most historians, however, have treated classicistic architecture and naturalistic constructivism as curious appositions. Their explanation for the reality—that in many cities the naturalistic (and often approved) lamb lies down with the classicistic (and frequently disapproved) lion—is twofold. First, classicism characterized the City Beautiful, not naturalistic constructivism. The juxtaposition of classicistic and naturalistic represents a sequential development: all landscape work is of pre-City Beautiful origin or inspiration, while only the classicistic buildings are in the City Beautiful mode. Second, the origins of landscape design are English while those of the classicistic are French and Italian[36].

These explanations have an appealing simplicity but they do not bear examination. First of all, combining the classicistic and the naturalistic was not new to the City Beautiful era. It was a favourite eighteenth- and nineteenth-century device. English landscape gardening as imported into the United States was not merely Reptonian or simply picturesque but a complex heritage incorporating French and Italian survivals. Classicistic designs appeared in 'romantic' landscapes and in 'natural' English garden scenes. Secondly, Olmsted, the dean of naturalistic constructivists, learned from the English but also from Jean Alphand and Baron Haussmann. Charles Eliot and George Kessler absorbed important continental influences. Thirdly, the Paris Universal Exposition of 1889 combined axiality, formality, and naturalistic constructivism, as did its American derivative, the Chicago Fair. Indeed, the Columbian Exposition was no stark contrast of green, blue, and overpowering white, demanding deference from the multitude. It was instead an illusion, a romantic medley of buildings, waterscapes, greenery, throngs, flapping flags, and playing bands. The fair's inspired combination of classicistic architecture and naturalistic constructivism disturbed few contemporaries. Nor did most of them object to later civic blendings of the two styles[37].

CIVIC CENTRES

Grouped public and semi-public buildings in civic centres formed the third major aesthetic commitment of the City Beautiful. Civic centre plans blossomed in the later City Beautiful era for several reasons. There was no way to bring the 'middle landscape' near the retail-commercial cores of most cities except in tandem with sweeping functional-aesthetic improvements. Land near retail-commercial centres was too dear for much of it to be given over to parks. The landscape architect's touch would have to be seen around useful, accessible buildings. Second, the hope of raising the city to a higher aesthetic plane by constructing separate, beautiful buildings was forlorn. Despite architect White's infectious optimism, making New York (or any other city) beautiful through random buildings ignored the fact that there were too many architects, and too many clients with simultaneous but divergent demands, for one aesthetic to encompass them all. Important elements of beauty—unity, proportion, harmony and symmetry—involving similarities of bulk, height, colour, and façade treatment, were impossible under the circumstances. A civic centre comprising structures of similar function could express their harmony while exerting a positive influence upon the surrounding property[38].

Third, civic centre plans were designed to supply the citizen with a symbolic as well as actual representation of his urban government. Planners of the progressive era believed in the socializing power of art. Burnham justified the Brobdingnagian proportions of the city hall dome in his *Plan of Chicago* by writing: 'The central administrative building, ... is surmounted by a dome of impressive height, to be seen and felt by the people, to whom it should stand as the symbol of civic order and unity ... its effect may be compared to that of the dome of St. Peter's at Rome'. Unless we keep a grip on ourselves we may be reading malevolent meanings into designs and statements such as Burnham's. Surely Burnham hoped for social control through architecture, but just as surely he hoped for the citizen's legitimate civic involvement and concern. In the age of the City Beautiful many American cities grew explosively, jammed by migrants having few civic attachments. Foreign immigrants—there were 781,217 in Burnham's Chicago in 1910—should be encouraged to develop local loyalties. Architectural symbolism could offer benign assistance in the transformation[39].

A single building, no matter how grand, did not express unity as well as the civic ensemble. City Beautiful architects emphasized the composition, the interplay of structure and space, and the possibilities of vista in their civic centres. They did not deny, on the other hand, the eminently practical reasons for centres: the need to rationalize expanding municipal and county governments, to draw together related civic activities, and to replace scattered, outmoded, or outworn public buildings. The civic centres have, until recently, stood for the whole, or almost the whole of the City Beautiful movement in the literature of architectural and planning criticism. Several critics who deplore the centres—'pompous' and 'autocratic' are among their hefty weapons—hasten to relieve their readers' minds with the news that few of the proposed centres ever were built. The failure to build is implicitly a certificate of ineptitude for the City Beautiful and a vindication of the aesthetic of the American public, which did not fall for the importation of such foreign nonsense. It is true that few City Beautiful civic centres were built. Those few usually deviated from the original plans in important and detrimental respects. But anyone with more than a passing acquaintance with the City Beautiful knows that civic centres emerged at midpoint in the movement's career. Often they appeared as partial statements in comprehensive plans. They were not insignificant to City Beautiful planners, but to judge the movement by the civic centre statement alone is unfair. The judgment also denies the City Beautiful's continuing influence on city planning[40].

Nor is it true, as the embittered Louis Sullivan declared in his celebrated autobiography, that the Columbian Exposition foisted classicistic

FIGURE 8.3. State Street, Harrisburg, in about 1913, looking east to the Pennsylvania State Capitol, completed in 1906.

architecture on the country. In this charge Sullivan was abetted, albeit unwittingly, by Burnham's declarations that City Beautiful civic centres were inspired by the Chicago Fair. Sullivan's charge, that the fair clouded the public mind with the classic and throttled the development of native American architecture, rings false to anyone who thinks about it for a few minutes. Thomas E. Tallmadge challenged it in 1927, three years after Sullivan's autobiography appeared, and the challenges have continued. They may be summarized as follows: The fair did not end Sullivan's career, or Wright's, or the careers of the Chicago or Prairie Schools. Sullivan continued to design, Wright built prairie houses into the teens, and Chicago School buildings appeared to the eve of World War I. Sullivan's Transportation Building at the fair, beneath its mediocre exterior, was structurally less advanced than others. Sullivan was a toplofty drunkard who damaged his own career, Wright a feisty maverick, and neither had in the early twentieth century developed city planning ideas congenial to the local elites who chose city planners. Shifts in Chicago School emphasis from commercial to residential design, or public infatuation with other arts than architecture, also explain the expiration of that style[41].

These challenges may be expanded in several directions. Taking Sullivan first, he was not a high-quality planner of anything. Sullivan entertained few notions of the city as ensemble, while the Burnham firm excelled him in interior building design. In his lyrical-to-bombastic *Kindergarten Chats* Sullivan did not ask the capitalist to shut up shop but rather to develop a

FIGURE 8.4. The model of a City Beautiful monumental ensemble. This is the Pennsylvania State Capitol again, this time looking west towards the rear façade. Architect Arnold Brunner completed the plan for Capitol Park under state auspices in 1916, and the model may date from that time. The arrangement of buildings, bridge and open space is essentially what was constructed, although the differences imposed by later designers tend to descredit, unfairly, the City Beautiful plan. Large wings were added in the final design of the foreground buildings, giving each of them a mixed blessing of bulk. The area comprising the balustrade, grand staircase, and plaza to the rear of the Capitol remains an asphalt parking lot, an extreme sacrifice of aesthetics to convenience. Happily, a later expansion of state government offices of contemporary design was placed to the north (or the right-hand side of the model) in a way that avoids stylistic clashes with the earlier group.

social conscience in architecture. It is difficult to imagine a building more congenial to American capitalism than the skyscraper, the style of which Sullivan did so much to advance, or an institution more representative than the bank, small examples of which he designed in the declining years of his practice. As for Wright, nothing save his personal lapses stayed his work. Wright was in full career as America's reigning architectural genius when he died, nearing ninety-two, in 1959. Wright's plans, when they did come, were scarcely urbanistic. No antidote for pressing urban problems, they visualized instead a suburbanized middle-class utopia held together by ubiquitous automobiles, telephones, and televisions[42].

So far as the Chicago School goes, its demise has as much to do with its own design sclerosis as with anything else. William H. Jordy has remarked on the inability of Chicago architects to develop new wall and window treatments after 1900. Sullivan, though he continued his innovation in detail, achieved his last breakthrough, the Schlesinger, Mayer department store, in 1899. These failures of vision and imagination are as serious as any of those charged against the architects of the City Beautiful. As for the Prairie School, some of its practitioners fed upon City Beautiful ideas. Mark L. Peisch's sensible study notes the positive impact of the Columbian Exposition upon several Chicago architects and the use, in Walter Burley Griffin's 1913 plan of Canberra, of City Beautiful devices such as axes, groupings, and waterscapes[43].

The Chicago Fair and the City Beautiful, far from impeding the rise of the skyscraper, had virtually no impact on the design of tall buildings. City Beautiful design was unconcerned with impressive exterior heights, save for domes. City Beautiful planners left commercial-retail cores to their own devices, except for individual building designs and schemes for functional definition and traffic relief. City Beautiful architects were designing low buildings more useful for the governments of their day than were skyscrapers. Classicistic styles infrequently decorated tall buildings. When they did, they tended either to an attenuated Renaissance, or if more obtrusive, to become lost in mass and silhouette as the building rose. Talbot F. Hamlin's straight-forward, popular discussion of the 'American style' of half a century ago argued convincingly that the 'American' quality of the skyscraper lay in its proportions, not in its ornamental detail. As Lewis Mumford deftly phrased it, tall commercial architecture is for 'angels and aviators', not for the terrestrial critic. Neither the City Beautiful nor any other movement influenced the main run of skyscraper design as much as technology, ground rent, labour costs, and tax policy. Sullivan's statement reflects the pain of a picturesque secessionist whose designs and ideas had failed to conquer. Nor had the classicistic conquered. Both styles continued, before and after 1893, borrowing from one another as well as battling. Both helped to prepare the path for the architectural resurgence of the 'international style' and its successors[44].

POLITICS OF THE CITY BEAUTIFUL

The politics of the City Beautiful assumes equal importance with its ideology and aesthetics. City plans cannot be fully appreciated apart from their implementation, and implementation involves politics. A defect in United States planning history is that it slights the politics of implementation and deals instead with the description, explanation, and criticism of planning elements. This caveat should not be construed to mean that politics has been ignored. The political history of planning has shown us some planners in political situations and it has discussed some planners in managerial-political roles. In general, it has done little to suggest why some plans failed of realization, were partially successful, or were initiated almost immediately. Without investigations of planning politics by scholars who know their way around in planning history we shall be left with our segmented view of planning development. We must tie the ideology and aesthetics of planning to political dynamics if we are to hope for a systematic understanding of planning from inception to realization. City Beautiful planners alone, with their circumscribed authority, were unable to see their plans through. They were, usually, outsiders called into service by local organizations. They enjoyed virtually no independent access to the public. As a rule they had little to do with the campaigns for their plans' implementation, although they might appear during campaigns at the behest of the sponsoring organizations[45].

City Beautiful politics have been studied enough to suggest some common themes in the campaigns for the initiation of comprehensive planning. First of all, planning began in a city because the commercial-industrial-professional elite became aware of the need for it. This awareness arose partly from local problems: unkempt streets, a polluted water supply, the instablity of elite residential sections, the building over of traditional 'squares' or 'groves' serving the public in the absence of public parks, or other situations. But these problems were endemic, if exacerbated by rapid growth. The late nineteenth century's rising leisure and literacy contributed by assuring direct and vicarious comparisons with more advanced cities. Local elites were self-interested in the future of their communities and they were self-aware. They knew about public improvements and elite activities in other cities through travel, acquaintanceships, and reading.

Each local group acted through its commercial club or a similarly-named organization, or through an *ad hoc* group of business leaders, or through both. Almost always a small committee, whether or not formally designated, handled important details such as selecting the planner or planners and mapping the strategy of public acceptance. The committee assumed several essential functions. It acted to persuade any members of the elite who were unconvinced of the problem; to investigate the legal basis for civic improvement and, if necessary, to secure additional ordinances or state enabling acts; to conduct preliminary negotiations with the expert or experts who would draw the plans, and to arrange for the expert's expenses by attaching him to the city payroll, or by financing his work through private funds. Elite members donated heavily to the fund, but sometimes they raised popular subscriptions to increase the public's interest and sense of participation. After a time the planner submitted his report. In the early City Beautiful age these documents, though analytical, were visually limited. Rapid advances in printing art produced more elaborate documents, climaxing in the visually sumptuous *Plan of Chicago* and the virtuoso technicality of Virgil Bogue's *Plan of Seattle* (1911). Almost always the plan called for public funding through bonds or similar obligations. The plan narrative usually mentioned the possibilities of piecemeal construction under the guidance of the entire conception, a wise concession, considering the high total cost.

Once the planner had submitted his report, work for the plan's realization began. Campaigns for public acceptance usually revolved around a bond issue vote to launch the first construction. The plan itself was public property, but local elites did not intend to rest with documents. They pushed for translating the pictorial representations into realities. Their campaigns employed similar devices from city to city. Newspaper publicity was an important feature. Sympathetic editors who shared the outlook of the local elites accepted information from the campaign organization and not infrequently placed their own reporters on assignment to a campaign. The newspaper publicity included close attention to the details of the plan; assurances that the plan's features were designed for all, not just some segments of the city's population; reviews of similar projects in other cities, American and European, with enumerations of their advantages if completed; implicit and explicit competitive comparisons with those cities; interviews with proponents of the plan; reports on the activities of the proponents, and refutation and ridicule of opponents' objections.

The campaign sometimes involved a flurry of pamphlets and door-to-door vote solicitation. Almost always it included neighbourhood meetings, carefully staged. There, talented proponents showed lantern slides of existing urban situations, usually disgracefully ugly and defiled, and contrasted these with renderings of the proposed improvements. City-wide rallies, the so-called mass meetings, often provided an emotional impetus or climax to the campaign. In these events the major proponents, perhaps even the experts themselves, made platform appearances in situations even more contrived than the neighbourhood meetings. Sometimes the mass meetings featured speakers calculated to work the audience into a high emotional pitch. Special visual appeals were common: supporters of the Harrisburg plan decked out a large streetcar in a banner proclaiming 'Don't Give Your Own Town a Black Eye'. The car ran on different routes, covering the city on the day before election day[46].

These privately-conducted, quasi-revivalistic, prototypically progressive campaigns were not passkeys to construction. Witness the two-to-one failure of Seattle's Bogue plan at the polls in an election that brought several reform candidates into office. Note the crushing defeat of John Nolen's plan for Reading, Pennsylvania, where socialists galvanized working-class opposition. In New York an eminently practical City Beautiful plan languished perhaps because its supporters insisted on tying it to the city government instead of pursuing their own campaign. The tactical error looms as large in the failure of the plan as the fact that some of its design incidents looked like those at the Chicago Fair, or that the 'city practical' zealot Benjamin C. Marsh attacked it for not including housing. Robinson's plan for Raleigh also suffered a stillbirth, partly because the Woman's Club, the sponsoring group, failed to campaign or to rally businessmen to the cause[47].

Our knowledge of the public acceptance of the City Beautiful is growing but is deficient in some areas. The occupational, residential, ethnic, and denominational characteristics of the movement's elite were firmly upper class, Western European in origin, and Protestant. Not surprisingly, voters in elite wards overwhelmingly approved City Beautiful improvements. Sometimes favourable majorities diminished or were lost as assessed valuations or rentals declined, sometimes not. An early City Beautiful campaign in Harrisburg saw a 1902 bond issue carry nine of ten wards, with many wards voting above or below the city-wide favourable mean in little apparent relationship to their assessed valuations. In 1910, however, a similar campaign failed dramatically in Reading with upper-income wards generally favouring the improvements, low-income wards generally opposing them. More instances of voter behaviour should be examined before generalizations are forthcoming. It does appear that the first planning bond issue election was critical for the future of the City Beautiful in a given city. If the issue passed, or if the city council took quick action, subsequent improvements seem to have been more readily approved[48].

CONCLUSION

A valid appreciation of the City Beautiful movement must begin with understanding it as its advocates understood it. The movement was, first, an effort to grace American cities with beauty, a sorely needed feature in the nineteenth century. It was, second, a conscious effort to merge classicistic beauty with naturalistic constructivist landscape and with essential functional elements. It combined aesthetic appreciation with some knowledge, and sometimes a keen perception, of political and legal necessities. It was, finally, comprehensive in its vision. It conceived the city and its inhabitants to be organisms, having a life and growth susceptible to definition, rationalization, and control.

Of course the City Beautiful suffered from defects. It did little directly with housing, with utilities except as adjuncts of beautification, and with a range of urban concerns now included within the purview of planning. These shortcomings may be explained, if not excused, by sterner notions of individual responsibility than are fashionable now, by a view of housing as a private matter or as the domain of its own expert corps, by the sensible view that strictly 'engineering' matters should be subordinate to comprehensive solutions, and by an optimistic commitment to the creative social power of the city and the people in it. Attacks against the City Beautiful based on the appalling maintenance or destruction of once-grand City Beautiful artifacts, on growth or change that has outmoded City Beautiful plans, on the inadequacies of partially completed plans, or upon crimes in parks, are unrealistic. These problems result from demographic and social revolutions unimagined when City Beautiful practitioners designed[49].

The criticisms pale beside the extraordinary vision of the City Beautiful. It left us with buildings breathtaking in grandeur and workmanship, the like of which we shall not know again. It left us with urban landscapes lovelier than those it found, with a host of recreational, street, traffic and aesthetic reforms, and with abundant suggestions for further change. Our legacy from the movement is two-fold. First, City Beautiful enthusiasts came to terms with one reality of our time: increasing numbers of people had no alternative to urbanization. That reality required a fresh examination of the city and the needs of its inhabitants. Second, those inhabitants required symbols of the city, beautiful surroundings, or access to beautiful areas. Their needs could be met only by beautifying portions of the city, not alone for the aesthetic or psychic benefits but for practical, utilitarian reasons that are as important now as they were then.

NOTES

1. Major studies mostly critical of the movement include Churchill, H. S. (1945) *The City Is the People.* New York: Harcourt, Brace & World, pp. 68–9; Jacobs, J. (1961) *The Death and Life of Great American Cities.* New York: Random House, pp. 24–5; Fitch, J. M. (1966) *American Building,* 2nd ed. Boston: Houghton Mifflin, pp. 210–13; Hamlin, T. (1947) *Architecture: An Art for All Men.* New York: Columbia University Press, pp. 248–9; Reps, J. W. (1965) *The Making of Urban America.* Princeton: Princeton University Press, p. 524, and (1967) *Monumental Washington.* Princeton: Princeton University Press, p. 193. Assessments refusing to condemn the movement entirely are Adams, T. (1935) *Outline of Town and City Planning.* New York: Russell Sage Foundation, pp. 173, 174–5, 181, 184, 196–206; Mumford, L. (1932) The plan of New York. *New Republic,* 71 (22 June), p. 154; Walker, R. A. (1950) *The Planning Function in Urban Government,* 2nd ed. Chicago: University of Chicago Press, pp. 7–8, 12–20. Partially sympathetic treatments include Burchard, J. and Bush-Brown, A. (1961) *The Architecture of America.* Boston: Little, Brown, pp. 273–81, 295–6, and Newton, N. T. (1971) *Design on the Land.* Cambridge: Belknap Press of Harvard University Press, pp. 413–26. Scott, M. (1969) *American City Planning Since 1890.* Berkeley: University of California Press, pp. 76, 78, stresses the movement's concentration on beautification, although there is as much material refuting as supporting his claim in the preceding pages. See also Tunnard, C. (1968) *The Modern American City.* New York: Van Nostrand Reinhold, pp. 46–66, 73. Two studies outside convenient historiographical groupings are Burg, D. (1976) *Chicago's White City of 1893.* Lexington: University Press of Kentucky, pp. 296–321, and Hines, T. S. (1974) *Burnham of Chicago: Architect and Planner.* New York: Oxford University Press, pp. xvii–xxii, 74, 141–2, 158, 163–6, 172–3, 367–9. Burg sees positive social values in the visual order of the Columbian Exposition, although he, with Hines, finds the City Beautiful's origins in the Chicago Fair. Both authors demonstrate the worth of Burham's city planning, but overstate his leadership in the movement. Revisionist studies include Peterson, J. A. (1967) The Origins of the Comprehensive City Planning Ideal in the United States, 1840–1911. Unpublished PhD. thesis, Harvard University, Cambridge, and (1976) The city beautiful movement: forgotten origins and lost meanings. *Journal of Urban History,* 2 (August), pp. 415–34; Wilson, W. H. (1964) *The City Beautiful Movement in Kansas City.* Columbia:

University of Missouri Press, and Boyer, P. (1978) *Urban Masses and Moral Order in America, 1820–1920*. Cambridge: Harvard University Press, pp. 182–7, 261–76.

2. Recent major studies of Olmsted include Roper, L. W. (1973) *FLO: A Biography of Frederick Law Olmsted*. Baltimore: Johns Hopkins University Press; Fein, A. (1973) *Frederick Law Olmsted and the American Environmental Tradition*. New York: Braziller; Bender, T. (1975) *Toward an Urban Vision: Ideas and Institutions in Nineteenth-Century America*. Lexington: University Press of Kentucky, pp. 161–87, and Blodgett, G. (1976) Frederick Law Olmsted: landscape architecture as conservative reform. *Journal of American History*, 62 (March), pp. 869–89.

3. Simutis, L. J. (1971) Frederick Law Olmsted's Later Years: Landscape Architecture and the Spirit of Place. Unpublished PhD. thesis, University of Minnesota, Minneapolis, and (1972) Frederick Law Olmsted, Sr.: a reassessment. *American Institute of Planners Journal*, 38 (September), pp. 276–84. Cleveland, Jackson, J. B. (1972) *American Space*. New York: Norton, pp. 76–7.

4. Buffalo, Simutis, L. J. (1972) *ibid.*, p. 282. Kessler, Glaab, C. N. (1963) *The American City: A Documentary History*. Homewood: Dorsey, pp. 257–63, and Wilson, W. H. (1964) *The City Beautiful Movement in Kansas City*. Columbia: University of Missouri Press, pp. 46–52, 89–90, 122–4. Manning's and others' reports, Harrisburg League for Municipal Improvements (HLMI) (1901) *The Plain Truth About the Improvements*, 2nd ed. Harrisburg.

5. Definitions of outdoor art, American Park and Outdoor Art Association (APOAA) (1898) *Second Report*. Boston, pp. 112–23; (1903) *Year Book and Record of the Seventh Annual Meeting*. Rochester, p. 50, and (1904) *General Addresses at the Seventh Annual Meeting*. Rochester, pp. 6–11. Founding, APOAA (1897) *First Report*. Louisville, pp. 68–71.

6. Peterson, J. A. (1967) The Origins of the Comprehensive City Planning Ideal in the United States, 1840–1911. Unpublished PhD. thesis, Harvard University, Cambridge, pp. 182–3, and Simutis, L. J. (1971) Frederick Law Olmsted's Later Years: Landscape Architecture and the Spirit of Place. Unpublished PhD. thesis, University of Minnesota, Minneapolis, pp. 196–200, 206–7.

7. Peterson, J. A. (1976) The city beautiful movement: forgotten origins and lost meanings. *Journal of Urban History*, 2 (August), pp. 420–5; Good, J. M. (1901) The how of improvement work. *Home Florist*, 4 (January), pp. 42–4; Proceedings of the annual convention, 1901 of the American League for Civic Improvement. *Home Florist*, 4 (October), 1901, p. 65, and American League for Civic Improvement (ALCI) (1903) *Nation-Wide Civic Betterment*. Chicago, p. 1.

8. Good, J. M. (1901) The how of improvement work. *Home Florist*, 4 (January), pp. 1–34, 44, quotation p. 33; Proceedings of the annual convention, 1901 of the American League for Civic Improvement, inside front cover, pp. 1–2; ALCI (1903) *Nation-Wide Civic Betterment*. Chicago, pp. 23–6, 50–6, 70–1; McFarland, J. H. (1904) *How to Plant the Home Grounds*. Philadephia: Curtis Publishing, and (n.d.) *How to Form a Beautiful America Club*. n.p.; Huggins, K. A. H. (1967) The Evolution of City and Regional Planning in North Carolina 1900–1950; Unpublished PhD. thesis, Duke University, Durham, pp. 23–30, and Wilson, W. H. (1975) More almost than the men: Mira Lloyd Dock and the beautification of Harrisburg. *Pennsylvania Magazine of History and Biography*, 99 (October), p. 492.

9. Peterson, J. A. (1976) The city beautiful movement: forgotten origins and lost meanings. *Journal of Urban History,* 2 (August), pp. 416–20.

10. *Ibid.,* and Peterson, J. A. (1967) The Origins of the Comprehensive City Planning Ideal in the United States, 1840–1911. Unpublished PhD. thesis, Harvard University, Cambridge, pp. 185–9. Pre-Beaux-Arts collaboration, Kidney, W. C. (1974) *The Architecture of Choice: Eclecticism in America, 1880–1930.* New York: Braziller, pp. 24–8. Richardson, Hitchcock, H. (1966) *The Architecture of H. H. Richardson and His Times,* 1st M.I.T. paperbound ed. Cambridge: M.I.T. Press, pp. 110-17, 136–44, and Van Rensselaer, M. G. (1967) *Henry Hobson Richardson and His Works.* Park Forest: Prairie School Press, pp. 51–3, 59–66. McKim, Moore, C. (1929) *The Life and Times of Charles Follen McKim.* Boston: Houghton Mifflin, pp. 69–94. Municipal Art Society, Kantor, H. A. (1971) Modern Urban Planning in New York City: Origins and Evolution, 1890–1933. Unpublished PhD. thesis, New York University, New York, pp. 29–104, and (1973) The city beautiful in New York. *New–York Historical Quarterly,* 57 (April), pp. 149–71.

11. Kidney, W. C. (1974) *The Architecture of Choice: Eclecticism in America, 1880–1930.* New York: Braziller, pp. 24–8. Whitehall, W. M. (1968) *Boston: A Topographical History,* 2nd ed. Cambridge: Belknap Press of Harvard University Press, pp. 172–3, 194–5, and illustrations 196, 197. Hines, T. S. (1974) *Burnham of Chicago: Architect and Planner.* New York: Oxford University Press, pp. 139–96, 312–45.

12. APOAA (1900) *Proceedings . . . 1900,* part 3. Boston, pp. 85–95, and Wilson, W. H. (1964) *The City Beautiful Movement in Kansas City.* Columbia: University of Missouri Press, p. 125. Merger, ALCI (1903) *Nation–Wide Civic Betterment.* Chicago, pp. 2–3, and Harlean James to Hans Huth, 17 May 1951, Papers of the American Planning and Civic Association, Department of Manuscripts and Archives, John M. Olin Library, Cornell University. G. P. Putnam's Sons, New York, published Robinson's book.

13. McFarland to Charles H. Kilborn, 28 May 1908, J. Horace McFarland papers, box 15, manuscript group 85, Pennsylvania State Archives, and speech, The crusade against ugliness, box 14. Downtown changes, Scott, M. (1969) *American City Planning Since 1890.* Berkeley: University of California Press, p. 154, and Toll, S. I. (1969) *Zoned American.* New York: Grossman, pp. 74–116, 159–63, 172–87. Smoke, Grinder, R. D. (1973) The Anti–Smoke Crusades. Unpublished PhD. thesis, University of Missouri, Columbia. Rivers, Wilson, W. H. (1975) More almost than the men: Mira Lloyd Dock and the beautification of Harrisburg. *Pennsylvania Magazine of History and Biography,* 99 (October), p. 491, and Ginger, R. (1965) *Altgeld's America.* Chicago: Quadrangle, pp. 23–4. Park statistics, U.S. Department of the Interior, Census Office (1895) *Report on the Social Statistics of Cities in the United States at the Eleventh Census: 1890.* Washington: Government Printing Office, p. 35.

14. U.S. Census Office, *ibid.,* p. 19. Slabaugh, W. M. (1903) Civic improvement in the city of Omaha and its environs. ALCI (1903) *Nation–Wide Civic Betterment.* Chicago, pp. 36–9.

15. Shuey, E. L. (1901) Commercial bodies and civic improvement. *Home Florist,* 4 (January), p. 35. McFarland, J. H. (1904) Beautiful America. *Ladies Home*

Journal, 21 (January), p. 15. Robinson, C. M. (1903) *Modern Civic Art, Or The City Made Beautiful.* New York: G. P. Putnam's Sons, p. 346.

16. Harmony, Robinson, C. M. (1903) *Modern Civic Art, Or The City Made Beautiful.* New York: G. P. Putnam's Sons, pp. 355–75. Quotation, ALCI (1903) *Nation–Wide Civic Betterment.* Chicago, p. 2. Bacchante, Moore, C. (1929) *The Life and Times of Charles Follen McKim.* Boston: Houghton Mifflin, pp. 90–4.

17. Beauty and utility, Peterson, J. A. (1967) The Origins of the Comprehensive City Planning Ideal in the United States, 1840–1911. Unpublished PhD. thesis, Harvard University, Cambridge, pp. 102–6; Wilson, W. H. (1964) *The City Beautiful Movement in Kansas City.* Columbia: University of Missouri Press, pp. 2–6; Moore, C. (1921) *Daniel H. Burnham,* vol. 2. Boston: Houghton Mifflin, p. 102; McFarland, Abstract of an illustrated address on the crusade against ugliness. J. Horace McFarland papers, box 14, manuscript group 85, Pennsylvania State Archives, and Beautiful America. *Ladies Home Journal,* 21 (January), 1904, p. 15. Harrisburg, HLMI (1901) *The Plain Truth About the Improvements,* 2nd ed. Harrisburg. Hunt plan, Wilson, W. H. (1964) *The City Beautiful Movement in Kansas City.* Columbia: University of Missouri Press, pp. 112–3. Brunner, American Civic Association (n.d.) *Program of the Seventh Annual Convention.* n.p., p. 7.

18. Weinstein, J. (1968) *The Corporate Ideal in the Liberal State: 1900–1918.* Boston: Beacon, pp. ix–x, 94–5, and Wiebe, R. H. (1967) *The Search for Order: 1877–1920.* New York: Hill and Wang, pp. 149–55, 160–1, 169–76.

19. Olmsted, F. L., Jr. and Kimball, T. (eds.) (1970) *Frederick Law Olmsted: Landscape Architect, 1822–1903,* vol. 2. New York: Blom, pp. 45–7, 214–32. Kessler, Wilson, W. H. (1964) *The City Beautiful Movement in Kansas City.* Columbia: University of Missouri Press, p. 48. Harrisburg, HLMI (1901) *The Plain Truth About the Improvements,* 2nd ed. Harrisburg, p. 10. Robinson, C. M. (1903) *Modern Civic Art, Or The City Made Beautiful.* New York: G. P. Putnam's Sons, pp. 280–1. Quotation, Moore, C. (1921) *Daniel H. Burnham,* vol. 2. Boston: Houghton Mifflin, p. 147.

20. Hines, T. S. (1974) *Burnham of Chicago: Architect and Planner.* New York: Oxford University Press, pp. 317–9, 321, 324, 352, and Peterson, J. A. (1967) The Origins of the Comprehensive City Planning Ideal in the United States, 1840–1911. Unpublished PhD. thesis, Harvard University, Cambridge, pp. 342–7.

21. Olmsted, F. L., Jr. and Kimball, T. (eds.) (1970) *Frederick Law Olmsted: Landscape Architect, 1822–1903,* vol. 2. New York: Blom, p. 46; Olmsted, F. L. (1870) *Public Parks and the Enlargement of Towns.* Cambridge: American Social Science Association, pp. 18–36; *Harrisburg Telegraph,* 6 June, 1901; and Moore, C. (1921) *Daniel H. Burnham,* vol. 2. Boston: Houghton Mifflin, p. 101. Recreation, Wilson, W. H. (1964) *The City Beautiful Movement in Kansas City.* Columbia: University of Missouri Press, pp. 50, 123–4, and (1975) More almost than the men: Mira Lloyd Dock and the beautification of Harrisburg. *Pennsylvania Magazine of History and Biography,* 99 (October), p. 494. McFarland, J. H. (1910) Chicago's answer. *Outlook,* 22 (October), pp. 443–52. Conflict between park advocates and recreation experts, Finfer, L. A. (1974) Leisure as Social Work in the Urban Community: The Progressive Recreation Movement, 1890–1920. Unpublished PhD. thesis, Michigan State University, East

Lansing, pp. 121–6, 132; Burnap, G. (1916) *Parks: Their Design, Equipment and Use.* Philadelphia: J. B. Lippincott, p. 168, and Curtis, H. S. (1917) *The Play Movement and Its Signifcance,* reprint ed. Washington: McGrath Publishing, pp. 126–7, 129–30, 315. Olmsted's critics, Jackson, J. B. (1972) *American Space.* New York: Norton, pp. 215–9, and Peets, E. in Spreiregen, P. D. (ed.) (1968) *On the Art of Designing Cities.* Cambridge: M.I.T. Press, pp. 187–8.

22. Robinson, C. M. (1903) *Modern Civic Art, Or The City Made Beautiful.* New York: G. P. Putnam's Sons, p. 246, and Jeffreys–Jones, R. (1974) Violence in American history: plug uglies in the progressive era. *Perspectives in American History,* 8. Cambridge: Charles Warren Center, Harvard University, pp. 486–9. Progressives and community, Wilson, R. J. (1968) *In Quest of Community.* New York: Wiley, and Quandt, J. B. (1970) *From the Small Town to the Great Society: The Social Thought of Progressive Intellectuals.* New Brunswick: Rutgers University Press, pp. 1–30, 58, 126–33, 151.

23. Quotation, Robinson, C. M. (1903) *Modern Civic Art, Or The City Made Beautiful.* New York: G. P. Putnam's Sons, p. 3. Impact of Chicago, Wilson, W. H. (1964) *The City Beautiful Movement in Kansas City.* Columbia: University of Missouri Press, pp. 21–3. Impact of European cities, Moore, C. (1921) *Daniel H. Burnham,* vol. 2. Boston: Houghton Mifflin, pp. 100–3. Faith in progressive leader, Steffens, L. (1931) *The Autobiography of Lincoln Steffens.* New York: Literary Guild, pp. 470–81.

24. Shaw (1895, 1901) *Municipal Government in Continental Europe.* New York: Macmillan, pp. 6–13, 290–1, 401, and quotations, p. 410–11.

25. Howe, F. C. (1913) *European Cities at Work.* New York: Scribner's, pp. ix, 7, 219–42, 253. McFarland to Richard B. Watrous, 5 June 1913, box 10, McFarland Papers; Jones, H. M. (1971) *The Age of Energy: Varieties of American Experience, 1865–1915.* New York: Viking, pp. 245–53; Kaplan, J., (1974) *Lincoln Steffens.* New York: Simon and Schuster, pp. 38–9; Mann, A. (1956) British social thought and American reformers of the progressive era. *Mississippi Valley Historical Review,* 42 (March), pp. 672–92; Lubove, R. (1977) Frederick C. Howe and the quest for community in America. *Historian,* 39 (February), pp. 270–91 and Ekrich, A. A., Jr. (1974) *Progressivism in America.* New York: New Viewpoints, pp. 3–15, 19–33, 96–8.

26. McFarland, J. H. (1903) The great civic awakening. *Outlook,* 73 (18 April), pp. 917–20, and (1906) The nationalization of civic improvement. *Charities and the Commons,* 17 (3 November), pp. 231–4.

27. Howe, F. C. (1905) *The City: The Hope of Democracy.* New York: Scribner's, pp. 239–48. Progressive change and planning, Scott, M. (1969) *American City Planning Since 1890.* Berkeley: University of California Press, pp. 47–109; U.S. Congress, Senate Committee on the District of Columbia, (1910) *Hearing . . . on . . . City Planning,* 61st Congress, 1st session, (11 March); and Marsh, B. C. (1909) *An Introduction to City Planning.* New York: author. See also Lubove, R. (1959) The twentieth century city: the progressive as municipal reformer. *Mid–America,* (October), pp. 195–209.

28. Reed, H. H. (1959) *The Golden City.* Garden City: Doubleday, p. 100, and Huth, H. (1957) *Nature and the American: Three Centuries of Changing Attitudes.* Berkeley: University of California Press, pp. 183–4. Downing, A. J. (1967) *A Treatise on the Theory and Practice of Landscape Gardening,* reprint of 1859 ed.

New York: Funk & Wagnalls, and (1969) *The Architecture of Country Houses.*
New York: Dover. Rural cemeteries, Bender, T. (1975) *Toward an Urban Vision:
Ideas and Institutions in Nineteenth–Century America.* Lexington: University
Press of Kentucky, pp. 80–5, and Harris, N. (1966) *The Artist in American
Society: The Formative Years, 1790–1860.* New York: Braziller, p. 201. Mariposa
and Yosemite, Roper, L. W. (1973) *FLO: A Biography of Frederick Law Olmsted.*
Baltimore: Johns Hopkins University Press, pp. 233–90. Niagara, *ibid.,* pp.
378–82, 395–8, Riverside, *ibid.,* pp. 318, 322–4, and Fein, A. (1973) *Frederick
Law Olmsted and the American Environmental Tradition.* New York: Braziller,
pp. 32–5. Biltmore, Roper, L. W., *ibid.,* pp. 415–9. Trees' environmental role,
Fein, A. (ed.) (1967) *Landscape into Cityscape.* Ithaca: Cornell University Press,
pp. 234, 266, 273.
29. Boston, Scott, M. (1969) *American City Planning Since 1890.* Berkeley:
University of California Press, pp. 17–23. Robinson, Huggins, K. H. (1969) City
planning in North Carolina, 1900–1920, part 1. *North Carolina Historical Review,*
46 (October), pp. 381–7. Kessler, Presnall, P. C. (1972) Beginnings of City
Planning in Dallas, Texas. Unpublished thesis, North Texas State University,
Denton. McFarland, Huth, H. (1957) *Nature and the American: Three Centuries
of Changing Attitudes.* Berkeley: University of California Press, pp. 184, 186–8,
189–91, and *Harrisburg Patriot,* 4 October, 1948. White, Baldwin, C. C. (1976)
Stanford White, reprint ed. New York: Da Capo, p. 5. Shuey, E. L. (1898)
Outdoor art and workingman's homes, in APOAA (1900) *Proceedings . . . 1900.*
Boston, pp. 112–23; Patterson, J. H. and Shuey, E. L. (1900) The improvement
of grounds about factories and employee's homes, in APOAA *Proceedings . . .
1900.* Boston, pp. 42–5, and McFarland, J. H. (1913) How to improve railroad
stations and their surroundings. *American City,* 9 (November), pp. 440–4.
30. Burham, Hines, T. S. (1974) *Burnham of Chicago: Architect and Planner.* New
York: Oxford University Press, pp. 153–4, 168, 182–8, 332–3, and Burnham, D.
H. and Bennett, E. H. (1909) *Plan of Chicago.* Chicago: Commercial Club, pp.
43–60, and Reps, J. W. (1967) *Monumental Washington.* Princeton: Princeton
University Press, pp. 109–38. Robinson, Tunnard, C. (1968) *The Modern
American City.* New York: Van Nostrand Reinhold, pp. 46, 159, and Peterson, J.
A. (1967) The Origins of the Comprehensive City Planning Ideal in the United
States, 1840–1911. Unpublished PhD. thesis, Harvard University, pp. 342–5.
Nolen, Hancock, J. L. (1964) John Nolen and the American City Planning
Movement. Unpublished PhD. thesis, University of Pennsylvania, Philadelphia,
pp. 323–33, 508–16.
31. Meeks, C. L. V. (1956) *The Railroad Station.* New Haven: Yale University Press,
pp. 1–2, 24, and (1950) Picturesque eclecticism. *Art Bulletin,* 32 (September),
pp. 229, 234. Romanesque, Hitchcock, H. (1966) *The Architecture of H. H.
Richardson and His Times,* 1st M.I.T. paperbound ed. Cambridge: M.I.T. Press,
and Tallmadge, T. (1927) *The Story of Architecture in America.* New York:
Norton, p. 197.
32. Quotation, Tunnard, C. (1968) *The Modern American City.* New York: Van
Nostrand Reinhold, pp. 47–8. Cf. Scully, V. (1969) *American Architecture and
Urbanism.* New York: Praeger, pp. 142–3.
33. Jordy, W. H. (1972) *American Buildings and Their Architects: Progressive and
Academic Ideals at the Turn of the Twentieth Century.* Garden City: Doubleday,

pp. 333–42; Burchard, J. and Bush–Brown, A. (1961) *The Architecture of America.* Boston: Little, Brown, p. 280, and Granger, A. H. (1972) *Charles Follen McKim,* reprint ed. New York: Blom, pp. 23–5. Criticism of McKim, Larkin, O. W. (1960) *Art and Life in America,* rev. ed. New York: Holt, Rinehart and Winston, pp. 337–8. Atwood quotation, Hoffman, D. (1973) *The Architecture of John Wellborn Root.* Baltimore: Johns Hopkins University Press, p. 221.

34. Quotation, Hudnut, J. (1961) Architecture and the spirit of man, in Coles, W. A. and Reed, H. H., Jr. (eds.), *Architecture in America: A Battle of Styles.* New York: Appleton-Century-Crofts, p. 245.

35. Vance, J. E., Jr. (1973) The classical revival and rural-urban conflict in nineteenth century North America. *Canadian Review of American Studies,* 4 (Fall), pp. 149–68, and Baldwin, C. C. (1976) *Stanford White,* reprint ed. New York: Da Capo, p. 222. Early, J. (1965) *Romanticism and American Architecture.* New York: Barnes, pp. 27–49, 157–8; Harris, N. (1966) *The Artist in American Society: The Formative Years, 1790–1890.* New York: Braziller, and Hamilton, G. H. (1970) *19th and 20th Century Art.* New York: Abrams, pp. 11–45, 47, 150–8. Burnham's romantic view of Greece and Rome, Moore, C. (1921) *Daniel H. Burnham,* vol. 1. Boston: Houghton Mifflin, pp. 126–8, 150.

36. Newton, N. T. (1971) *Design on the Land.* Cambridge: Belknap Press of Harvard University Press, pp. 353–71; Hoffman, D. (1973) *The Architecture of John Wellborn Root.* Baltimore: Johns Hopkins University Press, pp. 225–6; Fein, A. (1970) The American city: the ideal and the real, in Kaufmann, E., Jr. (ed.) *The Rise of an American Architecture.* New York: Praeger, pp. 102, 104; Scully, V. (1969) *American Architecture and Urbanism.* New York: Praeger, pp. 136–7; Barlow, E. (1972) *Frederick Law Olmsted's New York.* New York: Praeger, pp. 8, 49–50; Spreiregen, P. D. (ed.) (1968) *On the Art of Designing Cities.* Cambridge: M.I.T. Press, pp. 68–9; Peterson, J. A. (1967) The Origins of the Comprehensive City Planning Ideal in the United States, 1840–1911. Unpublished PhD. thesis, Harvard University, pp. 178–80, 197–8, 356–9.

37. Harris, N. (1966) *The Artist in American Society: The Formative Years, 1790–1860.* New York: Braziller, illustrations 4, 5; Bing, S. (1970) *Artistic America, Tiffany Glass, and Art Nouveau.* Cambridge: MIT Press, p. 135; Garrett, W. D. *et al.* (1969) *The Arts in America: the Nineteenth Century.* New York: Scribner's, illustration 153, p. 213, Newton, N. T. (1971) *Design on the Land.* Cambridge: Belknap Press of Harvard University Press, pp. 182–232, 273, illustrations 141, 142, 144, 146, 148–9, 152, 154, 158–60, 169–70. Kessler, Wilson, W. H. (1964) *The City Beautiful Movement in Kansas City.* Columbia: University of Missouri Press, p. 41. Fair, Hoffman, D. (1973) *The Architecture of John Wellborn Root.* Baltimore: Johns Hopkins University Press, pp. 222–9, and illustrations 163–7.

38. Marx, L. (1967) *The Machine in the Garden.* New York: Oxford University Press, and Lapping, M. B. (1972) The Middle Landscape and American Urban Theory. Unpublished PhD. thesis, Emory University, Atlanta. White, Baldwin, C. C. (1976) *Stanford White,* reprint ed. New York: Da Capo, pp. 2, 4. Cf. Tunnard, C. (1968) *The Modern American City.* New York: Van Nostrand Reinhold, pp. 65–6, and Moore, C. (1921) *Daniel H. Burnham,* vol. 1. Boston: Houghton Mifflin, p. 206.

39. Burnham, D. H. and Bennett, E. H. (1909) *Plan of Chicago.* Chicago: Commercial Club, p. 116; Harris, N. (1966) *The Artist in American Society: The Formative*

Years, 1790–1860. New York: Braziller, p. 168; Aitken, R. I. *et al.* (1926) *Arnold W. Brunner and His Work.* New York: American Institute of Architects, pp. 29–30; Lubove, R. (1959) The twentieth century city: the progressive as municipal reformer. *Mid–America,* October, p. 198, and U.S. Department of Commerce, Bureau of the Census (1913) *Thirteenth Census of the United States Taken in the Year 1910,* vol. 2. Washington DC: Government Printing Office, p. 504.

40. Burnham, D. H. and Bennett, E. H. (1909) *Plan of Chicago.* Chicago: Commercial Club, pp. 115–7; Wilson, W. H. (1964) *The City Beautiful Movement in Kansas City.* Columbia: University of Missouri Press, pp. xii–xv, 45–6, 108–9; Fitch, J. M. (1966) *American Building,* 2nd ed. Boston: Houghton Mifflin, pp. 239–40, and Hines, T. S. (1974) *Burnham of Chicago: Architect and Planner.* New York: Oxford University Press, pp. 166–71, 193–5.

41. Sullivan, L. (1956) *The Autobiography of an Idea,* reprint of 1924 ed. New York: Dover, pp. 321–5; Tallmadge, T. (1927) *The Story of Architecture in America.* New York: Norton, pp. 196–7; Crook, D. H. (1967) Louis Sullivan and the golden doorway. *Journal of the Society of Architectural Historians,* 26 (December), pp. 250–8; Tselos, D. (1967) The Chicago fair and the myth of the 'lost cause'. *Ibid.,* pp. 259–68; Hines, T. S. (1974) *Burnham of Chicago: Architect and Planner.* New York: Oxford University Press, pp. 98–100; Burg, D. (1976) *Chicago's White City of 1893.* Lexington: University Press of Kentucky, pp. 303–9. Wright, Scully, V. (1969) *American Architecture and Urbanism.* New York: Praeger, p. 138, and Hines, T. S. (1973) The paradox of 'progressive' architecture: urban planning and public building in Tom Johnson's Cleveland, *American Quarterly,* 25 (October), pp. 445, 447.

42. Rowe, C. (1976) *The Mathematics of the Ideal Villa and Other Essays.* Cambridge: M.I.T. Press, pp. 96, 98–9. Sullivan, L. (1947) *Kindergarten Chats.* New York: Wittenborn, pp. 38–9. Wright's planning ideas are in his *The Living City.* New York: Horizon, 1958.

43. Jordy, W. H. (1972) *American Buildings and Their Architects: Progressive and Academic Ideals at the Turn of the Twentieth Century.* Garden City: Doubleday, pp. 63–70, 83–179. Peisch (1964) *The Chicago School of Architecture.* New York: Random House, pp. 4, 13–5, 18, 32–3, 70, 105–24, 144–5, illustration 28.

44. Tunnard, C. (1968) *The Modern American City.* New York: Van Nostrand Reinhold, pp. 89–90, 92. Hamlin (1929) *The Enjoyment of Architecture.* New York: Scribner's pp. 266–97; Mumford, L. (1955) *Sticks and Stones,* 2nd ed. New York: Dover, p. 174.

45. Exceptions to the lack of implementation studies are Hancock, J. L. (1964) John Nolen and the American City Planning Movement. Unpublished PhD. thesis, University of Pennsylvania, Philadelphia, pp. 306–7, 334–49, 487–559; McCarthy, M. P. (1970) Chicago businessmen and the Burnham plan. *Journal of the Illinois State Historical Society,* 63 (Autumn), pp. 228–56, and (1972) Politics and the parks: Chicago businessmen and the recreation movement. *Ibid.,* 65 (Summer), pp. 158–72; Wilson, W. H. (1964) *The City Beautiful Movement in Kansas City.* Columbia: University of Missouri Press, pp. 25–39, 55–90, 98–103, 120–36; Reps, J. W. (1967) *Monumental Washington.* Princeton: Princeton University Press; Zangrando, J. S. (1974) Monumental Bridge Design in Washington, DC, as a Reflection of American Culture, 1886 to 1932.

Unpublished PhD. thesis, George Washington University, Washington, and Wilson, W. H. (1979) Harrisburg's successful city beautiful movement 1900–1915. Unpublished paper.

46. Harrisburg example, McFarland, J. H. (1903) The Harrisburg achievement. *Chautauquan,* **36** (January), pp. 401–4, and Zueblin, C. (1904) The Harrisburg plan. *Ibid.,* **39** (March), pp. 60–7.

47. Hancock, J. L. (1964) John Nolen and the American City Planning Movement. Unpublished PhD. thesis, University of Pennsylvania, Philadelphia, pp. 334–44; Sale, R. (1976) *Seattle: Past to Present.* Seattle: University of Washington Press, pp. 95–103; Kantor, H. A. (1973) The city beautiful in New York. *New-York Historical Quarterly,* **57** (April), pp. 149–71, and Huggins, K. H. (1969) City planning in North Carolina, 1900–1920, part 1. *North Carolina Historical Review,* **46** (October), pp. 381–7.

48. Hancock, J. L., *ibid.,* Sale, R., *ibid.,* and Wilson, W. H. (1964) *The City Beautiful Movement in Kansas City.* Columbia: University of Missouri Press, pp. 69–90, 120–33, and Wilson, W. H. (1979) Harrisburg's successful city beautiful movement 1900–1915. Unpublished paper.

49. Jacobs, Jane (1961) *The Death and Life of Great American Cities.* New York: Random House, pp. 24–5, 74–111, 144, 171–2, 402–3, and Burchard, J. and Bush-Brown, A. (1961) *The Architecture of America.* Boston: Little, Brown, p. 276.

9

Cities and evolution: Patrick Geddes as an international prophet of town planning before 1914[1]

HELEN MELLER

It is important to remember that, before 1904, Patrick Geddes had not been directly engaged in town-planning activities, although he was sympathetic to the ideas of those who were creating the modern town-planning movement[2]. He was, first and foremost, a natural scientist and an evolutionist who felt that he had a biological message for his fellow men that they could ignore only at their peril. The message itself was clear and simple. The twin processes of industrialization and urbanization of the nineteenth century had created a vast new potential in the evolutionary pattern for mankind. It was a potential, however, which, unlike evolutionary patterns in former ages, could be realized only by conscious and deliberate thought. The rise of science and technology had helped to create both the worst conditions known to man, and also the power to control life and environment to an unprecedented extent. Geddes's life was a one-man crusade to try and awaken a response to this challenge, which he considered of vital importance since he understood, as a biologist, that evolutionary changes were not always progressive. Inability to adapt to change, to accept responsibility for the future, could lead to social degeneration, to the decline and fall of 'modern civilization'.

Geddes's career as a prophet of the future, with an answer to modern problems, developed gradually from a number of activities he instigated in pursuit of his burning interest in the application of evolutionary theory to society[3]. His message may have been simple, but the means to achieve the desired objective of a higher civilization were quite the opposite. Control and development over the human organism and its environment required a degree of scientific understanding of the human condition, and of the factors which produced it, which were certainly beyond the limits of contemporary knowledge.

The need for new knowledge on man and society had become more widely recognized in the period 1880–1914, and it proved to be a very formative period in the social sciences in Europe and America[4]. In Britain, the academic establishment was rather less responsive, and Geddes had to pursue his evolutionary interests outside the framework of academic life. However, he believed firmly that his biological training gave him an especial insight into social conditions and he was optimistic that voluntary activities could reach a wider cross-section of people. In spite of his optimism, he rarely underestimated the challenge he had set himself. As the movement towards town planning gained momentum in the first decade of the twentieth century, he lent it his full support. Yet he was relieved when the first piece of town-planning legislation in Britain, the Housing and Town Planning Act of 1909, was so tentative and unambitious[5]. He believed that current knowledge was still far from adequate for the successful implementation of town-planning schemes, not only in the understanding of technical details, but, more importantly, in solving the whole complicated problem of self-direction in the future, of which town planning was but a small part.

Thus the position of Geddes as an international prophet of town planning has to be seen against the background of first, his personal and longstanding campaign to arouse people to an awareness of the evolutionary trends of modern society; and, secondly, his endeavour to provide new and relevant knowledge of the human condition which could become the basis for future action. The former brought him into contact with many different groups and individuals, nationally and internationally, who were in some ways concerned about the state of society, and were anxious for reform or development. Geddes found that it was these people who were ready to consider his advice and warnings for the future.

When, for instance, he prepared his plan for Dunfermline in 1904, at the instigation of the Carnegie Dunfermline Trust, he marked his entry into direct planning practice by seeking the advice of over 200 people. Those he consulted included Canon S. A. Barnett of Toynbee Hall, Sidney and Beatrice Webb, Alfred Marshall, John Hobson, J. Ramsey MacDonald and Frederic Harrison; and, in the U.S.A., John Dewey and Frederick Law Olmsted and many others[6]. It was a deliberate attempt to get a response from already interested individuals who would then provide a seedbed for

Geddesian evolutionary ideas. Not all were prepared to follow this 'evolutionary' pattern, but it led Geddes to become involved in a great number of activities, and to acquire a world-wide circle of friends. His longer-term international influence was to be transmitted largely through them.

This voluntary, and sometimes amateur, support for Geddes became more and more vital as other channels for transmitting his ideas dried up. Geddes not only had to work outside the realms of academic life, he also adopted a highly idiosyncratic method of tackling his second major endeavour, to provide new and relevant knowledge of the human condition as a guide to future action. Starting from a biological understanding of man as body and mind, and hostile by nature to purely academic activity, he became convinced that new insight could not be gained without new methods. He was prepared to go back to fundamentals, to create a theory of knowledge itself, in the hope that, by becoming self-conscious on this deeper level, he would find the path which would lead towards the new kinds of knowledge that he sought.

This was not an unusual quest for the generation of young scientists who encountered the concept of evolution, as students, in the exciting decades of the 1860s and 1870s[7]. The small group of dedicated students who came to T. H. Huxley at this time, to learn from the master, often displayed less caution in their enthusiasm for working out the implications of evolutionary theory than Huxley himself. As he was to write in 1880, in his essay 'On the Coming of Age of *The Origin of Species*: 'History warns us that it is the customary fate of new truths to begin as heresies and to end as superstitions'[8]. The problem which Geddes and one or two of his fellow students at the Royal School of Mines, such as C. Lloyd Morgan[9], were prepared to face, with the optimism of youth, was of gigantic proportions. Knowledge, they argued, and the understanding of creation and change, had been transmitted through the generations by book knowledge, supplemented by religious belief. Now they had to apply the new understanding that the concept of evolution had given them to question not only the validity of traditional knowledge but also the validity of the very methods by which knowledge was created.

What they sought, in effect, was nothing less than a new cosmology, a reinterpretation, in the light of evolutionary theory, of the relationship between philosophy and natural science. The development of modern science since the Industrial Revolution had been dominated by a mechanistic point of view. As Durant has observed: 'The priority of mathematics and mechanics in the development of modern science and the reciprocal stimulation of industry and physics under the common pressure of expanding needs, gave to speculation a materialistic impulse: and the most successful of the sciences became the models of philosophy'[10]. What the evolutionists wanted was to bring Life, the 'elan vital', to a central position in philosophical speculation. In their revolt against materialism, some were prepared to go to the opposite extreme and adopt a view of the 'elan vital' as an all-powerful force, of mystical origins and beyond the bounds of reason. They became known as 'vital' biologists and, relating their concept of the natural sciences to philosophy, some, including Geddes and Lloyd Morgan, stumbled along a path leading from 'vital' biology towards anti-intellectualism and a new scientific humanism.

The leading apologist of this philosophical standpoint was Henri Bergson, whose major work, *Creative Evolution,* published in 1907, brought him international fame[11]. However, for many years before that, he had been experimenting on ways of trying to understand the 'elan vital' which, given its irrationality, demanded a totally new approach to knowledge. Bergson was able to capture and classify the ideas behind the attempts made by those, like Geddes and Lloyd Morgan, who sought to attack the philosophical stance of mechanistic materialism. Their target was especially the 'three rheumatic joints of the materialist mechanism: between matter and life, between body and mind, and between determinism and choice'[12], and they sought new ways of coming to an interpretation of these. For Geddes, this was actually a practical necessity, since he believed that only a deeper knowledge of life and its creative force would enable man, in the future, to direct or influence his destiny. A concern for the practical implications of Evolution for Progress in the future was the centre of his scientific humanism.

New ways of gaining knowledge, however, were most clearly spelled out by Bergson. He asserted that the business of science was to explain reality, the business of philosophy was to know it, and one knows by direct intuition and not by the use of the intellect. To grossly oversimplify, instinct was the creative element; intellect was of a lower order, to be used merely as a means to interpret and classify; and intuition (which was a developed instinct with self-awareness) was the counterbalance to the mechanical, devitalizing process of the intellect. Geddes's ideas lacked the clarity of Bergson's, though in many respects they ran in parallel with them. But this view of knowledge was the starting point of Geddes's attack on modern academic institutions, especially universities[13]; and also of his deep belief in the educational benefit of a rural childhood. In 'natural' surroundings, the instinct and intuition are sharpened by close experience of Nature, which if followed by enlightened and practical training in the natural sciences, would result in an understanding of Life[14]. This 'vitalist' approach to an understanding of the universe also developed a practical capacity for the direction of society towards higher evolutionary goals. This is what Geddes understood as planning.

The problem was to translate this concept of Life into practical planning activity. For guidance on how to set about such work, Geddes had to have a clearer understanding of evolutionary stages. He, and his friend Lloyd Morgan, were to invent the concept of 'emergent evolution', a concept which owed as much to the idea of entelechy as advocated by the vitalist Hans

Driesch, as it did to the 'elan vital'[15]. The central core of their argument was that evolution occurs by discrete steps. These steps were equivalent to chemical emergence; the various observable properties of a chemical compound cannot be predicted from the observable properties of the elements of which it is made up. The task of the emergent evolutionist, therefore, was to recognize when two or more separate elements came together to form something new, a new stage in evolution; and then, even more of a challenge, to ferret out, using all available means including instinct and intuition, the possible combinations which could control, or at least form, the future.

The influence of Geddes's evolutionary approach on his planning philosophy was fundamental. It made him totally different from both the utopian planners like Ebenezer Howard, and the practical architect-planners, such as Raymond Unwin[16]. Howard's vision was of an ideal, which had to be deliberately created from the very beginning and bore little relation to the historical evolution of modern, large cities, or the needs and demands of society as it was then constituted. The architect-planners were limited to working with the housing reformers on selected and small-scale improvement schemes. They aimed to fulfil the highest possible expectations, within economic limits, of modern housing ('light and air', in Nettlefold's quotation, not just 'gas and water')[17]; and at the same time to satisfy their aesthetic sense in the orderly use of space, and design of building. What Geddes offered, however, was both a philosophical and practical understanding of the totality of modern city life in all its complexity. He saw the trends in modern urbanization as the evolutionary pattern of the future and he was prepared to try and analyse them, starting with a clean slate, and observing them at first hand. As an evolutionary scientist, he wanted, metaphorically speaking, to put the modern city under his microscope. From the mass of detail he thus accumulated by acute observation, he would discern the evolutionary steps of the city's past which had led to its present, in the passionate belief that only when this was done could one start to speculate about, and plan for, the future. To help him in this work, however, he needed to invent a method of translating the accumulated knowledge into such an evolutionary framework.

With his lack of respect for approaching problems only through book-learning, Geddes was willing to meet this challenge by inventing an intellectual device, which he hoped would incorporate both thought and action. The device was a diagrammatic method of notation which he called his 'thinking machine', which enabled him, so he thought, to codify his observations and knowledge, thus pointing up the dynamic factors in the evolutionary process[18]. The development of his 'thinking machine', however, was to lead him down a path where the academic could not follow. The subject-matter of his studies was nothing less than the social life of the city, yet, in his determination to be comprehensive, the elements which made up that social life—economic and social structure, social institutions based on race, religion and culture, etc.—could not be analysed in any depth. Indeed, they could be referred to only on a very general and superficial level. The following is a typical Geddesian analysis of social structure[19]:

Citizen

People	Emotionals	
Chiefs	Intellectuals	

Guildsman (left side)   Friar (right side)

Student

Geddes was unrepentant about the level of generality at which he worked. His interest in sociology, as such, extended only to the problems of reinterpreting the concepts of the natural sciences in a human context. It was not his intention to make sociology into an intellectual discipline for university study, and he was not in sympathy with the efforts of Durkheim, Weber, Pareto and others to define the subject[20]. He believed that the purpose of sociology was to inform social action. He drew strength not from contemporary sociologists, but from his great mentors in the social sciences, Auguste Comte and Frédéric Le Play. He was also very receptive to the ideas of Herbert Spencer, who had already, as a natural scientist and evolutionist, attempted a universal synthesis of all knowledge and had been at his peak of influence in the 1870s, in Geddes's impressionable student years[21].

Geddes hoped, however, to supersede the work of Spencer. He was repelled both by Spencer's 'architectonic' instinct[22], which made him pursue a logical interpretation of the universe, and his method of academic work, in the protected world of his own study. Geddes wanted to affirm the importance of the 'elan vital', and to reveal it through a practical programme of action. Such an approach precluded the possibility of creating any general theory or absolute position as Spencer had done. Geddes did not believe in absolutes. As an evolutionist first and foremost, and concerned with shaping future action directly, he saw constant change as the norm. He believed that his method, whilst never leading anywhere specific like Ebenezer Howard's vision of *Tomorrow*, was the only way of discovering and understanding the nature of city development and the process of social evolution. His motto, *Vivendo discimus*—by living we learn—sums up his view.

Geddes was able to continue developing his 'thinking machines' for the rest of his life. He was never to be completely satisfied with his results as his perceptions always outran his ability to put them down on paper[23]. But failures of technique did not prevent him from undertaking the urgent task of an active evolutionist and transmitting his ideas and their implications for society as widely as possible. He had a particularly vivid vision of the challenge posed by the events of the nineteenth century. He believed that the Industrial Revolution and its aftermath had created a situation in which Man was in slavery to the very machines he had created. His life and future were now controlled by economic forces which took no account of biological factors, which were of supreme importance to humanity's well-being and better evolutionary development[24].

Geddes was also hostile to political solutions to economic and social inequalities. Talk of political revolution, he maintained, was not the answer. It would not make one jot of difference to the biological circumstances of those who fought and died for it[25]. What was wanted was a new understanding of biological factors, the 'elan vital', a Vital Revolution. 'Such Vital Revolution', he wrote, 'is thus far from "Revolution" in the familiar sense: for these, with their appeals to force, are all mechanistic. It cannot in fact be too clearly noted that the French Revolution was at the opening of the Industrial Age even in France: and that that of Bolshevism is similarly inaugurating the mechanistic proletarian doctrine and practice in Russia. Whereas here we are in the beginnings of a veritable Revivance, which seeks not to take a single human life, but to aid and emancipate life from the hard and heavy mechanistic pressures of the Industrial Age: and to release it upon the upward road of a true and vitally renewing phase of Evolution. What shall we call this incipient phase of renewal? What better than the Revivance?'[26].

Yet if political revolution was not the answer, revitalization, social reconstruction, revivance, depended on the self-awareness and determination of the community at large. In an urbanized society, this meant the urban community, and Geddes was ready to regard citizenship and work for the local community as attempts at self-directed evolutionary effort, which was the antithesis of totalitarianism[27]. Thus for him, the key problem for a planner was to gain a consensus of support for future social developments from the whole community. He considered this to be the central problem, the most important part of the whole exercise of planning. Planning was not a matter of ironing out the technical and physical problems of modern city life. It was a matter of opening people's eyes to their biological nature, treating with respect the interaction of the human organism with its environment, and engaging people in their own development activities, since the only objective of importance was the social evolution of the species[28].

It was the urgency he felt for the need to transmit these views which encouraged Geddes to embark on a number of activities which were to bring him an international reputation, and lead him to a central role in the town-planning movement. It is, however, significant that he achieved the former long before he became identified with the latter, and it was this which was to make him into the 'prophet' rather than the mere propagandist of the town-planning movement. It is thus relevant to an understanding of his special role to trace briefly the steps by which he made his national and international reputation and the activities which brought him most into the public eye.

In the 1880s, Geddes (who was twenty-six in 1880) gained a national reputation for his voluntary work in Edinburgh. He earned his living as an extramural lecturer in the natural sciences at the School of Medicine and as a demonstrator in Botany at Edinburgh University. Four times in the course of the decade he applied for chairs in the natural sciences at Scottish universities[29], and his failure to secure one (the last failure was the hardest, the Chair of Botany at Edinburgh in 1888) was, perhaps, the price he paid for the amount of energy and time he devoted to his social work and pursuit of social evolution. To the uninitiated, the kind of work he was engaged in—for example, voluntary social reform societies like the Environment Society, the improvement of slum housing, extramural educational activities, and the founding of university residences for students (as a preliminary to involving them in the life of the community)—was very similar to that going on in London and other large cities[30]. The 1880s was a decade when the need for action over the social conditions of cities was widely recognized[31]. But the rationale behind Geddes's 'social' work went beyond the hope of undoing some of the damage inflicted on society by mass urbanization and industrialization. Edinburgh had grave social problems in the 1880s, yet it was not a 'shock' city of the Industrial Revolution. It was an historic town, its form largely dictated by influences from its pre-industrial past. Geddes's romantic imagination was deeply moved by his contemplation of the glorious days of Edinburgh's past, as capital of Scotland and intellectual centre of Europe. Such emotional commitment, moreover, was allied in his case to the scientific interest of an evolutionist. It was a combination which gave him the stimulus to pioneer a new kind of social activity in, and study of, his chosen city.

As a natural scientist, T. H. Huxley had, in his famous description of evolution in nature, used the Thames basin as his environmental context[32]. As a would-be social scientist, Geddes hoped to use Edinburgh and its region as his environmental context for a study of the evolution of society. He got some early encouragement for this project in 1884, the year he helped to found the Environment Society, which also happened to be in the tercentenary of Edinburgh University. To mark this latter event, Geddes helped to produce a small pamphlet giving biographical details of Edinburgh scholars who had achieved great eminence[33]. Poring over these individual case histories, he found outstanding evidence of Edinburgh's 'golden age' of social and cultural achievement which had taken place in the century after 1740[34].

If Geddes had been an historian, he might have asked himself why so many men of genius had flourished at this time and why a decline had set in during his own lifetime. But the questions of a social evolutionist were significantly different. The question was not 'why' but 'how'[35]. How had such a thing happened? What does that tell us about the favourable interaction of organism and environment? To test his answers, he wanted to experiment by recreating the 'right' juxtaposition of stimulating environment with responsive organism to see if he could get the same result. Much of the inspiration for his voluntary social work stemmed from this desire. For instance, his concern for slum improvement was not based only on a concern for the poor. The slums happened to be in the Royal Mile, the heart of the old city, which had once been the environment of great men. Similarly, the university residences for students which he established in 1887, modestly at first (only seven students in three small flats in former slum courts), were more than an indication of his concern for student welfare. His ambition was to create a little Bohemia of students, artists, and literary and other creative people in the same place, the same buildings even, which had housed those who had contributed so much to Edinburgh's 'golden age'.

As he actively pursued his evolutionary viewpoint, he became, like all reinterpreters of the past with a vested interest in the present[36], fixated on certain elements in the city's and university's cultural heritage which he felt most closely answered the question of how Edinburgh's 'golden age' had come about. Three elements were of particular importance. The first and second were related to Edinburgh's contribution to knowledge through the publishing ventures of city firms. The first was the publication of encyclopaedias, in which the city had gained an international reputation with the publication of the *Edinburgh Encyclopaedia* by Blackwood's between 1808 and 1830; the second was the development of cartography, which had been pursued with great skill and pioneering spirit by the family firm of Bartholomew's, established in 1797. The third element, however, was to be found in the university rather than in the city. In the 'golden age' the university had been concerned to keep abreast with modern knowledge, and a Franco-Scottish college had been established at the Sorbonne. Scotland's greatest intellectual genius, Adam Smith, had, indeed, studied the work of the French encyclopaedists in Paris. What Geddes, the evolutionist, made of these elements was as follows: first, the concept of the encyclopaedia had an especial attraction for one aiming at a synthesis of all knowledge. The potential of such a classification of knowledge dominated his thinking on how to transmit his ideas, and particularly on how to organize museums and exhibitions, which were to become his chosen methods. The museum was to be an 'Encyclopaedia Graphica'; his town-planning exhibition an 'Encyclopaedia Civica'. His enthusiasm for this approach was fortuitously reinforced by a new interest in encyclopaedia publication which sprang up in Edinburgh and elsewhere in the late nineteenth century. The Edinburgh firm of W. & R. Chambers, particularly, attempted to exploit the potential of a newly-literate mass market by publishing, first, *Information for the People* (1857) and then, from 1874 onwards, a national, (and, in 1902, international) full encyclopaedia[37]. It was kept up to date by revision every five years and included generous sections on the natural sciences, many of them written by Geddes. He contributed articles to the *Chambers Encyclopaedia* and to the

Encyclopaedia Britannica on evolution, Darwinian evolution, sex, reproduction, variation and selection, parasitism and other subjects of key interest
to an understanding of evolution in the natural sciences[38].

His passion for geography and the work of Bartholomew's sprang from his
grasp of the potential of cartography for presenting information in totally
new ways, thus enabling a different kind of study to be undertaken. Facts
before theory were essential and cartography provided the best method of
displaying a wide range of information visually. Geddes was to gain a
reputation as a pioneer geographer in Britain since he was one of a very small
band, the most important of whom was H. J. Mackinder, who, in the late
1880s and 1890s, sought to extend the range of geographical studies in
Britain[39]. The aim was to take such studies beyond the 'explorers' stage',
towards a scientific study of every aspect of the environment—a study
already well established in continental Europe. There was, however, a
divergence of interest between Geddes and Mackinder. Mackinder looked to
Germany for his inspiration and was most deeply concerned with the political
implications of new geographical knowledge[40]. Geddes looked to France,
his intellectual home, and was most concerned with regional geography and
the interaction of geographical and social factors which produced
evolutionary trends.

Geddes found guidance for his studies of social evolution in the work of
the great French social scientist, Le Play, and his school. In particular, the
influence of Le Play's disciple, M. Demolins, was to encourage Geddes to
place especial emphasis on geographical factors when he set to work to
interpret the Le Play formula for social studies, 'Place, Work, Folk'[41]. He
was forced to seek such guidance abroad because, at that time, 'scientific'
social science in Britain was dominated by the practical social ameliorists,
the social statisticians and the political economists, none of whom was
concerned with a biological or ecological approach to social problems[42].
Geddes considered this to be a failure of British intellectual life, a product of
the out-of-date response of English universities to modern knowledge. The
Bergsonian theory of knowledge, if adopted, would revolutionize study and
bring all students to a new evolutionary approach in their different
disciplines. Geddes was interested in a bio-psychological approach to
learning, directed towards life-enhancement and the cultivation of individual
talent, as well as to the accumulation of knowledge. His opinions of British
academic life were not softened by his witness of the struggles of his master,
T. H. Huxley, to establish the natural sciences as a proper academic subject,
to reform the University of London, and to advise the Royal Commission on
the reform of Scottish universities.

Geddes, of course, wanted to go much further than his master, directing
his reforming zeal not only towards the content of education but also the
form. He wanted to pioneer a 'vitalist' approach to education at every level,
from the elementary school to the university. He followed Huxley's

pioneering work in encouraging the teaching of the natural sciences in elementary schools, which he considered to be of vital importance[43]. But this was not enough. The teachers themselves had to be made aware of evolutionary principles and 'vitalist' methods of nurturing the talents of their pupils. Much of Geddes's own talent lay in his ability to give a practical form to his ambitions and he was quick to pick up the idea, first developed in the United States by the American Chautauqua Society, of setting up a summer school. Such a school was ideal for educational experiments since it was voluntary and open to all, and had the advantage of being free from normal academic pressures. His summer school of 1886 was the first in Britain, but he kept his academic objectives at a fairly modest level, instructing his few volunteers (some of them elementary school teachers) in the advances in the natural sciences and taking them for practical work to Edinburgh University's marine station at Granton, which he had helped to set up in 1884[44]. These activities, however, did not help the present university undergraduates and for these, especially those living in his student residences, Geddes wanted to add the enlightening experience of foreign contact and travel.

In the early 1890s, he initiated a scheme to revive the Franco-Scots College at Paris, in the very same building which had housed it before[45]. He did not succeed in this latter part of his plan, but an exchange scheme between Scottish and French students was set up and flourished over the decade. Some of the Edinburgh students, such as A. J. Herbertson, who was to play a crucial role in the development of geographical studies in Britain, under the leadership of Mackinder at Oxford, benefited much from their French contacts. Geddes himself also benefited to the extent that his ties with French academics and social scientists were renewed and developed[46]. He was able to draw on the services of M. Demolins and many others to help him expand his summer schools in the 1890s. Above all, he brought the great French geographer, Elisée Reclus, to Edinburgh in 1892 and 1896, and the Edinburgh summer schools achieved international status[47].

Geddes, himself, also contributed directly to their fame for in the early 1890s he took the bold step of launching himself, finally, as a social evolutionist as well as an expert on evolution in the natural sciences. In 1889 he had published his first full-length scientific work, in collaboration with one of his most able students, J. Arthur Thomson, on the subject of sex. Entitled *The Evolution of Sex,* the book gained for its authors a certain notoriety for daring to tackle such a subject. But it went through three printings and two different editions in Britain, was published in America in 1890, and was translated into French two years later[48]. In this study, Geddes and Thomson explored the concept of evolution in relation to the biological organism and, in some controversial concluding chapters, Geddes speculated on the biological determinants of male and female roles in the human species[49].

Having advanced on this front, Geddes also intensified his studies on the other main evolutionary element, the environment. Guided by the Le Play formula, 'Place, Work, Folk', he and his helpers subjected Edinburgh to an intensive study, translating 'Place' as the geographical location, 'Work' as occupation, and 'Folk' as families, social groups and individuals of talent. These were the formative years for what Geddes was later to describe as the Edinburgh Survey[50]. In his summer schools of the 1890s, in his Outlook Tower Museum, in his Town and Gown Association and his private initiative, Patrick Geddes & Colleagues Co. (a firm dedicated to publishing the best literature and art to be found in Edinburgh), Geddes mounted a broad-based attack to discover the evolutionary potential of the city[51]. Both actively studying the evolution of Edinburgh's past and trying to influence the evolutionary trends of the city for the future, Geddes did not endear himself to the city's social or academic establishment. But from the work undertaken for the Edinburgh Survey, Geddes was able to develop a generalized technique, the Regional Survey, which was to be his most important practical contribution to the town-planning movement[52].

In the 1890s, however, the town-planning movement was still very much embryonic, and Geddes was more interested in publicizing and educating people with his evolutionary ideas. The central method on which he pinned his faith, more than all the host of his other activities, was his idea of an Index Museum[53]. In many respects, however, the birth of what he considered to be his most creative idea was to prove, in the end, the most still-born. He was never able to organize an Index Museum, the Outlook Tower in Edinburgh being only a small part of the grand design. Yet it was this idea which led to his passionate interest in museums and exhibitions which, in turn, was to lead him into organizing the great international summer school at the Paris Exhibition of 1900, which firmly established his international reputation[54]. It also brought him the expertise he was to use in his Cities and Town Planning Exhibition, his most important contribution to the town-planning movement, at the high peak of his influence between 1910 and 1914.

The objective of his idea of an Index Museum was certainly ambitious. It was dedicated to a visual classification of all knowledge. 'First of all, more than an ordinary museum', Geddes wrote, 'it is not only an encyclopaedia but an *Encyclopaedia Graphica*. That is, we may think of it as an Encyclopaedia of which the articles may be imagined printed separately, and with their illustrations and maps condensed and displayed as an orderly series of labels; labels to which specimens are then as far as possible supplied, so that over and above the description, the image, the interpretation of the thing, you can see the thing itself in reality if possible, or in reproduction or model as the case may be'[55]. Just as the planning of a conventional encyclopaedia was a complicated task, so the planning of an *Encyclopaedia Graphica* created many problems. 'Most difficult of all, the plan, the order must be no longer alphabetical or empirical, but rational; that is, in conformity at once with reason and with observation, with philosophy and with the order of nature.'

The Index Museum, in effect, was a philosophy of science, expressed in visual form. As Geddes wrote: 'since Philosophy and Nature find their common thought in Evolution, the curator is thus a philosopher in the concrete mood, and the philosopher but a curator in the abstract one'[56]. Geddes believed firmly that the greatest human ideas, ideals and achievements could be presented visually and he saw his museum work as the 'concrete' counterpart of academic study, a vital part of university work. But its educational value was not limited to academic circles. In the tradition of the 'modern' encyclopaedists, Geddes felt that the diffusion of knowledge, through the creation of Index Museums in large cities, was of vital importance. 'It cannot be too strongly emphasised', he wrote, 'that such a material expression of the evolutionary order of things as can be realised no less fully in a modest provincial museum than in the greatest, is actually needed to develop throughout our populations a correspondingly improved mental order . . . Were a provincial college or city once provided with any one Index Museum such as this, it would be in this respect provincial no longer. It would on the contrary be possessed of a museum literally metropolitan to the metropolis itself—that is a museum which it would be for the metropolitan institution to reproduce at the very centre of its organization, and this alike for the sake of its officials, its students and its public'[57].

The convolutions of his contorted prose get more and more elaborate as he struggles to express his ideas. For him, museums and exhibitions were of key importance as a method of synthesizing modern knowledge in many fields. Above all, they provided a crucial, and much sought-after, meeting-place between the natural and social sciences. All the strenuous efforts of the academic social scientists and evolutionists, such as Herbert Spencer and Lester F. Ward, had failed to achieve this association[58], and Geddes felt that his 'practical' exhibition method was justified by the work of his masters. Darwin and Huxley had visibly demonstrated their grasp of the concept of evolution with examples and illustrations. In the social sciences, Le Play and his followers used exhibitions as a means of ascertaining the economic and social advances of their day, prior to making their recommendations on what was necessary to achieve 'social peace'.

Le Play's disciples organized the 1889 Paris Exhibition, which Geddes attended, along the lines pioneered by the master in the 1867 Paris Exhibition. A leading exhibit was set up by Cheysson, Professor of Political Economy at the Ecole Libre des Sciences Politiques, and an old Le Playist, to illustrate the master's dearest wish, the road to 'social peace'[59]. Geddes was deeply impressed by its evolutionary approach: the analysis of how the present had grown from the past, and the understanding of both, before social prescriptions for the future were made. The key problem though, as he saw it, was to move people to take action for the future in a united and effective way. It was a problem not only of knowledge, but also of social morality, which is why, when Geddes undertook his practical activities, he did so with the fervour of a moral crusade. His fascination with M. de Bloch's exhibit on 'War' at the 1900 Paris Exhibition was not due entirely to his concern over the imminence of European conflict[60]. He was inspired by the idea that in wartime the community responds as one, in a cooperative effort of common concern and comradeship. His dream was to awaken that spirit and comradeship, that concern for the efficient use of men and resources, in peacetime, in aid of the social reconstruction of the future.

Geddes's vision was that his Index Museum would be a moral powerhouse for the community. His contempt for the solutions to modern problems put forward by politicians of whatever complexion, from far right to far left, caused him to put his faith in such an institution and the direct social activities which it would encourage. The direction of social evolution would be determined by the morality and culture of the people, once the biological limitations of food and reproduction had been met. An Index Museum would stimulate the pursuit of culture and harness the moral aspirations of young and old. 'In a word', he wrote, 'the Museum may be the culture-centre of its city, its region, and its time; the focus, at once receptive and radiant of its civilisation'[61]. It was an uplifting prospect, but Geddes, the practical Scot, was always willing to seize at any chances that offered themselves, however modest, to make a start.

His first and most successful attempt to establish a museum happened by chance. A building at the top end of the Royal Mile in Edinburgh, consisting of a tower with a camera obscura on its roof (used to entertain tourists in earlier days with its panoramic view over the city) came up for sale in 1892. Geddes set about acquiring it before he had thought what to do with it. However, the camera obscura gave him his key. He invented the idea of a regional museum, covering the area encompassed by the mirrors of the camera obscura, which could be used to interest local people and then involve them in their own history and present conditions. The concept of the regional museum was similar to that of the Index Museum in that it was based on evolutionary principles. The Outlook Tower, however, was to have as its mainspring, not the philosophy of science, but 'scientific' geography. As Geddes himself put it: 'The idea is no longer that of arts and sciences but of Place and People, and these in widening horizons. Our synthesis has thus no longer an abstract classification, a philosophy of science, by which to determine its planning; its basis is a concrete one. It is that of geography instead of philosophy: it is the concrete World-All, instead of the abstract'[62].

The Outlook Tower was the nearest Geddes ever got to his dreams of influencing the future through the development of a museum and culture-institute. But the success of his summer schools, held there from 1895[63], led him towards a new idea which was greatly to boost his international reputation. In 1900, a great, end-of-the-century, world international fair was planned in Paris. Geddes conceived the idea that such an exhibition could provide him with the raw material for a great, evolutionary study of the world, an Index Museum on the largest scale. He aimed to set up his 1900 summer school in Paris, on an international basis, to pursue such a study, and to encourage international contact and cooperation in utilizing the educational potential of the occasion. He got financial backing from a Scottish industrialist, Sir Robert Pullar from Perth; he sounded out the British Association, and its French equivalent, at their respective annual congresses in September 1899 at Dover and Boulogne; and he visited the United States, bringing about the formation of an Anglo-American group. Different national groups were affiliated to an 'International Association for the Advancement of the Sciences, Art and Education', and for the duration of the exhibition, the Geddesian international summer school administered a large-scale operation with numbers of distinguished guests and lecturers[64].

In the course of four months, the school organized 134 special congresses[65]. Emile Bourgeois, an active member of the French group, outlined the extent of the activity in a speech at the end of the school. Eight hundred classes had been held in 120 days, making an average of just over six per day, with attendance varying from forty to fifty people, and sometimes reaching three hundred. About a hundred professors taught in four rooms, and the administrative staff consisted of eight secretaries and ten other workers. 'Il y a plus d'une université qui dans un semestre ne donne pas une telle carrière' was Bourgeois's verdict[66]. Instruction was given in four languages among six 'nations', though the French classes attracted by far the largest numbers of students. The Anglo-American group had, on the whole, a poor attendance which Geddes put down to the fact that the kind of English-speaking tourist who came to the Exhibition was likely to be more interested in entertainment than instruction.

As the Exhibition drew to a close, however, Geddes conceived an ambition to save more of it than had been saved from international exhibitions in the past. London's Great Exhibition of 1851 had provided profits for funding both museums and educational work under the auspices of a specially created Science and Art Department, and this tradition had been observed on later occasions. In America, the holding of international exhibitions had proved a fruitful source for the founding of permanent museums, for instance in Philadelphia and Chicago. However, in 1900, in Paris, Geddes wanted more than this. He wanted to maintain the international spirit of his summer school on a permanent basis by encouraging each nation to donate its pavilion to a body which would become responsible for setting up a series of Index Museums in each of them, as a great contribution to evolutionary studies. In the expansive mood of 1900, this idea nearly came to fruition. But the legal battles over the land and future control held up proceedings and gradually the initial support from the different nations fell away. He did not give up, though, and he resuscitated the 'International Association for the Advancement of the Sciences, Art and Education' the following year, at the very much more modest international fair at Glasgow. He hoped to go to the St. Louis Exposition of 1903 but by then he, and his association, had run out of money. In 1903, hoping to establish a permanent Index Museum in his adopted city, Geddes applied for the Directorship of the Edinburgh Museum of Science and Art. But he failed to get it, and he failed again in a bid to secure the principalship of the College of Science at Durham. Yet to offset these failures, he had the triumph of the international summer school in Paris in 1900, which had brought him an international reputation; and it helped him to forge useful contacts with many leading social reformers and social scientists, united by a common concern for the future.

The nature of his reputation was to be of great importance to Geddes when he became more deeply involved in the town-planning movement. He had identified himself completely with the concept of social reconstruction, his development of the Le Playist objective of 'social peace'. This concept was to prove particularly attractive to a special group of administrators, the small band of liberal-minded British governors of colonial territories. Two Scotsmen, Lord Pentland, Secretary of State for Scotland, and subsequently Governor of Madras, and Lord Aberdeen, Viceroy of Ireland, were directly responsible for providing Geddes with a context for his town-planning activities which was to further his international reputation in this area. His career as an international prophet of town planning thus grew directly out of his work as a social evolutionist, and even the activity he became most famous for, his Cities and Town Planning Exhibition, was closely moulded on the ideas he had been working out for the past thirty years, as to how best he could help to bring an understanding of the concept of evolution to wider public.

The two main contributions Geddes made to the town-planning movement between 1903 and 1914 were his concept of the Regional Survey and his Cities and Town Planning Exhibition. He got only one small chance to undertake practical planning directly. The Carnegie Trust at Dunfermline, with a £500,000 bequest to spend, invited him to design a layout for Pittencrief Park. Geddes enthusiastically responded by providing a plan in which the park was to become the centre of the social life of the whole town, with its special culture-institutes and schemes for citizen involvement in environmental improvements[67]. The Trustees were both amazed and unimpressed by his work, by his insistence on the idea that planning was a continuous and evolutionary process and by his advice that they must invest the £500,000 and spend only the income on small-scale schemes in perpetuity[68].

Geddes's career, however, received a boost in a different sphere when the British Sociological Society was founded by his friend and admirer, V. V. Branford, in 1903. The Sociological Society briefly enjoyed a spectacular success as many eminent politicians, social reformers, and academics hoped that sociology might produce some answers to modern social problems. Interest, as quickly, faded when it became apparent that these were vain hopes[69]. But, meanwhile, Geddes had seized the chance to put forward his version of sociology as a preliminary to social action, in a couple of papers entitled 'Civics: as applied sociology'[70]. It was a generalized version of his Edinburgh regional survey technique, based on the Le Play formula of 'Place, Work and Folk'. The geographical concept of the region, the importance of the community and its relationship with its environment, the need to involve people in their own development towards higher evolution, were the well-established ideas of the Geddesian evolutionist repertoire. Yet now they began to strike a chord of response from the small, but growing, number interested in town and country planning. Geddes was able to form a Civics Committee within the Sociological Society, to undertake survey work and to promote his ideas on the priorities for planning activities.

It was, however, Geddes's second contribution, the Cities and Town Planning Exhibition, which did more to boost his international reputation in the town-planning movement. His chance to develop once again his interest in exhibition work came in 1910, with the organization of an international exhibition by the Royal Institute of British Architects to publicize the passing of the Housing and Town Planning Act of 1909. City and housing exhibitions had been held with increasing frequency in a number of European countries, particularly in Germany. Britain lagged very much behind in this respect and four-fifths of the R.I.B.A. exhibition came from abroad[71]. Much of the British content was accounted for by the Edinburgh exhibition from the Outlook Tower and Geddes was appointed the director of the exhibition. He saw here a chance to reactivate the techniques he had developed at the Paris Exhibition, using the City and Town Planning Exhibition as his raw material, his Index Museum. This time, however, he also invented a way of keeping the exhibition together, and maintaining his supplementary explanatory activities over a longer period than the duration of a single exhibition. He persuaded the National Housing and Town Planning Council to give him moral support for a scheme to make the exhibition a movable one which, Geddes argued, could visit large cities by invitation and thus reach far greater numbers than the London exhibition. Finance was to come from the cities which offered the invitations[72]. Geddes had the pleasure of getting his first invitation from the city which had hitherto responded most apathetically to his schemes, Edinburgh. The exhibition was opened, amid general acclaim, by Lord Pentland.

It was seen in Edinburgh by Lady Aberdeen, wife of the Viceroy of Ireland. She was anxious for Geddes to take the exhibition to Ireland since, in 1911, she was President of the Women's National Health Association, and responsible for the administration of the Royal Sanitary Institute Congress to be held in Ireland that year[73]. Through his exhibition work and his personal contacts, Geddes became deeply involved with the Irish Question. He believed passionately that a solution to the problem lay in improvements in economic and social life, and in the environment of city and countryside[74]. He was responsible for setting and judging the competition for a future plan for Dublin and he awarded the first prize to Patrick Abercrombie. He did not think that Abercrombie's Beaux-Arts-type plan could be easily implemented, but Abercrombie had attended meetings of the Civics Committee of the Sociological Society and he was an ardent supporter of the Regional Survey technique[75].

Geddes found much personal encouragement in all these activities after his many failures. In 1912, he completed the manuscript of his monograph, *Cities in Evolution,* the only general work on city development he was ever to write. It was not published, however, until 1915, as the editors and publishers of the series for which it was intended felt that it did not fit in with their other volumes. In this opinion they were probably right[76]. Geddes's idiosyncratic theory of knowledge, his determination to reinterpret all knowledge in an evolutionary synthesis, and the intellectual devices of his 'thinking-machines' meant that without prior understanding of his viewpoint and objectives, his work appeared nearly unintelligible. Yet his ability to observe modern social conditions, and his unrivalled first-hand knowledge of cities (gained on his many journeys abroad), brought him those flashes of insight with which he was able to dazzle his disciples and, sometimes, his students. It was recognition of his ability to stimulate and excite his audience which brought him his greatest international accolade, when he took his City and Town Planning Exhibition to the International Exposition at Ghent in 1913, and was awarded the Gold Medal there. The exhibition was particularly directed towards a concern for social conditions and urban development and attracted town planners, municipal administrators, civil servants, and professional and business people, from Europe and America. The founding of the International Garden City and Town Planning Association was an outcome of the exhibition, though it was destined to hold only one international congress before the First World War[77].

Geddes's ambitious attempt to explain the origin of modern conditions and to provide ideas for prescriptive measures thus found a favourable audience. His exhibition had an air of chaos, with its galleries packed with wide-ranging material, illustrating virtually the whole history of the world[78]. Yet all was arranged in an evolutionary sequence with a cell, or thought-room, at the end, for the observer to translate his experience into definite proposals for social action. To offer guidance and help in this process, there was Geddes himself, ever ready to talk with passion and enthusiasm about his ideas. A visit to his exhibition created a sense of promise, hope, and fresh insight which earned him the top prize over the other, better organized and produced exhibits. It was a personal tribute to him since his success depended entirely on his special techniques and his presence. It was the high-point of his career as an international prophet of town planning before 1914.

Yet Geddes's success in the town-planning movement was, in effect, a by-product of his ambition to convert the world to a new evolutionary understanding of modern society and progress. His success in this respect was much more limited. Universities, particularly, failed to take any heed of his pleas about the urgency of undertaking not only studies of new subject matter, in the natural and social sciences, but also of adopting new methods of creating knowledge, outside the library and the study. Before 1914, his work in sociology and geography, designed to uncover evolutionary trends and to influence the direction they should take in the future, misled as many people as it inspired. His supporters in the Sociological Society, who largely formed the backbone of the loosely organized Regional Survey Association[79], found themselves on a path which was to lead to the domination of British sociological studies by cranks and enthusiasts for a generation[80].

Even Geddes's Cities and Town Planning Exhibition was not universally acclaimed. Large cities like Manchester and Birmingham, with honourable records in the development of better housing and conditions for the poor, refused to have anything to do with Geddes and his propaganda campaign[81]. The First World War, moreover, cut off Geddes's hopes of winning them over, slowly, to his side. From 1914 to 1924, Geddes undertook his exhibition work in India, where a colonial context, and a pre-industrial sense of time, were more suited to his evolutionary and 'vitalist' approach to planning problems. Here, he also had a chance to undertake planning schemes for nearly forty cities, and the publication of his work in a series of reports provided the young British town planners with actual examples of Geddesian planning as a practical guide to his ideas. Geddes had taken the Comtist dictum to heart: 'Know in order to foresee, and foresee in order to provide', and it was also one which was close to the hearts of those trying to establish the town-planning movement on a professional basis. His a-political stance and devotion to Social Reconstruction were also important in providing a rationale for planning activities, which the disruption and destruction of the First World War were to emphasize.

Yet when Geddes returned to Europe, via America, in 1923, he found he was unable to regain the level of public interest he had enjoyed so briefly between 1910 and 1913. In his last years, he was to write his final book in collaboration with J. Arthur Thomson, a biological textbook entitled *Life: Outlines of Biology*. Thomson provided the lucid account of the natural sciences and Geddes tried to put his evolutionary philosophy down for the last time and as clearly as possible. He could not refrain from writing, though, that 'after long and perplexed thinking', he was unable to understand 'how it has come to be that Life, and its evolutionary developments and expression, still so generally fail to interest either the experts of the physical world or the scholars of the humanities'[82]. He had stood out against what he saw as the 'mechanistic' tendencies of his age, and he had tried to show how important an understanding of, and a respect for, the life sciences was for the future. There was no way of containing the 'elan vital', only evolution towards a higher state or total degeneration. Geddes was not sure, in spite of all his efforts, that he had got his message across.

NOTES

1. Research for this paper has been carried out as part of a project for a modern reassessment of the life and work of Sir Patrick Geddes, supported by a grant from the S.S.R.C.

2. Tracing the evolution of Geddes's ideas and activities is made more difficult by Geddes himself. Although he published a great deal, his work was mostly in short articles, even outlines for lecture courses, much of which is rather inaccessible. Some important material is to be found in the remnants of the Geddes collection at Strathclyde University, and in the Geddes papers at the National Library at Edinburgh. The books he published between 1880 and 1914 were:
   1. *The Evolution of Sex* (1889) with J. Arthur Thomson (revised ed. 1901);
   2. *City Development: A Study of Parks, Gardens and Culture Institutes. A Report to the Carnegie Dunfermline Trust* (1904) (reprinted by the Irish University Press, 1973);
   3. Two popular works for the 'Home University Library' series, both in collaboration with J. Arthur Thomson (a) *Evolution* (London: Williams and Norgate, 1911), (b) *Sex* (London: Williams and Norgate, 1914);
   4. *Cities in Evolution: An Introduction to the Town Planning Movement and to the Study of Civics* (London: Williams and Norgate, 1915).

3. Four books and numerous articles have been written on Geddes's life and social message. These fall into three categories: those concerned with preserving and promoting the ideas of the Master, e.g. Defries, A. (1927) *The Interpreter: Geddes, the Man and his Gospel.* London: Routledge; Boardman, P. (1944) *Patrick Geddes: Maker of the Future.* Chapel Hill: University of North Carolina Press (a new, much revised, edition is to be published shortly); and, to a lesser extent, Mairet, P. (1957) *A Pioneer of Sociology: Life and Letters of Patrick Geddes.* London: Lund Humphries; those interested in Geddes's pioneering perception of 'ecological humanism', a term used by P. T. Bryant in his introduction to B. Mackaye, *From Geography to Geotechnics.* Mackaye acknowledges his debt to Geddes, whom he met in 1923, for the term 'geotechnics'. See also Stalley, Marshall (ed.) (1972) *Patrick Geddes, Spokesman for Man and the Environment.* New Brunswick: Rutgers University Press; finally, those concerned with Geddes the town planner. Here, emphasis tends to be placed on his practical planning techniques, e.g. Tyrwhitt, J. (ed.) (1947) *Patrick Geddes in India.* London: Lund Humphries; and Goist, P. D. (1974) Patrick Geddes and the City. *Journal of the American Institute of Planners,* **40**, pp. 31–8.

4. For the best account of the development of the social sciences in France, which influenced Geddes most, see Clark, T. N. (1973) *Prophets and Patrons: The French University and the Emergence of the Social Sciences.* Cambridge, Mass.: Harvard University Press.

5. Geddes, P. (1915) *Cities in Evolution: An Introdu*[
   Movement and to the Study of Civics. London: Williams

6. The correspondence has been preserved in the Ge[
   National Library of Scotland.

7. For a discussion of this see Collingwood, R. G. (1945)
   Oxford: Clarendon Press, Introduction and pp. 133–74, a[
   (1963) *Man on his Nature.* Cambridge: Cambridge University [

8. Quoted from Bibby, C. (1959) *T. H. Huxley: Scientist, Humani[*
   London: Watts, p. 90.

9. C. Lloyd Morgan was appointed in 1883 lecturer in geology an[_oology at
   Bristol University College, and became the principal of the college in 1887. His
   main works included *An Introduction to Comparative Psychology* (1894), *Habit and
   Instinct* (1896), *Instinct and Experience* (1912), and *Emergent Evolution* (1923).
   He lectured in the 1890s at Geddes's Edinburgh Summer School.

10. Durant, W. (1962) *Outlines of Philosophy: Plato to Russell.* London: Ernest Benn,
    p. 386.

11. For a sympathetic discussion of Bergson's contribution to philosophy see
    Muller, H. J. (1964) *Science and Criticism: The Humanistic Tradition in
    Contemporary Thought.* New Haven: Yale University Press, pp. 246–50.

12. Durant, W. (1962) *Outlines of Philosophy: Plato to Russell.* London: Ernest Benn,
    p. 387.

13. A relatively lucid account of the kind of university Geddes wished to see
    developed is given in a small pamphlet, *On Universities in Europe and India, and
    a Needed Type of Research Institute, Geographical and Social—Being Five Letters to
    an Indian Friend* (Madras, 1915) (reprinted from *The Pioneer,* 14 August 1901,
    and *East and West,* (September 1903). Geddes called his concept 'the post-
    Germanic university'.

14. Geddes wanted a bio-psychological and evolutionary approach to education. A
    school on these lines, the Ecole des Roches, was run in the 1890s by M.
    Demolins, the Le Playist disciple, 'to inculcate an elite with particularistic
    values' (Clark, T. N. (1973) *Prophets and Patrons: The French University and the
    Emergence of the Social Sciences.* Cambridge: Harvard University Press, p. 108)
    Geddes educated his own children at home and was an ardent supporter of the
    Boy Scout movement.

15. C. Lloyd Morgan did not however publish his monograph, *Emergent Evolution,*
    until 1923.

16. See Creese, W. (1966) *The Search for Environment: The Garden City Before and
    After.* New Haven and London: Yale University Press.

17. Nettlefold, J. (1908) *Practical Housing.* Letchworth: Garden City Press, p. vi.

18. Geddes's clearest exposition of his 'thinking-machines' is to be found in 'Life
    theory in outline and notation', in *Life, Outlines of Biology.* London: Williams
    and Norgate, 1931, pp. 1401–15.

19. This particular example is to be found in the Geddes papers, MS10656, National
    Library of Scotland.

20. For the development of sociological studies see Lukes, S. (1975) *Emile
    Durkheim: His life and work.* Harmondsworth: Peregrine Books, pp. 392–8. It
    was Durkheim, and not Geddes, who was invited to submit a paper on the
    subject of sociology and its role in the social sciences at the first conference of

ritish Sociological Society (*Sociological Papers*. London: Macmillan & Co.,
05, pp. 195–201).

 .. Spencer published the first volume of *The Principles of Sociology* in 1876, vol. 2 in
1882.

22. For Spencer on evolution see Peel, J. D. Y. (1971) *Herbert Spencer: The Evolution of a Sociologist*. London: Heinemann, pp. 131–65.

23. Lewis Mumford, in 'Mumford on Geddes', *Architectural Review*, August 1950, p. 81, suggests that 'Geddes was primarily a scientist, shy of committing his thoughts to writing, lest the provisional and dynamic and tentative became static and absolute'.

24. An early statement of this view is to be found in three lectures Geddes gave to the Royal Society in Edinburgh in 1884, published under the title *Analysis of the Principles of Economics* (pamphlet, London and Edinburgh: Williams and Norgate, 1885).

25. See another early pamphlet, *On the Conditions of Progress of the Capitalist and of the Labourer*. Edinburgh: Cooperative Printing Co., 1886.

26. From a typewritten document, headed 'Philosophy of the Movement—Branford's and more of us' (n.d.), Geddes Collection, Strathclyde University.

27. This is the basic message of his two papers to the Sociological Society entitled 'Civics: as applied Sociology', Parts 1 and 2 (*Sociological Papers*. London: Macmillan & Co., 1905).

28. This he had already worked out in the 1880s in another pamphlet, *Cooperation versus Socialism*. Manchester: Cooperative Printing Society, 1888, p. 24, where he concludes: 'our modern tragic antagonism—of capitalism with its sadly unideal practice, and socialism with its sadly unpractical ideals—must alike steadily rise and merge into a truly practical—yet nobly idealised—everyday life of true, that is, full and developed, cooperation ... in the struggle into the Culture of Existence'.

29. The extent of his international contacts in the scientific world was demonstrated in his bulky applications which, since he had no degree, consisted of letters of support from those whom he had met or worked under in his 'wander-years' in Europe. See letter of application and testimonials for Edinburgh, 1881, and St. Andrews, 1882, Geddes papers, National Library of Scotland.

30. An important example was the setting up of Toynbee Hall University Settlement in the East End of London, under the wardenship of Canon S. A. Barnett, in 1884.

31. See Hennock, E. P. (1976) Poverty and social theory in England: the experience of the 1880s. *Social History,* 1(1), pp. 67–91.

32. Huxley, T. H. (1877) *Physiography*. This was the model, yet Geddes, as a 'vital' biologist, wanted to challenge the two master concepts of Huxley's approach, the concepts of mechanism and struggle-for-life. See Geddes, P. and Slater, G. (1917) *The Coming Polity*. London: Williams and Norgate, p. 5.

33. Geddes, P. (ed.) (1884) *Vivi Illustres*. Edinburgh: Pentland.

34. See Smout, T. C. (1973) *A History of the Scottish People 1560–1830*. Bungay: Collins/Fontana, Chapter 19, 'The Golden Age of Scottish Culture', pp. 451–83.

35. Childe, G. (1963) *Social Evolution*. London: Collins/Fontana, p. 25.

36. William Morris's idealization of Medieval England is another example.

37. Allison, R. (1964) *Encyclopaedias: Their History Through the Ages.* New York and London: Hafner, p. 188.
38. He wrote these articles in the 1880s and early 1890s.
39. See Stevenson, W. I. (1975) *Patrick Geddes and Geography: Biobibliographical Study.* University College, London, Department of Geography Occasional Papers, no. 27.
40. His most famous paper, 'The geographical pivot of history', was published in the *Geographical Journal,* 23, 1904.
41. Demolins's masterpiece, *Comment la route crée le type social,* stressed geographic factors as the ultimate source of social organization.
42. See Abrams, P. (1968) *The Origins of British Sociology.* Chicago, University of Chicago Press, pp. 8–52. Others who acknowledged their debt to Le Play in the 1880s included Charles Booth and Cardinal Manning.
43. Geddes's main contribution in this respect was to run voluntary courses for teachers on the natural sciences and geography. This was one of his main objectives in his early summer schools; see 'Memorandum to County and Burgh Councils and School Boards on vacation courses of science', P. Geddes and five others, 1891. Geddes and J. Arthur Thomson were largely responsible for getting biology accepted as a subject in the Scottish Code of Education, 1899.
44. Granton Marine Station was founded by John Murray, Professor of Zoology at Edinburgh from 1879, who was to become founder of the modern science of oceanography (Kerr, Sir J. G. (1952–3) Edinburgh in the history of zoological science. *Advancement of Science,* 9, p. 22).
45. Geddes wrote about this to his friend James Mavor, lecturer in political economy at Glasgow University. Mavor replied: 'Has the air of James Court [Geddes' home in a slum court in the Royal Mile] so mesmerised you that you must follow their steps in every particular?' (letter from Mavor to Geddes, December 1, 1889. Geddes papers, MS10569, National Library of Scotland).
46. In 1889 a special chair of Botany at Dundee University had been created for Geddes by the philanthropist, J. Martin White. Geddes was required to be at Dundee only for three months of the year, leaving him free to pursue his evolutionary studies and to travel.
47. Geddes wrote a biographical obituary of Elisée Reclus, 'A Great Geographer: Elisée Reclus, 1830–1905', for the *Scottish Geographical Magazine,* September and October 1905 (reprinted as a pamphlet, 1905).
48. Boardman, P. (1944) *Patrick Geddes: Maker of the Future.* Chapel Hill: University of North Carolina Press, p. 125.
49. See Conway, J. (1970) Stereotypes of femininity in a theory of sexual evolution. *Victorian Studies,* 14, pp. 47–62.
50. See 'Edinburgh and its region', *Scottish Geographical Magazine* (1903), and 'The Civic Survey of Edinburgh', *Transactions: The Town Planning Conference, 1910,* pp. 537–74 (reprinted by the Outlook Tower Association, Edinburgh, 1911).
51. See Mairet, P. (1957) *Patrick Geddes: Pioneer of Sociology.* London: Lund Humphries, Chapter 7, pp. 51–70. Geddes also went to Cyprus in 1896 to try and solve the Armenian problem by concentrating on economic and social factors. He got little response from the Colonial Office.
52. For a recent discussion of this, see Goist, P. D. (1974) Patrick Geddes and the City. *Journal of the American Institute of Planners,* 40, p. 33.

53. Geddes wrote a monograph on the subject which remained unpublished (typescript in the Geddes Collection, Strathclyde University), entitled *Museums: Actual and Possible.*

54. Chapter 8 of the monograph was entitled 'The Index Museum on the largest scale: its application in an International Exhibition'.

55. *Ibid.,* chapter 6, p. 1.

56. *Ibid.,* chapter 2, p. 2.

57. *Ibid.,* chapter 7, p. 1.

58. Ward's *Dynamic Sociology* had been published in 1883, his *Outlines of Sociology* in 1898.

59. See Clark, T. N. (1973) *Prophets and Patrons: The French University and the Emergence of the Social Sciences.* Cambridge: Harvard University Press, pp. 108–14.

60. Geddes saved the exhibit by getting his Outlook Tower members to transfer it to the War Museum at Lausanne (see Geddes, P. and Slater, G. (1917) *Ideas at War.* London: Williams and Norgate, p. 31), and Geddes then started his own 'war exhibition' at the Outlook Tower which was to be an important element in his Cities and Town Planning Exhibit at the Ghent International Fair in 1913.

61. *Ibid.,* chapter 1 (Museums actual and possible), p. 1.

62. *Ibid.,* chapter 9 (An incipient regional museum; its Outlook Tower), p. 1.

63. For a eulogistic response to the Outlook Tower, see the article by Charles Zueblin, from the University of Chicago, 'The World's first sociological laboratory', *American Journal of Sociology,* March 1899, pp. 577–92.

64. Among those whom Geddes invited to participate were: Henri Bergson, the Reclus brothers, Peter Kropotkin, Henri Lafontaine, Jean de Bloch, Jane Addams, Lester F. Ward, the Swami Vivekananda, Sister Nivedita (Margaret Noble), Jagadis Bose (the scientist from Calcutta), and a small contingent from the Edinburgh Outlook Tower.

65. The 'encyclopaedic' nature of the proceedings can be assessed by the subjects of the congresses. These were as follows: Art (6 congresses), Mining engineering and applied science (14), Maritime affairs (5), Maths, physical and chemical sciences (6), Natural science (6), Agriculture and forestry (11), Medicine, hygiene etc. (12), Anthropology, archaeology and history (8), Education (14), Technical and commercial education (4), Geographical and colonial questions (3), Industry and commerce (8), Property and finance (10), Literature and the press (5), Labour and corporations (9), Women (2), Philanthropy (11), Peace (1).

66. Boardman, P. (1936) *Esquisse de l'oeuvre éducatrice de Patrick Geddes.* Montpellier: Pierre-Rouge, p. 99.

67. He published his plan as a monograph, *City Development: A Study of Parks, Gardens, and Culture Institutes. A Report to the Carnegie Dunfermline Trust.* Edinburgh, Geddes & Co., 1904.

68. Geddes papers, MS10536, National Library of Scotland.

69. Halliday, R. J. (1968) The sociological movement, the Sociological Society and the genesis of academic sociology in Britain. *Sociological Review,* 16, pp. 377–98.

70. Published in *Sociological Papers.* London: Macmillan & Co., 1905.

71. Raymond Unwin, who was largely responsible for the Exhibition, visited exhibitions in Dusseldorf and Berlin to collect material. The greatest town-

planning competition ever had just been held for laying out the whole area around Berlin (*Architects and Builders Journal,* September 28, 1910 and *Town Planning Review,* 1, 1910, p. 167).

72. Geddes held a symposium on 'Town Planning' at one of the Guildhall Conferences of the Garden Cities and Town Planning Association and lobbied all interested parties with a questionnaire, 'Shall There be a Permanent Exhibition of Town Planning?'. For various responses see *Garden Cities and Town Planning,* 1, 1911, pp. 223–4.

73. It is interesting to note that, in 1904, when Geddes had lobbied J. Ramsey MacDonald about civic exhibitions, MacDonald had replied: 'A civic section at an Exhibition which appeals to all and sundry, as the St. Louis Exhibition does, is most excellent, but we do not have St. Louis Exhibitions every day or every year. On the other hand, we do have Sanitary Congresses, Public Health gatherings ...' (letter from MacDonald, 9 November 1904, Geddes papers, MS10536, National Library of Scotland).

74. 'With a hundred thousand pounds well spent in carrying out the beginnings of all this—aye, even half of it—there would have been no Sinn Fein Revolution of 1916. I do not merely suggest this: I know it! And from both sides, from all concerned.' Defries, A. (1927) *The Interpreter: Geddes, the Man and his Gospel.* p. 181.

75. In a letter to his daughter, September 14, 1922, Geddes wrote: 'Certainly I knew Dublin far better than Abercrombie etc.—knew his plan was impracticable. So were they all, more or less, and this was the best one for educating public to what town planning schemes—and drawings—are like! We had no option but to decide as we did: but we *did not recommend its carrying out* ... I told Abercrombie privately his survey was less adequate than it should have been ...' (Geddes papers, MS10502, National Library of Scotland).

76. A letter from G. H. Perris, Assistant Editor, Home University Library, 18 March 1912, sets out their views (Geddes papers, MS10555 f.163, National Library of Scotland).

77. For an account of this and a list of participants see *Garden Cities and Town Planning,* 4, 1914.

78. For a first-hand account of this see Defries, A. (1927) *The Interpreter: Geddes, the Man and his Gospel.* Chapter 2, pp. 57–90.

79. A Regional Survey Committee to co-ordinate work in the United Kingdom was formed in Edinburgh at Easter 1914, and in London at Christmas 1914.

80. Glass, Ruth (1955) Urban sociology. *Current Sociology,* 4(4).

81. Letter from T. R. Marr, ex-Outlook Tower and currently warden of Manchester University Settlement and city councillor, to Geddes, 7 June 1912. Manchester City Council is 'in the grip of reactionaries and it is well nigh impossible to get them to even talk about town planning, and less possible to get them to think of spending money on a town-planning exhibition'. Marr suggests that Geddes should try Dusseldorf (Geddes papers, MS10566, National Library of Scotland).

82. Thomson, J. A. and Geddes, P. (1931) *Life: Outlines of Biology.* London: Williams and Norgate, p. 1417.

Index

225